RIDING THE JETSTREAM

RIDING THE JETSTREAM

**The story of ballooning:
From Montgolfier
to Breitling**

John Christopher

Foreword by Brian Jones OBE

JOHN MURRAY
Albemarle Street, London

First published in 2001
by John Murray (Publishers) Ltd,
50 Albemarle Street, London W1S 4BD

A catalogue record for this book is available from the British Library

ISBN 0-7195-6051-9

Typeset in 11/13 Adobe Garamond by Servis Filmsetting Ltd, Manchester
Printed and bound in Great Britain by Butler & Tanner Ltd, Frome and London

DEDICATED TO THE MEMORY OF
FJ AND RB CHRISTOPHER

— I did it guys.

CONTENTS

ACKNOWLEDGEMENTS

First and foremost I must thank all the pilots and their teams for their help over the last decade, for talking to me about their projects and for making the years of the global balloon race such an exciting time – even though none of them ever offered me a place on a flight. In particular, thanks go to Alan Noble, Per Lindstrand, Brian Jones and Victoria Osborne from Breitling.

Special thanks to my unofficial mentor, that doyen of ballooning, accomplished author and general man of wise words, Anthony Smith. To Mike Shaw of Curtis Brown for his faith in me and to Caroline Knox of John Murray and editor Antony Wood for their guidance and support throughout.

I am grateful to the many people and organizations who gave permission to use their photographs and illustrations and these sources are acknowledged with the illustrations. In particular I wish to thank Chas Breton who has provided me with so many pictures over the years including the one for the cover. My thanks also go to those who either provided additional information or helped to check the manuscript including John Ackroyd, John Gray, Mike Kendrick and Barbara Moreton, and to Mike Willoughby for his help with filling in a few gaps in my reference library. All quotations are taken from my interviews and conversations with those involved and from their own accounts or direct statements to the media.

Then there are three special people without whom this book would never have got finished. My love and very special thanks go to Ute, but also to Anna and Jonathan for putting up with all those times when daddy's head was off somewhere in Morocco, Switzerland or halfway across the Pacific, when it should have been dancing with the Teletubbies.

JC

FOREWORD BY BRIAN JONES

To have finally ridden the jetstreams full circle brings an intense feeling of pride and privilege, tinged with a sense of guilt. Bertrand Piccard and I have been fêted in ways of which a mere mortal could never dream. The truth is, of course, as with most great adventures, that success is due not only to the people up front, but to the team backing them up. Technicians, meteorologists, air traffic controllers and communications team members each contributed that vital piece which makes the jigsaw whole. The support of family and loved ones is also an indispensable element.

Many of the great firsts, whether in aviation or other forms of exploration and adventure, begin with an individual passion and willingness to confront the unknown. By the time the idea matures, it has often become a competition between several likeminded souls. So it was with the race to circumnavigate the world in a balloon.

To understand ballooning is to feel closer to nature. There is very little control in a balloon. One embarks on a journey with no known destination, no certainties of direction and no point in attempting to control or fight against what nature has in store.

In this captivating book, John Christopher, from a unique position as journalist, historian and balloon pilot, has been able to give an informed account of more than twenty attempts by various teams. One feels the mounting excitement as year after year the records are stretched until finally, at the turn of the century, the ultimate challenge was met. John's story answers all the questions

– how, when, where, who and why. Moreover, it puts the round-the-world race firmly into the context of the grand history of ballooning – a form of flight which precedes the Wright brothers' invention of the powered aeroplane by 120 years. I thought I was pretty well informed about the fascinating world of ballooning. Having read and thoroughly enjoyed this account, I am now.

In the ultimate balloon, our *Breitling Orbiter 3*, Bertrand and I were blessed by the winds of providence. Our sincere wish is that the lasting legacy of this extraordinary flight will be the 'Winds of Hope' – a foundation that we set up with the prize money to highlight and alleviate the plight of children suffering in unreported circumstances in this beautiful but often sad world of ours.* After all, what use is history if it can't influence the future?

Brian Jones
Breitling Orbiter 3

* The website of the Winds of Hope Foundation is www.windsofhope.org

AUTHOR'S PREFACE

'It beats working in an office.' That's what I tell people when they ask me if I enjoy my job as a balloon pilot. And yes, I really do. Nothing can compare with the experience of flying a balloon. Floating high above the mortal world, or so it seems from that god-like perch, with each town, village, hillside and woodland laid out like details on a fantastic patchwork quilt. Every year thousands of ordinary people take to the skies to taste this adventure for themselves, and I am frequently asked how their joyrides compare with those of the other high achievers – the global balloonists. Where to begin?

For the most part the 'ordinary' hot-air voyager is content to float just a few thousand feet above the countryside, gently meandering at the mercy of the wind at speeds ranging from perhaps 15 mph down to absolutely zero, on a flight lasting around 60 minutes or so, in an aerial carriage which is little more than an over-sized laundry basket, the only means of staying aloft being to blast raw flame into that huge bubble of air wrapped up in its colourful coat of nylon. The 'jetstream jockeys', on the other hand, ride in high-tech capsules suspended beneath large helium-bloated balloons which are heated only to maintain or alter their height. Travelling in an aerial fast lane, they hope to dash along at speeds of 150 mph or more at the sort of altitude normally frequented by passenger airliners, flying non-stop for two or even three weeks as they endeavour to encircle the globe risking all in the pursuit of adventure, fame and glory. How did that gentle air-child of the Montgolfier brothers evolve into these extreme machines?

While some of the global pilots have already given accounts of their individual attempts, this book sets out to paint the big picture – tracing the essential stepping stones that led to the conquering of aviation's last great challenge. The story begins with the birth and early development of ballooning, the scientists' urge to study the atmosphere spurring the aeronauts on to take their craft to new heights and, most importantly, to learn the means of surviving in a hostile environment. By the nineteenth century the balloon had become little more than a fairground attraction, and then the thrill-seeking Edwardian jet-set took it up and pushed it to fly further and further, all in the name of sport – a golden age for ballooning which was brought to an end by war. It was when the military took an interest in balloons that the jetstream wind was first identified and exploited – as a means of delivering airborne bombs. And it was in the dark days of the Cold War that military research inadvertently sparked the imagination of a new generation of aeronauts keen to pit themselves and their machines against the elements and each other, finally, so late in the day, conquering the great oceans. Only when all these strands came together did balloonists discover the means and the will to push for the final goal of global circumnavigation.

Back in the 1960s when the astronauts were striving for the Moon, I was just a schoolboy – a child of the space age, born one year before the first *Sputnik* orbited the Earth and thirteen years old when Armstrong and Aldrin planted their footprints on the lunar soil. When the global balloon race began in earnest in the early 1990s I was a little more grown up. A professional balloonist flying for Virgin by this time, I was also in the very fortunate position of editing the *Aerostat* journal on behalf of the British Balloon and Airship Club, and consequently I found myself at the hub of this new adventure, able to follow the inside story from its inception to its dramatic conclusion. Almost uniquely I was equally welcomed by the competing teams, not just as a journalist but as a fellow balloonist, and the result was a period of great excitement as each successive season brought new twists and turns of fortune. In March 1999 when Bertrand Piccard and Brian Jones lifted off from Switzerland at the start of their epic flight, I was there to see them off. And when the *Breitling Orbiter 3* passed the finishing line almost twenty days later I was among the first to fax them my congratulations before ringing my friends and family, unable to contain the terrific news: 'They've done it! They've done it!'

With a laugh my sister told me that I sounded as if I had done it myself. And in many ways she was right, for I had ridden every inch of the way with them in that tiny red capsule. I too had been part of this great global balloon quest over the past decade. But more than that, when those two men stepped out onto the Egyptian sand they weren't alone – they were standing on the shoulders of each and every balloonist dating back to the Montgolfier brothers and their initial leap of faith in man's ability to do the seemingly impossible. This book is a testament to their courage and the remarkable story of riding the jetstream, a twenty-day flight and a 216-year-long journey.

John Christopher

Part one

INTO THE SKIES

'How posterity will laugh at us, one way or the other! If half a dozen break their necks, and balloonism is exploded, we shall be called fools for having imagined it could be brought to use: if it should be turned to account, we shall be ridiculed for having doubted.'

Horace Walpole, 1785

1 THE WAY TO THE SKIES

1783, France

Mankind's first brave forays into the heavens were among those rare milestones of human endeavour that seem to leapfrog the normal conventions of historical progression. This was 1783. The bloody days of the French Revolution were still to come, Ludwig van Beethoven was thirteen and Napoleon Bonaparte only one year older. It was fifty years before the first railways set the industrial age in motion, and more than a century before the advent of powered flight. Yet it is perhaps more remarkable still that while many historians have painted a romanticized picture of the first aeronauts as a noble breed of intrepid young pioneers striving to break the shackles of gravity, the reality was much more down to earth. The invention of the balloon was the direct result of some healthy ignorance combined, very nearly, with criminal involvement at the highest level.

The latter half of the eighteenth century had seen great strides in the scientific knowledge of the physical world, resulting among other things in a growing understanding of the properties of gases. In 1766 the Englishman Henry Cavendish had discovered the gas he called 'phlogiston' or 'inflammable air', and which we now know as hydrogen. Although highly explosive when mixed with even the smallest quantities of oxygen, hydrogen is nonetheless the most readily available of the gases possessing molecules which are less dense than the cocktail we know of as 'air'. In other words, it is 'lighter-than-air', and inquiring minds throughout Europe began working along similar lines of research to harness this new discovery. But even some of the most educated of these minds' perception of the true nature of hydrogen was sometimes a little confused; none more so than in the case of two brothers, wealthy papermakers from the little town of Annonay in the south of France.

There is an abundance of myths offering various scenarios for that most famous eureka moment, the invention of the balloon. But it is unlikely that Joseph Montgolfier was actually inspired by Madame Montgolfier's chemise gently rising as it dried in front of the fire. For him the urge to experiment had come in the more prosaic form of Joseph Priestley's book *Experiments and Observations on Different Kinds of Air*, which had been translated into French in 1776. This sparked, so to speak, his own observation that as smoke and cinders invariably rise above a burning fire, the process of combustion must in itself be generating quantities of this mysterious 'inflammable air'. In fact Montgolfier – the name literally means 'master of the mountain' – had initially conducted experiments in which he attempted to fill small paper and cotton globes with hydrogen, but invariably the tiny molecules of this gas seeped out through the pores of paper and fabric like water through a sieve. Undeterred, he then turned instead to a different source of lift and attempted to inflate small balloons over the blackest, smelliest bonfires he could muster – damp straw, wool, old shoes and even decomposing meat were said to be best fuel – in order to capture a substance he confusingly referred to as 'rarefied air'. And as luck would have it, the billowing sooty smoke did actually serve to block the pores of the fabric and thus he succeeded in capturing the lifting properties not of any gas as such but of the all-important heated air, or as it is known nowadays, hot-air. What Joseph Montgolfier didn't appreciate is that as a given volume of air is heated it expands and the spaces between the molecules increase, thus making it less dense and therefore lighter than the same volume of ordinary air which it has displaced. A little ignorance got him a long way.

Joseph was joined in his experiments by his younger brother Etienne, and the two Montgolfiers were soon ready to go public with their discovery. On Thursday 5 June 1783 they organized a demonstration in the town square of Annonay, which today is a sprawling industrial town that is still home to the Montgolfier paper mills. In recent years their direct descendants have organized an annual reenactment to mark this auspicious day and in 1992 I was fortunate enough to take part in one of these while attending the annual Annonay balloon festival. I joined many of the local inhabitants dressed in splendid period costume for the occasion. The atmosphere in the sunny town square was one of carnival, as it must have been two centuries earlier, but as the replica paper and cotton balloon was unloaded from its simple wooden cart the mood quickly changed to one of hushed reverence. Measuring 25 feet high, the yellow and red bag was hoisted upright between two wooden poles to suspend it above a surprisingly small mound of burning straw. And, as with any balloon's inflation, in that moment when the inanimate heap of fabric stirred and swelled into a living, breathing creature, a powerful magic cast its spell. Although the latter-day Montgolfiers didn't want to release their precious replica, it did not take much imagination to roll back the years and to envisage the awe that this primitive flying machine must have inspired the first time it soared silently to an estimated 6,000 feet and then drifted for ten minutes in the gentle breeze before coming down to earth one and a half miles away.

The Montgolfier brothers were not alone in their aerial ambitions, however. Affronted by the prospect of two provincial paper-makers stealing their thunder, and not quite believing their claims anyway, the Parisian Academy of Sciences attempted to restore its prestige by encouraging a rival line of aeronautical research. Taking up the challenge was the thirty-seven-year-old physicist Professor Jacques Alexandre César Charles, who possessed a much clearer grasp of the composition and properties of hydrogen gas (although at first even he presumed that the Montgolfiers were still trying their hand with hydrogen, their experiments in Annonay being far removed from the scrutiny of the Parisian scientific establishment, and the lifting properties of hot-air still being generally misunderstood). With the aid of his own set of illustrious brothers, the two Roberts, Jean and Noël – who had perfected an essential technique for coating fine silk with a solution of rubber to make it impermeable to gas – he set to work on the world's first gas balloon.

As the two rival camps each sought to demonstrate the superiority of their approach, mainly through the launching of small test balloons, their activities stirred up a whirlwind of excitement and anticipation throughout Parisian society and each new step was greeted with a clamour of amazement and disbelief. It was the equivalent of the space race two centuries later and, as with modern concerns about the effects of flying in space, they too were worried about sending men up into the unknown – the uncharted province of the upper air, an 'aerial ocean' as some regarded it. These fears, of course, appear entirely illogical when it is considered that many people already lived quite happily at altitudes thousands of feet higher than that the balloonists were likely to attain, and that mountaineers had climbed considerably higher by this time and lived to tell the tale. But many scientists at the time reasoned that the layers of the atmosphere might follow the earth's contours and accordingly, in a move that anticipated Nasa's spacefaring dogs and monkeys, the first living creatures to ride in a flying machine – a Montgolfière balloon launched in Paris in September 1783 – were a cockerel, a duck and a sheep.

This flight propelled the Montgolfier brothers into the lead and soon they were ready to send a human 'aeronaut' aloft. But although the three animals had survived their balloon ride completely intact, King Louis XVI nevertheless decreed that the candidates to undertake man's first giant leap into the unknown should be found among the prison inmates – risking their lives in exchange for a pardon. It is fortunate for the reputation of balloonists everywhere that the King was persuaded otherwise by the twenty-six-year-old daredevil and Academy member Jean-François Pilâtre de Rozier, who had recruited the assistance of fellow aristocrat François Laurent, Marquis d'Arlandes, and together they volunteered for the task.

On 21 November 1783, the 79,000 cubic-foot paper and cotton envelope of the Montgolfiers' hot-air balloon, magnificently decorated in blue and gold with the signs of the Zodiac, was hoisted over a pit of burning straw, old shoes and rancid meat. Not surprisingly the whole of Paris held its breath – in awe as much as to keep out the obnoxious fumes – and at 1.54 pm the restraining ropes were cut and the balloon rose up from the Château La Muette in the Bois de Boulogne and so began the history of manned flight.

Riding in a wickerwork gallery encircling the base of the balloon, de Rozier and the Marquis were equipped with pitchforks to feed faggots of straw into the iron basket carried within the balloon's open mouth to maintain the supply of smoke, and as a precaution against embers setting their fragile craft ablaze they also carried several buckets of water and sponges fixed onto the end of long sticks. These two men were the very first air travellers, the first to taste that liberating moment of buoyant flight when the earth simply drops away. For them there was no sensation of rising, no surge of noisy engines or the thundering rush along a runway to get airborne – just pure silence and a rapid change in perspective as the hushed sea of upturned faces fell into the distance.

'The machine, say the public, rose with majesty,' wrote the Marquis after the flight. 'I was surprised at the silence and absence of movement which our departure caused among the spectators, believing them to be astonished and perhaps awed by the strange spectacle; they might well have reassured themselves. I was still gazing when M. Rozier cried to me – "You are doing nothing, and the balloon is scarcely rising a fathom." "Pardon me," I replied, as I placed a bundle of straw upon the fire and gently stirred it.'

For the onlookers the impact of what they saw was almost beyond belief, and to show that all was well de Rozier and the Marquis waved their hats and bowed as a gentle northwesterly breeze wafted the balloon towards the River Seine. But the two aeronauts had precious little time to spare in which to soak in the

21 November 1783: the first aloft – Pilâtre de Rozier and the Marquis d'Arlandes aboard the elaborately decorated Montgolfier hot-air balloon constructed of cotton and paper

unique pleasures of ballooning – that liberating freedom of three-dimensional travel, floating high above the mortal world, taking in the whole of existence with one turn of the head, and enjoying a godlike perspective on the tiny human-ants beneath your feet. Understandably, the Marquis was captivated by the novelty of his situation: 'Astonished, I cast a glance towards the river. I perceived the confluence of the Oise. And naming the principal bends of the river by the places nearest them, I cried, Passy, Saint-Germain, Saint-Denis, Sèvres!' Whereupon the coolheaded de Rozier pointed out that if he continued in that fashion the Marquis would be bathing in it soon and once more urged, 'More fire, my dear friend, more fire!'

After dodging the Parisian rooftops and staying aloft for an all too brief 25 minutes, the two aeronauts had their first lesson in what is perhaps the cruellest irony of ballooning – that such self-delusions of superiority are but pride before a fall, lest any aeronaut should get ideas above his station. Such is gravity's revenge! What goes up invariably comes down again and de Rozier and the Marquis were returned to earth with a thump at the Butte-aux-Cailles, just 9,000 yards from their starting point. 'Looking around and expecting to see the balloon still distended, I was astonished to find it quite empty and flattened,' wrote the Marquis. 'On looking for Rozier I saw him in his shirt-sleeves creeping out from under the mass of canvas that had fallen over him.'

It had been a modest first outing, with the balloon climbing to an estimated height of between 2,000 and 3,000 feet, and in which, miraculously, neither aeronaut died as a result of his elevated position. But calamity could have overtaken them at any moment, and when one considers the huge leap into the unknown that they were taking, and the ever-present risk of their craft catching fire, the bravery of these two pioneer test-pilots can only be marvelled at.

Robbed of their place in history as the first aeronauts, only eleven days later, on 1 December 1783, Professor Charles and Noël

Robert inflated their gas balloon in the Tuileries gardens. The only drawback with this type of balloon was the difficulty of generating sufficient quantities of hydrogen in the first place – a long tedious process involving the reaction of dilute sulphuric acid passed over iron filings. As the acid and iron mixture bubbled away the hydrogen fumes were piped into sealed casks, where they cooled; they were then fed into the balloon's envelope. It was complicated and it could take many hours to prepare a gas balloon for flight, whereas a hot-air balloon inflation took only a matter of minutes. It was also a very expensive process.

These problems aside, the ingenuity of Charles' balloon design has served as a virtual blueprint for gas balloons ever since. The wicker basket, or 'gondola' as it was shaped like a boat, was suspended by lines coming from a net which covered the plump hydrogen-filled envelope. This had at its base an open tube or appendix which acted as a safety valve, allowing excess gas to escape freely, thus preventing the balloon from popping as the gas expanded with reduced atmospheric pressure at height or the warming effect of the sun. To deliberately release or 'vent' a quantity of gas in order to make the balloon descend, Charles had fitted a simple wooden valve at the apex of the envelope. Opening inwards, it was held in place by the internal gas pressure and could be opened via a line passing through the envelope and out through the appendix down to the aeronauts in the basket underneath.

So great was the public interest in this second balloon launch that a crowd estimated at 400,000 strong had gathered to witness this miracle of flight for themselves. Among the spectators was Joseph Montgolfier, and in a gracious tribute from one pioneer to another, Charles invited him to come forward and handed him a small five-foot hydrogen-filled globe to be released as an indicator of the air currents above. 'It is for you, Monsieur, to show us the way to the skies.'

Charles then joined Robert in the basket. Together they unloaded nineteen pounds of sand ballast and the balloon took to the skies like a fish to water, quickly rising to 1,800 feet. 'Nothing

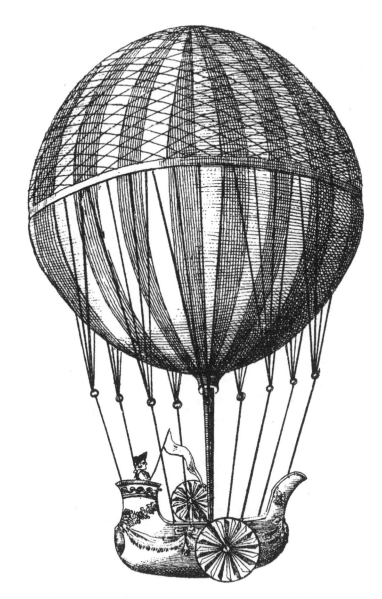

1 December 1783: Professor Charles established many of the basic principles of gas balloon design including the net, gas valve at the crown of the envelope and the open neck at its bottom. The only fundamental change to the design since his day has been to move the load-bearing ring closer to the basket

will ever equal that moment of joyous excitement that filled my whole being when I felt myself flying away from the earth,' Charles recounted afterwards. 'It was not mere pleasure; it was perfect bliss.'

The two aeronauts made a perfect landing two hours later near the small town of Nesle, having flown 27 miles from their starting-point. By that time the sun was setting, but, exhilarated by his experience, Charles couldn't resist the temptation to ascend again and after promising that he would return within thirty minutes he set off beneath the now flaccid balloon for a further flight solo. Relieved of his companion's weight, the balloon shot upwards at a meteoric rate, whisking Charles to an estimated height of 10,000 feet and causing him to suffer an acute earache, but also rewarding him with a spectacular view of a second sunset. 'I passed in ten minutes from the temperature of spring to that of winter. The cold was keen and dry, but not insupportable. 'And afterwards, offering an insight into his lofty isolation, he said, 'I could hear myself live, so to speak.'

It had been a magnificent tour de force, clearly demonstrating the gas balloon's superiority over the hot-air variety. It was much smaller in volume (hydrogen is about three times more efficient as a lifting medium), and as a pressurized sphere it was also more robust and for the most part lacked the inherent self-destruct properties of its fire-borne cousins.

Nothing in our modern lives, not even the Lunar landings, begins to measure up to the phenomenal impact that these first balloon flights had upon informed society. Throughout France and the rest of Europe 'balloon-mania' spread like wildfire. 'We think of nothing here at present but of flying,' wrote one observer. 'The balloons engross all attention.' Every fashionable item from furniture to clothing was crafted in the likeness of balloons or decorated with their image. Balladeers sang their praises, and the pioneering aeronauts such as de Rozier, the Marquis d'Arlandes, Charles and the Roberts in France, followed by Chevalier Paul Andreani in Italy, Vincenzo Lunardi in England and Pierre

Blanchard in America, were greeted like the pop stars of today as they risked life and limb in a series of trailblazing ascents. It was a time when people believed that if man could now fly then surely any accomplishment was within the realms of possibility. Some argued that even death itself might be escaped some day. These were indeed years of wonder.

2 TAKEN FOR A RIDE

Wednesday 7 January 1785, Dover

It was a fine crisp, clear day at Dover. Two aeronauts were preparing to fly across the English Channel to France, but instead of being a bold pioneering adventure this was in danger of becoming pure comic opera. The bantamweight Frenchman Jean-Pierre Blanchard, one of the new breed of professional balloonists seeking fame and fortune through their exploits, had joined forces with the wealthy patron Dr John Jeffries, a successful Boston-born physician practising in England and noted for his interests in science, especially meteorology. It was Jeffries who had paid the considerable sum of £700 to cover the costs of the trip. However, the egotistical Blanchard was not keen to share the limelight with anyone, and at the moment of launching the hydrogen-filled balloon seemed too heavily laden and incapable of bearing two men aloft. Apparently Blanchard had put on a lot of weight . . . in fact, he had actually got his tailor to sew lead weights into his clothing in an attempt to deny Jeffries his place in the basket. Such was the ignoble start of the relationship between balloonist and sponsor, and some might say that little has changed down the years.

A balloon, whether constructed in the eighteenth or the twentieth century, costs a lot of money, and only the wealthiest enthusiasts can afford to foot the bill themselves. From the very beginning most aeronauts have had to seek sponsorship or patronage to fund their

Dr John Jeffries, the long-suffering partner and patron of Pierre Blanchard, pioneered
the balloon as a platform for scientific observation of the atmosphere

adventures: a symbiotic relationship in which only one half gets to call the tune. The aeronaut's dilemma has always been to find that elusive sponsor – someone prepared to be taken for a ride and pay for it.

Having shown the way to the skies, in the process satisfying their own scientific curiosity, the Montgolfier brothers and Professor Charles soon retired from centre-stage to return to their other interests. (Joseph was the only Montgolfier brother to fly, and then only the once, and perhaps deterred by his painful earache Charles never repeated the experience either.) Filling the vacuum left by these great pioneers there emerged the professional aeronauts – half daredevil and half showman, and in some cases apparently only half informed in the finer points of aerostatics.

Although the Montgolfier brothers rightly received recognition for their trailblazing efforts, only the most die-hard proponents of the 'Montgolfière' balloon continued to practise that inherently precarious form of elevation and these hot-air borne craft virtually disappeared from the scene until modern times. Instead it was to the sturdier 'Charlière', the gas balloon, that the vast majority of aeronauts entrusted their lives and somebody else's fortunes. And with public interest at fever pitch and all that money burning holes in the pockets of the curious, it looked like a 'win-win situation' for those who would gladly accept money from wealthy patrons and also take it from the public who paid to see the balloons ascend.

Word of the incredible aerial advances taking place in France spread rapidly throughout Europe, although sceptics required a little more convincing. No less so than in England where the 'Frenchies' and their flying contraptions were regarded with a jaundiced eye and a widespread conviction that the whole business must be some sort of elaborate hoax. This distrust was partly exacerbated by money-grabbing charlatans who were milking the balloon's novelty value for all it was worth by announcing and selling tickets for ascents that never took place. So it was left to another foreigner – an Italian this time – Vincenzo or 'Vincent' Lunardi, in service to the Neapolitan Ambassador to the Court of St James, to introduce the art of aerostation to the backward English. Young and undeniably handsome, this colourful exhibitionist saw ballooning as his ticket to fashionable society, and in 1784 he set to work to build a gas balloon and with it his own public profile.

In order to raise funds to pay for its construction Lunardi displayed his red and white striped balloon envelope under the dome of the Lyceum Rooms in the Strand, London, where a staggering 20,000 visitors paid the not inconsiderable sum of five shillings to see it and the dashing young aeronaut. Despite several setbacks, eventually Lunardi raised sufficient funds to complete the balloon, pay the proprietor at the Lyceum and cover the expense of generating the hydrogen for a flight. Accordingly on 14 September 1784 a further 150,000 paying spectators thronged to the Royal Artillery Ground to cheer and jeer in turn as the interminable inflation process dragged on well past the advertised time for the ascent. Fearing a riot, and with the envelope still far from fully bloated, Lunardi climbed aboard the balloon's gondola taking with him his dog, a cat, some wine and a plentiful supply of food – no matter how short a flight, the early aeronauts were always lavishly provisioned – and both he and the balloon finally rose to the occasion.

'The effect was that of a miracle on the multitudes which surrounded the place . . . they rent the air with their acclamations and applause,' wrote Lunardi later.

Like many of his contemporaries Lunardi had given considerable thought to the problem of how to steer his balloon at will. Taking the analogy of the air as an aerial ocean quite literally, he equipped his gondola with an elaborate set of huge paddle devices by which he intended to row his way about the sky. He wasn't alone in this conviction, and others contrived to fly with such oars or even large sails attached to their balloons. But they were only deceiving themselves, for no amount of paddling, flapping or generally wafting around will make any appreciable difference to a balloon's movement: it goes with the wind. It's as simple as that. As one historian put it, 'The balloon is not the master of the atmosphere, on the contrary, it is its powerless slave.' The only way to steer a balloon is to take advantage of different air currents that might or might not exist at different heights on a given day. But that was a lesson that most would take a little longer to learn.

After Lunardi's safe return to earth – apparently he used his one remaining oar, the other having broken off earlier in the flight, to 'row' the balloon to his chosen landing field near North Mimms, Hertfordshire – the English public's distrust of balloons, ballooning and balloonists instantly turned to hero worship on a grand scale. The dashing young Italian epitomized the image of the brave aeronaut and, a flamboyant egotist by nature, he basked in the attention, especially from the ladies. But alas, it was to be short-lived. Two years later Lunardi met his nemesis at Newcastle-upon-Tyne when a young man, a well-meaning bystander, accidentally became entangled in one of the ropes which was holding the balloon down. He was hoisted into the air as the balloon took off, lost his grip and fell to his death in full sight of the crowds and his distraught parents. Lunardi, entirely blameless, was mortified by this tragic accident and when he became the target of the ensuing public derision he fled the country.

For most aerial showmen, the act of putting on a public display was enough in itself. Only a handful of the most adventurous sought to make a name for themselves by covering longer distances. The English Channel was the first great hurdle to overcome and such was its allure that only fourteen months after the very first manned balloon flight, three different groups of contenders were lining up like an early version of the modern round-the-world balloon race. Most Channel hoppers planned to launch from England with the larger continental land mass ahead of them, rather than the other way round, although either way required very careful observation of the wind currents before making a decision to launch.

Representing the French was Pilâtre de Rozier who had piloted the original Montgolfier-built balloon, teamed up with fellow countryman Jules Pierre Romain who had constructed their *Royal Balloon*. This was a highly unconventional hybrid design, half hot-air balloon and half hydrogen gas, shaped like a giant mushroom with an upper sphere of hydrogen capping a broad cylindrical hot-air chamber. Some sources suggest that the two component parts were separated by a small gap between them and not joined as shown in most contemporary illustrations of the balloon. What prompted this configuration is uncertain – presumably the designers hoped to take advantage of the best of both types of balloon – but the proximity of such a highly combustible gas with a source of ignition seems utter folly to anyone with an ounce of common sense and the comfort of hindsight. Indeed, de Rozier himself appeared to have had grave misgivings, but he could not back out, the honour of France was at stake, not to mention a considerable prize offered by the French government. It is an enduring irony that this type of balloon was to be forever linked to his name and is now known as a 'Rozière'.

Meanwhile two other teams were mustering their forces on the English coast. James Sadler, the first Englishman to fly a balloon, was thwarted in his attempt when fresh varnish caused his folded envelope to stick to itself. That left the way open to the multinational team of Blanchard and Dr Jeffries. Despite Blanchard's best endeavours to keep him out of the picture the doctor took his antics in surprisingly good humour, and on 7 January 1785 they departed at 1 pm for France. Almost immediately the balloon began to sink, either because it was overloaded or because the drop in temperature over the icy water had cooled the hydrogen, and they were forced to ditch all non-essential items – including more of those oars. This did the trick for a while, but as they neared the French coast the balloon was losing height again and this time some essentials, including most of their clothing, went overboard. In surprisingly good spirits the now shivering duo continued on their way until the balloon began to descend over dense woodland in the forest of Felmores a few miles south of Calais. With all the other ballast already disposed off there was only one solution left, and they became the first aeronauts to resort to what the Doctor describes as 'a curious expedient' – they pissed themselves out of danger, no doubt much to their relief. After landing, almost naked and freezing cold, the two men were greeted warmly by the locals and later fêted as heroes, with King Louis XVI generously rewarding Blanchard with a prize of 12,000 livres and a pension.

De Rozier and Romain, meanwhile, were still stuck in Calais, and it was not until 15 June that conditions were right for them to launch. The balloon climbed steadily to a height of 5,000 feet, at which point an impish breeze decided to push it back over French soil. Then flames suddenly leaped from the balloon's crown and in a flash it plummeted back to earth, taking both men to their deaths. It is thought that they may have vented hydrogen to bring the balloon lower and that this had ignited. So it was that the first aeronaut of all, and his new companion, became the first victims of air travel.

One problem for the fledgling aeronauts was that there just weren't enough wealthy Dr Jeffries to go round, and as public enthusiasm waned at the start of the nineteenth century they had to resort to ever more extravagant stunts to attract the paying crowds rather than tackle more ambitious flights. Soon they were dropping hapless animals by parachute, riding horses aloft and even sending their wives up in balloons, but still attendances declined. First to buck the trend was Charles Green, England's most dedicated and celebrated aeronaut, whose flying career began with his first flight at the age of thirty-six in 1821 and continued for thirty-one years, his five-hundredth flight being undertaken when he was nearly seventy years old. Although he wasn't averse to taking the odd horse up to earn money at public ascents, he also took the art of ballooning very seriously. It was Green who introduced the use of

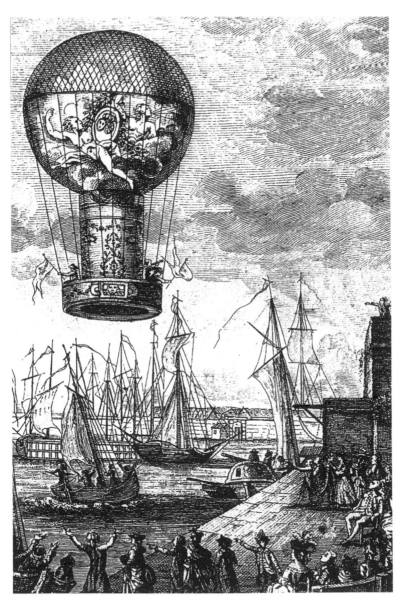

The original combination hot-air and gas balloon on its first and fatal last flight, an attempt to cross the Channel on 15 June in 1785. When it exploded Pilâtre de Rozier and Pierre Romain became the first casualties of air travel

town gas – carburetted hydrogen generated from coal – which, although not as efficient a lifting agent as hydrogen, was considerably cheaper and was abundantly available at the turn of a tap at the local gasworks. He also pioneered the use of the trail rope, a very effective device which slows a balloon's descent at the time of landing, the weight of this long rope being progressively taken up by the ground as the balloon lands.

Green's most celebrated flight began on 7 November 1836, when the *Vauxhall Gardens* balloon ascended from those very gardens in London and caught a north-west breeze that propelled it towards the English Channel. That evening he and his two companions, the writer Thomas Monck Mason and Member of Parliament Robert Hollond – who had funded the flight – enjoyed an agreeable in-flight dinner of cold beef, ham, fowl and tongue, washed down with wine, as they drifted over Calais. A little later they spied the blast furnaces at Liège before entering a period of such utter darkness that Mason described their passage as being like 'cleaving our way through an interminable mass of black marble which, solid a few inches before us, seemed to soften as we approached'. As the marble gave way to dawn's first light they realized that they were totally lost. In fact they were over the Duchy of Nassau in present-day Germany. Eighteen hours and some 380 miles from home, the balloon came to rest near the town of Weilburg. By today's standards it was a fairly modest flight, yet it had established a new long distance record that would stand for over 20 years.

Inspired by this success, Green next turned to the possibility of a transatlantic flight. By observing the movement of the clouds and weather systems he had identified a reasonably consistent west to east airflow at higher altitudes which roughly corresponded to the trade winds familiar to sailors. Twice he advertised for 'wealthy patrons of the art' to underwrite the project, and twice they failed to materialize. So instead the frustrated and now sixty-seven-year-old elder statesman of ballooning embarked on a long series of sentimental, positively 'final' balloon ascents to prepare for his retirement, and it was left to the American showman balloonists to tackle an ocean crossing.

On the other side of the Atlantic the balloonist John Wise had observed the same airflows: 'A current from west to east in the atmosphere is constantly in motion within the height of 12,000 feet above the ocean. Nearly all my trips are strong proof of this.' He was also a firm believer in the future of ballooning as a viable mode of transatlantic transport, having once stated: 'Our children will travel to any part of the globe without the inconvenience of smoke, sparks and seasickness, and at the rate of 100 miles per hour.' With backing from a wealthy Vermont businessman Wise decided to take his appropriate if unimaginatively named *Atlantic* for a pre-Atlantic test-flight. At dusk on 1 July 1859 the 120-foot-high gas balloon launched from St Louis. Alas, by the following afternoon it was to be found lodged halfway up a tree near Lake Ontario. Wise and three companions, fellow aeronaut John La Mountain, his backer O. A. Gager and a newspaper reporter, William Hyde, had encountered fierce gale force winds of up to 90 mph which had slammed the balloon through the forest, ripping it to tatters. But they had established a new distance record, having flown an incredible 809 miles in just under 20 hours, more than doubling Green's record, although this distance was still far short of that required to reach Europe.

John La Mountain rebuilt the *Atlantic*'s envelope, but he fared little better on his own test flight. Launching from New York, he ended up stranded for four days in the Canadian wilderness. Next up was the New Englander Thaddeus Lowe who launched from Cincinnati on 19 April 1861 and landed nine hours and some 350 miles later at Unionsville, South Carolina, where he was promptly arrested as a Yankee spy. Fortunately for Lowe a local man recognized him and he was released. But unfortunately for ballooning, the American Civil War put paid to any further serious attempts at pond-hopping for some time, and incredibly the Atlantic would remain unconquered until the 1970s, nearly two hundred years after the birth of ballooning. Instead of covering greater distances the upwardly mobile of the late nineteenth and early twentieth centuries were left to push the boundaries of ballooning in an entirely different direction.

3 IN THE NAME OF SCIENCE

At the time of Professor Charles' and Noël Robert's first gas balloon ascent, Benjamin Franklin was in Paris as the United States Ambassador and, more covertly, as a key member of the American Committee of Secret Correspondence. When confronted by a bystander with the question 'Of what use are these balloons?' he replied 'And of what use is a new-born baby?' Of course his response was meant to silence the unimaginative questioner, but because of their total reliance on the elements and in particular the wind, in reality balloons did seem to have only limited practical application. However, there is one endeavour in which balloons have excelled – exploring our planet's atmosphere.

Dr Jeffries had begun this branch of scientific study by carrying instruments on both of his flights, investigating, as he put it, 'the nature and properties of the atmosphere which surrounds us, and into which we had hitherto been unable to rise'. On his first sortie aloft, he sampled the upper air and measured its temperature, barometric pressure and humidity; while on the second he was too busy keeping out of the clutches of the English Channel to pay his experiments much heed. As had Professor Charles before him, Jeffries observed that the temperature and air pressure reduced with height. In 1803 the Frenchman Etienne Robertson noted that his breathing became more laboured in the thinner air. He also made the dubious claim that at height his head had swollen up so much that his hat no longer fitted him.

The pattern of the flights that ensued was intermittent. In

1808, for example, the Italian meteorologists Pascal Andreoli and Carlo Brioschi took a balloon to 25,000 feet, although neither experienced any hat problems. But as with other scientific endeavours, ballooning activities tended to come in waves – spurred on by a particular advance or by a climate of international rivalry – and they were frequently punctuated by tragedy. Over 40 years passed before the next concerted effort. In 1850 Jean-Auguste Barral and Jacques Bixio set off to study humidity at high altitudes. Unfortunately, while both men were accomplished in their own fields, Barral being a lecturer in chemistry and Bixio the editor of an agricultural journal, they had neglected to attend to the rudiments of ballooning. As they shot up like a rocket to 20,000 feet, their over-filled hydrogen balloon envelope began to swell, pushing downwards on the basket and its hapless occupants. Frantic efforts to retrieve the valve line caused the fabric to rip and down came Barral and Bixio, tossing everything overboard as if there were no tomorrow (and there nearly wasn't). Incredibly, the plucky duo gave it another go and climbed to 23,000 feet to become the first scientists to discover that high-altitude cirrus clouds consist of ice crystal. But their efforts were soon overshadowed by events taking place in England.

In September 1862, the latest high-profile ballooning duo – English aeronaut Henry Coxwell, who had abandoned a career as a dentist to follow in the footsteps of Charles Green, together with meteorologist James Glaisher – attempted to fly a balloon higher than ever before to study the temperature and moisture content of the atmosphere. Despite observing that the air was becoming thinner as they reached 26,400 feet, they were throwing out ballast to go even higher when Glaisher's vision began to fail – a tell-tale sign of the onset of hypoxia, the condition of torpor caused by a lack of oxygen. Summoning his partner for assistance, he discovered that Coxwell, climbing into the rigging in order to free the valve line which had become tangled, was also the worse for wear. His hands were numb with cold and if he didn't release some hydrogen quickly they both faced certain death as the balloon continued its climb. Eventually the line came free and Coxwell fell back into the basket. Barely able to move, he grabbed the line between his clenched teeth and jerked his head in desperation until the welcome hiss of escaping gas could be heard. They survived, but others were not so fortunate.

The altitude at which a human being requires an oxygen supply differs enormously from person to person. It can even vary for an individual depending on many factors including health and physical fitness. In broad terms it is generally recommended that oxygen should be carried on flights exceeding 10,000 or 12,000 feet above sea-level, but some people manage quite happily without it up to 20,000 feet or more. It is all a matter of acclimatization and in serious climbing circles it is now considered positively de rigeur to tackle Everest's formidable 29,000 feet oxygen-less. Admittedly it has a lot to do with the rate of climb. Whereas a mountaineer might take many days, if not weeks, to reach the summit, a balloon is capable of rising at 1,000 fpm (feet per minute) or more. American global contender Steve Fossett has habitually flown at altitudes up to 24,000 feet without using an oxygen supply, aside from times of physical exertion or during sleep. But he is the exception, an experienced mountaineer among other things, who puts great emphasis on acclimatizing himself before undertaking such flights.

Learning from Coxwell and Glaisher's near death experience, French scientists Joseph Croce-Spinelli and Theodore Sivel devised a simple breathing apparatus consisting of a mouthpiece connected via a tube to a small balloon inflated with normal air mixed with oxygen, and in April 1875 they joined the aeronaut Gaston Tissandier in *Le Zénith* to put their equipment to the test. At around 23,000 feet they sucked on their oxygen tubes for the first time. 'The effect is excellent,' Sivel scrawled in his log, and accordingly they jettisoned ballast in an attempt to attain 30,000 feet. But as they climbed Tissandier felt himself becoming lightheaded, demonstrating the onset of hypoxia as his brain became starved of oxygen, and when he reached for his breathing tube once more he found that he could no longer move his arm. He slumped into unconsciousness and by the time he came round the balloon was in a rapid descent. His companions were lying motionless on the basket floor. Tissandier blacked out again, to be roused by Croce-Spinelli and, feeling euphoric from the lack of oxygen, he then made the fatal mistake of throwing out more ballast, pushing *Le Zénith* back up to 28,000 feet at which point he blacked out for a third time. It was another hour before he regained consciousness and by this time the two scientists were clearly dead. 'I collected all my strength and endeavoured to raise them up. Sivel's face was black, his eyes dull, and his mouth was open and full of blood. Croce's eyes were half closed and his mouth was bloody.' Tissandier's considerable experience as an aeronaut enabled him to bring the balloon and its tragic cargo back to earth. The fact that he alone survived this ordeal by altitude is probably due in part to his own physical condition and to his greater experience in ballooning and consequent acclimatization to the conditions.

The tragedy of *Le Zénith* brought a virtual halt to atmospheric exploration until the beginning of the twentieth century, when unmanned balloons were sent to 30,000 feet to probe the lower edge of the stratosphere – an unexplored region and the point at which the air stops getting any cooler with height. This new research also confirmed earlier observations that prevailing wind currents existed at certain heights, suggesting to some that it might be possible to plot these airflows just as the mariners had plotted the great trade routes of the oceans. Perhaps a way could be found to direct a balloon to a specific destination at will – maybe even around the world?

National pride and prestige were also at stake, with several nations vying for the upper hand in stratospheric exploration. Where unmanned balloons went, men soon followed. In 1901 a German aeronaut established a new altitude record of 35,000 feet and in 1927 the United States Army topped that by sending Captain Hawthorne C. Gray up to 42,470 feet to determine the limits at which the human body can function. Unfortunately, on

April 1875: when their crude breathing apparatus proved inadequate the occupants of *Le Zénith* rapidly succumbed to the deadly effects of hypoxia. Only one survived

his return to earth Gray's balloon began falling out of control and he was forced to bale out – an action that denied him the record because the organization that governs all record-breaking attempts, the FAI (Fédération Aéronautique Internationale), established in Paris in 1905 by the embryonic national aero clubs to promote the new sport and science of flying, decrees that a pilot must stay with his craft from lift-off to landing. (It was for this reason that the Soviets lied about Yuri Gagarin's return to earth in 1961, as the first man in space had actually ejected to land separately by parachute.) Gray had another go and this time achieved 40,000 feet after writing this final entry in his log: 'Sky ordinary deep blue – sun very bright – sand all gone.' Tragically, even with his sophisticated equipment Gray had succumbed to the torpor of hypoxia, and the following day his lifeless body, still in the open gondola, was discovered on farmland in Tennessee where the balloon had come to rest.

Following this latest tragedy many scientists were convinced that a sealed casing was the only safe means of ensuring survival in such a hostile environment. Professor Auguste Piccard, a physicist more concerned with studying cosmic rays than with any notion of setting ballooning records, devised an airtight aluminium sphere, or capsule, in which to safely probe the new frontier. Approximately 7 feet in diameter, it was equipped with its own air supply fed by a cylinder of compressed oxygen which released two litres of the gas every minute and the air in circulation within the capsule was passed through a potash filter to remove the carbon dioxide. In May 1931 Piccard, together with his assistant Paul Kipfer, took their hydrogen-filled balloon to a new altitude record of 51,775 feet. On the way up the capsule developed an air leak which had to be sealed with grease and a length of hemp rope. Later it became intolerably hot inside the sphere – Piccard had painted one side of the capsule white and the other black in order to moderate the internal temperature by reflecting the heat of the sun when necessary, but the rotation mechanism which kept it properly orientated had jammed and the black side was absorbing

In the early 1930s Swiss physicist Auguste Piccard pioneered the use of the pressurized
capsule for high-altitude balloon research

too much heat. Worse still, as they prepared to descend they found
that the valve line had become twisted and the only way down was
to wait for the hydrogen to cool in the night. This it duly did and
the balloon was finally deposited on the slope of an Austrian
glacier, leaving them stranded until the morning.

At first sight Piccard's balloon bears an uncanny resemblance to the later global balloons, but in fact this is deceptive, for the 500,000-cubic-foot envelope contained only hydrogen and had no hot-air chamber. It was the business end – the pressurized capsule – that was Auguste Piccard's greatest legacy to his as yet unborn grandson Bertrand.

Piccard made a further ascent in 1932, setting another record of course, this time 53,152 feet in a flight that passed without incident: 'We could hardly have hoped for a more perfect journey. It was indeed so perfect that it became almost monotonous.' The only discomfort was the extreme cold – because the capsule had now been painted all white it reflected the sun's heat too efficiently and a frost formed inside as the temperatures dropped below freezing – and after a gentle landing the spherical capsule proceeded to roll about like a football.

Then it was the turn of Auguste's twin brother Jean who, together with his wife Jeanette, ascended to 57,000 feet in 1934. During the Second World War Auguste Piccard fled with his family from Belgium back to neutral Switzerland where he continued his research. In particular he was working on the design for his 'Bathyscaphe', a deep-sea submersible which floated under the water in much the same way as a balloon floats in the air. His son Jacques joined him on this project and together in 1953 aboard the vessel christened as *Trieste* they descended to over 10,000 feet beneath the Mediterranean. With the backing of the US Navy, in 1960 Jacques Piccard took the *Trieste* down to 35,800 feet within the Pacific's Mariana Trench, the deepest known place on earth. Auguste died in 1962, the last of a breed of scientists who could have an idea and see it through in practice. His twin brother Jean died within a year.

In part it was the exploits of the flying Piccards in the early 1930s that escalated a new tit-for-tat altitude race between two superpowers. In September 1933 the Russians' *Stratostat USSR* hydrogen balloon ascended with a two-man crew to 58,700 feet; two months later the Americans upped it to 61,221 feet with their

Auguste Piccard's stratospheric balloon of 1932 bears a striking resemblance to the
Breitling Orbiter 3 at first sight, but its 500,000-cubic-foot envelope was filled entirely
with hydrogen gas

Century of Progress, named after the world's fair in Chicago. The Russians retaliated the following year with 72,000 feet, but on their return the crew of three was killed when their steel gondola broke free and plunged to earth. In July 1935 the Americans came back but almost suffered a similar fate when their *Explorer* balloon's envelope failed in an attempt on 75,000 feet. They tried again in November with *Explorer II*, the first to use helium as a lifting gas, and this time achieved 72,395 feet. Interest in these high-rise excursions waned, however, and as the two governments garnered their resources with the prospect of a war on the horizon, they came to a halt. It would take the advent of the space race to break the ensuing hiatus.

By the late 1940s the development of new lightweight polythene envelopes had made it possible to send unmanned scientific payloads right to the edge of space and soon manned flights were resumed with the express purpose of testing the waters for future astronauts. In 1956 the US Navy's *Stratolab* took a crew of two in an open gondola up to 40,000 feet, and on another occasion to 76,000. In 1957 Captain Joe Kittinger of the US Air Force went to 96,000 feet, riding in a tiny cylindrical capsule and wearing a pressure suit that was so body-hugging he compared it to 'being loved by an octopus'. (Four years later Kittinger jumped out of a balloon at 102,800 feet – high enough to see the curving blue-purple divide between the atmosphere and the blackness of space – to freefall back into the atmosphere at speeds of up to 614 mph, eventually landing by parachute. He tells the story of how he lifted his feet as he reached the layers of cloud on the way down because it 'felt like the natural thing to do'.)

Undoubtedly these space-age aeronauts were the unsung heroes who paved the way to the stars long before any rocket-borne astronaut had left a launchpad. Ironically, these flights actually reached their zenith a month after Gagarin's historic orbit in 1961 when Americans Malcolm Ross and Victor Prather floated up to a staggering 113,740 feet. But this brief moment of glory turned to tragedy after their splashdown in the Gulf of Mexico. Prather, weighed down by his *Mercury*-style spacesuit, drowned just an arm's length away from the rescue helicopter's hook.

It had been the Victorian aeronaut James Glaisher who had summed up the unique value of the balloon as a platform for scientific observation: 'We have been enabled to ascend among the phenomena of the heavens, and to exchange conjecture for instrumental facts, recorded at elevations exceeding the highest mountains of the earth.' As well as dispelling some long held misconceptions regarding meteorology and the Earth's atmosphere, balloons had given scientists the opportunity to take measurements and to conduct tests at first hand long before any aeroplanes or rockets could achieve such heights. By the middle of the twentieth century most of our understanding of the properties of our atmosphere had been learnt through ballooning. Even today hundreds of unmanned research and meteorology balloons are released from every part of the planet on a daily basis.

4 HIGH SOCIETY

Apart from the occasional scientific forays aloft, by the end of the nineteenth century ballooning was for the most part regarded as a played-out fairground attraction. Yet it was to enjoy a remarkable renaissance when it was taken up as the latest plaything of the new wealthy young men of leisure, and for a few halcyon years balloon races became an essential feature of the Edwardian jet set – a hearty band of sporting aeronauts in whose hands the ballooning technology of the day would be pushed to its limit. Not surprisingly these activities attracted such distinguished figures as the aviator and co-founder of Rolls Royce, the Hon. Charles Rolls, and gentleman-aeronaut Frank Hedges Butler, co-founders of the Aero Club of the United Kingdom which controls the science and sport of aviation in this country. Those 'magnificent men in their flying machines' – but it was by no means an all-male preserve. The lady aeronauts were just as adventurous, as demonstrated by the Contessa Grace di Campello della Spina who ballooned over the Apennine Mountains on her honeymoon. 'Sport of the gods!' she declared after the flight. 'Who else flies over a sleeping world, through space, and knows the joy of motion without movement, without sound, without effort?'

'Without effort' was a moot point. For the moneyed Edwardian gentleman would hire a balloon from either Spencer Brothers balloon-builders at Highbury or Shorts in Battersea Park, London, at a cost of around nine guineas (the equivalent of £1,000 or so in today's terms) or maybe a bit more for a pilot if he needed one,

The Hon. Charles Stewart Rolls, pioneer balloonist, aviator and motorist, seen in this
studio photograph surrounded by the paraphernalia of Edwardian gas ballooning.
Rolls died in an aeroplane accident in July 1910
(*Royal Aeronautical Society*)

have it inflated for him with town gas at the local gas works and then take his often formally attired guests for a little jaunt. Upon landing he would give the locals a few shillings to have the balloon taken to the nearest railway station and it would be returned by train. In this way the balloon had become as much a fashion accessory as an adventure, and accordingly the stylish aeronaut could purchase beautifully crafted accessories such as rucksacks, flasks, hampers and megaphones for keeping in touch with the ground as well as the more practical niceties of sandbags, scoops for metering out the sand and even portable washbasins. The lady aeronauts were advised to furnish themselves with a change of underwear, a light volume of a favourite author and a small 'nécessaire', a receptacle to deal with any calls of nature. Ever since Blanchard's days balloonists have recognized the value of this liquid asset as ballast and it was invariably collected for disposal later in the flight – to be known euphemistically as 'golden rain'.

Members of this elite high society were the same people who embraced the other symbols of technological advance with equal gusto. They drove the newfangled automobiles, raced yachts and all too often got themselves killed flying aeroplanes. Ballooning therefore was a natural adjunct to their leisure activities and before long races were being organized throughout Europe by the newly formed aero clubs, catering to those who relished the excitement of competition tinged with the spice of danger. But how do you race balloons? As one contemporary put it: 'The length of a journey is a matter of accident; without the necessary wind, it is impossible for the greatest dexterity to be of any use. Skill can be shown if several balloons ascend at the same moment and it is a question as to who can remain in the air for the longest time.' In island Britain long distance was not always an option and instead the balloonists played variations on the 'Hare and Hounds' game where accuracy in following the leader was paramount. But not so on the continent.

When Count Henri de la Vaulx won one of the first long-distance races organized by the Aéro Club de France in 1900, he established an impressive new distance record of 1,193 miles flown in 36 hours. Launching from Paris, he had climbed swiftly to 18,000 feet where he rode the brisk winds eastwards all the way to Russia. Unfortunately at this time border-hopping balloonists were frequently regarded as spies and upon landing the Count was promptly incarcerated in one of the Tzar's jails for twenty-four hours. But conditions couldn't have been too dire as he confirmed on his return: 'The Russian officers persecuted me by opening so many bottles of French champagne that I was in great distress.'

Balloon competitions became increasingly common and although international races were still a rarity in 1905 the newly formed FAI established a set of uniform standards for competitive flying and record-breaking attempts – both for balloons and the handful of emergent aircraft. This more than anything conferred an official and international status upon the achievements of balloonists. In the same year a new patron and champion of the cause appeared in the form of the *New York Herald* publishing tycoon James Gordon Bennett. He was a larger-than-life character who had been cast out by his native New Yorkers after a string of incidents in which his eccentric lifestyle had overstepped the mark of polite society (once when drunk he had relieved himself into the grand piano at a party hosted by the family of his then fianceé). He moved to Paris to set up a French edition of the *Herald* and continued to run the New York version by cabled instructions. An avid sportsman, Gordon Bennett had already established a very successful trophy for automobiles and now he wanted to do the same for aviation. Fortunately for balloonists his proposal that all types of aerial craft were eligible to enter the race was amended by the FAI to exclude powered flight, and he later went on to establish another trophy specifically for aeroplanes.

In 1906 sixteen balloons representing seven countries lined up in the Tuileries gardens in Paris for the inaugural Coupe de Gordon Bennett long-distance competition. Among their ranks were some of the most skilful and well-off balloonists from Europe and America, including Count de la Vaulx and his rival Jacques Balsan

The Gordon Bennett balloon races became the premiere event in the gas ballooning calendar between the wars. In 1979 the Americans revived the competition and in the 1980s the Europeans also joined in the fun representing France, Rolls and Butler for Britain, and also the dapper Brazilian aviator Alberto Santos-Dumont, a pioneer of the small airship and the first man in Europe to achieve powered flight in an aeroplane. The balloons were launched at intervals determined by a lottery and initially the wind carried them south-west towards the Atlantic coast – not the best of starts – but at just the right moment it shifted and the flotilla of balloons turned north towards the more manageable waters of the English Channel.

More than half of the contestants balked at this first hurdle but seven braver souls flew onwards to England. Of these the winner, the American Army Lieutenant Frank P. Lahm, had the good fortune to make landfall over the middle of the southern coast and so he was able to continue flying much further than the others, until he too had to stop because of the North Sea and landed to the north of Hull. Lahm had flown for twenty-two hours, through one night, and had covered 402 miles. Two of the other contestants landed near the south coast, and the remaining four in Kent, Norfolk and Lincolnshire.

As the prospect of war drew nearer the heightened atmosphere of international rivalry provided the spur for several impressive new distance records. In 1913 the German balloonist Hugo Kauleu seized the crown from the French when he flew a sizzling 1,756 miles to Siberia, and the following year another German crew also flew to Siberia, pushing the distance record to 1,897 miles, one that would stand until 1977. The technology might have been more wicker work and cow intestines or rubberized fabric than high-tech, but here at last were some worthy flights which were within a hair's breadth of a transatlantic distance or, in global parlance, almost one-tenth of a circumnavigation. This was a second golden age for ballooning, and these gentlemen-aeronauts would have had little trouble in recognizing their counterparts in the likes of Richard Branson, Steve Fossett and the other millionaire adventurers of today.

Inevitably the First World War brought a pause in the proceedings. It wasn't until 1920 that the Gordon Bennett balloon races could be resumed and surprisingly they were contested with renewed vigour. However, in 1923 the competition suffered its greatest disaster. All started reasonably well with seventeen balloons assembled near the outskirts of Brussels, but as the aeronauts struggled to inflate the balloons they were lashed by torrential rain and violent gusts which hammered the balloons until one of them burst under the punishment. The Belgian officials consulted their rule-books and found that there was no provision for bad weather, so officials being officials and rules being rules they pronounced that the race must go ahead. Any sane balloonist would have called it a day, but in the heat of the competitive moment they all went for broke.

The angry sky was blackened with thunderclouds when the balloonists began their precarious ascents. Immediately an American balloon barged into one of the unlaunched Belgian entries, badly ripping its net and forcing the Belgians to retire. They were the fortunate ones. A French team decided to climb above the weather and after dropping 600 lb of ballast their balloon soared so high that they encountered blizzard conditions and the weight of the ice and snow sent the balloon hurtling back down again, forcing them to clamber into the rigging to avoid injury when the basket smashed into the ground. Others fared even worse. The Swiss balloon was struck by lightning, instantly igniting the hydrogen into a fireball and sending the two-man crew 1,000 feet to their deaths. Then a Spanish balloon was also struck, killing one pilot outright, and the other suffered two broken legs in the ensuing plunge to earth. Three hours into their flight the Americans had reached the Netherlands when they were also struck by lightning and the crew died as the balloon tumbled out of the sky. The final roll-call revealed that six balloons had been destroyed, five balloonists had been killed, five others were injured and two more had been rescued from the sea off the Danish coast.

In the remaining interwar years a further fourteen Gordon Bennett races were held despite the ascendance of the aeroplane. The last of the great pre-Second World War Coupe de Gordon

Bennett races took place in 1937 and it was won by the Polish pilot Antoni Janusz, and by convention the following year's event was to be hosted by Poland. But just one month before the balloons were due to launch, Hitler's forces invaded. War brought an end to the old world and an end to this golden era of ballooning.

After a gap of 42 years the Americans revived a similar gas balloon race, even hijacking the Gordon Bennett name, and within a few years it had once again become recognized as the premiere international gas balloon competition, and so it continues to this day.

5 WHEN THE BALLOON GOES UP

As with so many technological innovations, the balloon was not immune to the interest of the military and from its conception was exploited as an aerial platform from which to spy upon the enemy or to deliver bombs, propaganda and agents deep into hostile territory. Not for nothing did the expression 'The balloon's gone up!' come to indicate the start of hostilities, and the fortunes of that most peaceful form of aerial carriage, always at the mercy of the wind, have forever been linked to those of war.

Even before his balloons had left the ground, Joseph Montgolfier had envisaged his progeny as a means of launching a surprise attack upon the English forces that held Gibraltar. 'By making the balloon's bag large enough,' he reasoned, 'it will be possible to introduce an entire army, which, borne by the wind, will enter right over the heads of the English.' And as for Benjamin Franklin, the diplomat turned spy was anxious to keep track of political and military activities and wherever possible to strengthen the alliance between the French and the Americans. He summed up certain future military roles of the balloon when reporting that it 'may be sufficient for certain purposes, such as elevating an engineer to take a view of an enemy's army, works etc, conveying intelligence into, or from, or out of a besieged town, giving signals to distant places, or the like.' Which puts his famous comment, 'Of what use is a new born baby?' in context.

Theory was first put into practice on 2 June 1794 as the Dutch and Austrian forces advanced upon the French Revolutionary forces at the northern town of Maubeuge. From behind the wooded hills a large sphere climbed several hundred feet above the besieged town, and from its basket two French officers scanned the enemy's every movement through their telescopes. From the perspective of the twenty-first century, when every inch of the planet's surface has been scrutinized in the most minute detail, we are accustomed to the notion of aerial surveillance and it is hard to conceive the shock with which those soldiers must have greeted this new airborne adversary – the original 'eye in the sky'. If the pioneering balloonists had been lacking a sense of purpose, then warfare certainly provided one and the balloon had become its latest, if perhaps the most unlikely, recruit.

Despite its initial successes the balloon had a rather patchy career in Emperor Napoleon's army. A grandiose scheme for a three-pronged invasion of England complete with a flotilla of troop-carrying balloons arriving by air, a fleet of surface vessels on the Channel and, way ahead of its time, a tunnel passing underneath it, was never put into operation. And when Napoleon took a balloon with him on his Egyptian campaign he was not inclined to have it even unloaded from the ship.

More than half a century later it was on the other side of the Atlantic that the balloon really proved its worth. At the outbreak of the American Civil War in 1861 several of the established balloonists offered their services to the military, mostly on the Union side, and the initial rush into action was often chaotic as each undertook his own operational arrangements. Thaddeus Lowe, who had earlier held ambitions for an Atlantic flight and had been detained as a Yankee spy, was to outstrip his rivals. He won the ear of President Lincoln and consequently funding from the War Department was arranged for trial ascents. Two important innovations greatly aided this new air corps; the use of telegraph lines enabled the airborne observers to wire instant messages to the ground, and the development of a horse-drawn hydrogen generator made it possible to inflate a balloon in three hours. Admittedly fortunes were mixed, but the balloons did provide useful aerial

It is easy to scoff at this Napoleonic scheme for a fleet of aerial-borne invaders. But the French also planned to tunnel under the Channel to get their troops to England. So who's laughing now?

reconnaissance on many occasions. Once however, Lowe flew over the Confederate lines to be shot at by their troops and then drifted back again on a higher air current only to encounter 'friendly fire' from his own side mistaking him for an enemy spy.

The next theatre of war in which the balloon had a role was the Prussians' Siege of Paris in 1870–71 during which sixty-six balloons escaped from the beleaguered city – an essential life-line to the outside world carrying half a million letters and countless homing pigeons which would be sent back to the Parisians with vital micro-dot messages taped to their legs. The Prussians, antagonized by this exodus over their heads, retaliated with a swivel-mounted anti-aircraft gun, forcing the balloonists to make all future flights under cover of darkness. Remarkably, despite the dual hazards of hostile fire and the vagaries of the elements, all but eight of the balloons launched from Paris landed safely and in friendly territory. The longest flight was that of two aeronauts whisked 800 miles across the North Sea to central Norway.

Despite their good performance in the role of aerial surveillance in several other war zones, including the Boer War, by the early years of the twentieth century, with the ascendance of the aeroplane, it looked as if time was up for the balloon. However, the stalemate of entrenched warfare in the First World War brought the observation balloon into its own again in directing artillery shelling and watching the enemy's movements. German ingenuity transformed the traditional spherical shape into the elongated kite balloon which, with its stabilizing air-filled tail, could fly at greater heights and in much windier conditions. The appearance of these balloons became a sure harbinger of an imminent offensive and as an attractive stationary target they spawned a new style of flying ace, the 'balloon buster'. Consequently the defenceless observer became the only airman allowed a parachute – rigged on a fixed line, a policy based on the dubious assumption that aircraft pilots might not give their all if so equipped, and one that resulted in the pointless loss of many lives in a war that was epitomized by its wholesale carnage.

A British observation balloon is carefully moved into a new position during the Boer War

In the Second World War the sight of similar unmanned kite balloons made the beleaguered home front feel that little bit safer. Originally they were conceived of as a curtain straddling the sky – a row of barrage balloons linked by a drapery of cables – not such a clever idea as the cables often ended up wrapped around the homes of the people they were meant to defend. Instead the skies over London, and other industrial centres and ports, were peppered with hundreds of individual balloons, each operated by a dedicated team of men and, increasingly as the war went on, women. The main role of these balloons is often misunderstood. Yes, their cables would clip the wings of any marauding pilots foolish enough to fly into their embrace (and it has to be confessed, more than one allied aircraft also came a cropper in this way), but their primary function was to keep the bombers high in order to reduce their accuracy and to locate them within a predetermined height range in which the anti-aircraft guns could more easily pick them off. That they were more than an inconvenience to the Germans is evident by the counter-measures that they developed, such as protective wing shields that deflected the cable away from the engines and into strong cutters on the tips of the wings. But even though these devices worked moderately well in tests, their added weight made them unpopular among the Luftwaffe hierarchy.

To present a more user-friendly face to civilians, especially children who might have found them menacing, the balloons were portrayed in illustrated story books as either *Boo Boo the Barrage Balloon* or *Blossom* and *Bulgy*. But the barrage balloon also had a nasty streak and many offensive roles were devised for Boo Boo's chums. In one of these they were dispatched on favourable winds to the Continent trailing long cables designed to damage enemy powerlines and communications. There was a short-lived scheme known as the Free Barrage Balloon, dozens being sent aloft in the path of approaching enemy formations. Each balloon trailed an explosive device at the end of a long piano wire. In theory, when an enemy aircraft got caught on the wire it would slide across the wing until the explosives found their target. Unfortunately, such clandestine operations were also secret to the civilian population and on more than one occasion, the morning after a raid, people would find their homes draped with the wires. In some cases there was a real risk from explosives going off in the wrong hands, and so the scheme was soon abandoned.

The idea of a flying bomb was nothing new. The Austrians had used the balloon in this way in the Siege of Venice during the Italian War of Independence in 1849 when they launched a cloud of small balloon bombs fitted with time fuses, but the capricious winds turned them roundabout in mid-air, sending them back again. In the Second World War the Japanese became experts at this form of aerial bombardment. Incendiary devices were carried aloft by paper balloons equipped with rudimentary automatic ballasting systems and known as FuGos. Starting in 1944, more than 9,000 were launched to ride the transpacific jetstream with the intention of setting America's eastern forests ablaze and thus bringing its population to its knees. At first the American authorities believed that the balloons were being launched from on or near their own west coast as they could not believe that they had crossed the Pacific. The few devices found intact did not seem to carry enough ballast for a long Pacific crossing. Yet the analysis of that sand ballast by geologists proved beyond doubt that their origin was indeed in Japan, and the existence of the high-altitude fast jet-stream winds was also confirmed by secret US Air Force studies conducted to investigate the risk of fallout dispersion to the USA if an atomic bomb were dropped on Japan.

At least 285 of the FuGos are known to have reached the American mainland. However, the propaganda value was nullified by the US authorities who, remembering the widespread panic that ensued after Orson Welles's 1938 dramatization of a Martian invasion of New York, kept the news under wraps. It was also fortunate that the Japanese had made a fundamental error; the time of year when the jetstream is most reliable in the northern hemisphere is the winter – when the tilt of the earth's axis causes the warm tropical air to move northwards and push against the cooler arctic air moving downwards, creating the west to east jetstream currents – the very time when America's forest areas are either covered in snow or damp with rain water. The few FuGos that started small fires were dealt with by the emergency services and the American public remained blissfully unaware that it was being bombed. This secrecy turned one family picnic into tragedy when a woman and five children were killed after accidentally triggering a bomb that had come down near Bly in Oregon. These were the only deaths on the American continent resulting from enemy action during the Second World War.

During the Cold War years, unmanned balloons regularly rode the jetstream across Russian airspace carrying extensive photographic payloads to examine the Soviet Union's deepest reaches long before satellites roamed the skies. Launched in Germany, Turkey and occasionally Scotland, those that survived the long flight were picked up in the Pacific. Inevitably many of those that

didn't make it home came down in Russian territory and not surprisingly the Russians howled in protest, putting the remnants on
display in Moscow for all the world to see. The Americans'
response was that these were harmless weather balloons, but both
sides knew better and the Russians instigated a concerted fighter
defence against the invaders.

In the Second World War the British had sometimes used small
balloons to place another payload into occupied territory – their
agents. These hydrogen-filled balloons were usually inflated on
ships in the North Sea off the coast of German-occupied mainland
Europe. The 'passenger' would ride in a small basket or on a lightweight platform and at the appropriate location would vent gas to
bring the balloon to earth before stepping off, leaving it, and any
evidence of his arrival, to float downwind for many hundreds of
miles. The degree of success of these agent-carrying balloons is
hard to ascertain, but for their occupants the flight was just one of
many risks they faced on these clandestine missions. During the
Cold War years other bodies concerned with covert operations also
turned to the balloon to fulfil a similar function. Under cover of
the US Office of Naval Research (ONR), and ostensibly at least as
a means of rescuing downed fighter pilots, the CIA was taking a
closer look at this application. And from that research a new generation of hot-air balloons was born out of the combination of
modern lightweight materials with propane gas to supply the heat.
Unpalatable as it may be, the balloon, which had originally been
conceived as a child of warfare by Joseph Montgolfier, enjoyed its
greatest resurgence as a direct result of the Cold War and the needs
of the military.

At an abandoned and remote bomber-training base in Bruning,
Nebraska, the very first of the new balloons made its maiden flight
on 21 October 1960. It was a simple affair, an almost spherical
envelope with a volume of 27,000 cubic feet and constructed of a
translucent plastic film beneath which were suspended two small
liquid propane fuel tanks, a crude burner and a short piece of
wooden planking. Sitting astride this was Ed Yost. Working for the

General Mills Company, Yost had built high-altitude gas balloons to drop propaganda leaflets behind the Iron Curtain. Now he was to become the first 'propane man' – a latter-day Montgolfière pilot lifted aloft on pure hot-air.

With the burner working continuously Yost rode the balloon up to 500 feet where it levelled off and after ten minutes began a gradual descent. Following some modifications to the burner and the envelope, on its next outing Yost flew the balloon for one hour and fifty minutes and at one point attained an altitude of 9,000 feet, landing 39 miles from the starting-point.

Despite the team's successes, ONR did not pursue this line of development any further, but Yost and his colleagues had been quick to recognize the enormous recreational potential of their craft. Instead of using hydrogen or helium gas to get airborne – the former was highly explosive and the latter highly expensive – with a few gallons of easily obtained liquid propane anyone could take up ballooning. Yost had already formed Raven Industries to work on the ONR balloon and in 1961 the company launched the first modern hot-air balloons onto the market, simple craft that inspired other balloon enthusiasts and builders throughout America and Europe. Gradually the designs were refined, especially regarding the efficiency and all-important reliability of the propane burners, and hot-air ballooning flourished into the sport and industry that now spans the world. A new generation of young aeronauts, both men and women, took up this challenging new pastime, quickly discovering and relishing a new-found and affordable freedom of the air. Not surprisingly they were keen to push the envelope, to pit themselves against the elements and against each other.

6 PUSHING THE ENVELOPE

Despite the unquestionable historical credentials of the balloon, it was to that latterday upstart, the heavier-than-air flying machine, that the Atlantic ocean, the great barrier between the old and the new worlds, was to succumb. First across were the 'pond-hoppers', the US Navy's Curtis flying boats, and more famously ex-RAF pilot and navigator John Alcock and Arthur Witten Brown completed the job non-stop in June 1919 when their *Vickers Vimy* biplane, a converted First World War heavy bomber, ended up nose down in a bog after crossing the Irish coast at Clifden, Co. Galway. Then in 1926 Charles Lindbergh, an unknown airmail pilot from rural Minnesota, achieved a truly heroic solo crossing when he flew his monoplane *Spirit of St Louis* across the wide ocean to link the two great cities of New York and Paris. Immortalized in the public eye as the 'Lone Eagle', overnight Lindbergh became the most famous man on earth.

Not to be entirely left out, lighter-than-air craft had in fact notched up the first double crossing in 1919 with the British airship *R34* only a couple of weeks after Alcock and Brown's flight. (It is said that in those more gentlemanly times a sense of good sportsmanship delayed the airship's flight until after Alcock and Brown had succeeded.) Pioneered by the German Count Ferdinand von Zeppelin, these cigar-shaped aerial leviathans consisted of a lightweight rigid frame which contained within it a number of individual gas cells or balloons. Accommodation for the crew was within the lower hull itself and the control cars and engine pods were suspended underneath it. The *R34* was actually a copy of a felled First World War Zeppelin. Complete with the first transatlantic stowaways, one crewman and one cat, it flew from east to west, refuelled in America and flew back again. By the late 1920s and early 1930s the Zeppelin company had established scheduled transatlantic passenger flights by airship decades ahead of any airliners and all in a degree of comfort unequalled to this day. It was a halcyon era of airship travel and one that came to a dramatic and abrupt end with the fiery destruction of the *Hindenburg* at Lakehurst, New Jersey, in 1936. Whatever the initial spark that caused the fire, the fact of the matter was that the hydrogen had ignited and the image of the airship's dying moments was seared on the public's collective consciousness forever.

But what of balloons? Several Victorians had made plans to take on the Atlantic but each had either become embroiled in the American Civil War or been thwarted by the lack of sufficient financial backing. One exception was jubilantly announced in 1844 when the *New York Sun* published the report of a transatlantic balloon flight from Wales to South Carolina, but this turned out to be a hoax penned by Edgar Allan Poe. Incredibly it was not until the 1950s that a serious assault on the Atlantic Ocean was mounted, and it would be almost two centuries after the first balloon flight that someone actually succeeded.

Despite its unforgiving nature, its cold and deadly embrace, the Atlantic and the challenge to cross it by balloon has for some inexplicable reason always held a magnetic attraction for a particular breed of dreamers – impulsive explorers with little or no previous experience of ballooning. There was always an underlying perception that flying a balloon with the prevailing wind from the USA to Europe couldn't be that difficult – a foolhardy notion that cost some their lives. So it was that the first team to set off in a balloon across the wide waters was made up of four British mariners who were complete newcomers to ballooning. Colin Mudie had devised a 15 foot boat/gondola – sturdy enough to survive a

splashdown if need be and capable of then being sailed to safety –
to be suspended beneath a 53,000-cubic-foot silver and black
hydrogen-filled balloon of conventional design and collectively
christened *The Small World.* Despite being given a bad press by the
Hindenburg incident, hydrogen is still widely used for gas ballooning, especially in Germany where its supply is cheap and plentiful
compared with inert helium which is much more expensive. If
handled correctly hydrogen is perfectly safe for balloonists' purposes and my own experiences with gas ballooning have all been
with hydrogen-filled balloons.

With his wife Rosemary, together with Bushy Eiloart and son
Tim, Mudie ascended from the Canary Islands off north-west
Africa in December 1958, bound for the Americas on the South
Atlantic trade winds that travel from east to west. A degree of con-
troversy continues to surround their flight – after all, launching
from an island wasn't quite the done thing – but officially at least
they flew *The Small World* for four days and covered 1,200 miles
of ocean before ditching in a violent storm and completing the
remaining stretch as a boat. Undeniably it had been a brave
attempt and their greatest contribution to transoceanic ballooning, the design of the ocean-going gondola, was a feature copied
on most subsequent attempts.

In the 1960s the Atlantic escaped virtually scot-free with one
attempt aborted when the balloon burst during inflation and
another was left high and dry when the balloon became becalmed
after achieving a meagre fifty miles at sea. By the 1970s, however,
the resurgence of interest in hot-air ballooning had spawned a new
generation of ballooning enthusiasts including a clutch of transatlantic hopefuls who were soon setting off from America at the rate
of two a year and in an ever-increasing variety of craft.

First to go was an American couple, Rodney and Pamela
Anderson, who as complete newcomers to ballooning also
recruited the British balloonist Malcolm Brighton to join them on
the flight. They had equipped themselves with a hybrid balloon in
an attempt to emulate Pilâtre de Rozier's combination gas and hot-

air concept of two centuries earlier. Traditionally the gas balloon had been regarded as the only solution for long-distance flights, but flying one is a delicate balancing act between conserving a finite supply of gas, to be valved off when it has expanded in the heat of the day, and of ballast to be disposed of during the cool of the night when the gas contracts. The result is a vicious circle with a one-way downward spiral. If either gas or sand run out, then it is all over. At least that was the received wisdom. The Andersons' balloon, *The Free Life*, built by Mark Semich of Semco Balloons in the USA, harnessed inert helium gas, instead of the deadly hydrogen that de Rozier had used, contained in an internal envelope or cell which was itself enclosed within an outer skin to be filled with heated air. This would act as a replenishable form of heat ballasting to maintain altitude and although the theory was sound, unfortunately the heater system for the air space failed in the haste to get the balloon launched on 20 September 1970. Just 30 hours later a last radio message from *The Free Life* indicated that they were east of Newfoundland and going down in a storm. The rest was silence and no survivors or wreckage were ever found.

Three years later the American balloonist Bobby Sparks set off in another Semich-built hot-air/helium combination balloon, *Yankee Zephyr*. Once again the flight terminated in a violent storm, although Sparks was fortunately rescued. Undeterred, he tried again two years later, this time complete with a stowaway – his chief crewman who had failed to let go. The unexpected additional weight did not help matters and when the envelope began to leak Sparks found himself in the water once more.

All these flights had been relatively low-altitude affairs. The first attempt with the intention of entering the jetstream winds began in February 1974 when another American balloonist, Thomas Gatch, ascended in *Light Heart*, a pressurized spherical capsule hoisted aloft beneath a cluster of ten helium balloons. Despite several radio contacts over the following days with airliners passing high above the Atlantic, and a sighting by a freighter at 25° N and 32.5° E – almost three-quarters of the way to Africa – the balloon disappeared. An immediate air and ground search was initiated in the eastern Sahara, but it is most likely that Gatch was lost at sea. One year later the American publishing tycoon Malcolm Forbes, of *Forbes Magazine*, together with co-pilot Tom Heinsheimer, prepared to lift off from California with a similar string of helium balloons. But in gusty conditions the *Windborne* became unmanageable and the diligent crew cut the balloons free before anyone was injured.

By contrast the next four attempts were all with conventional helium-filled balloons. In June 1976 the American Karl Thomas was airborne in *Spirit of '76* for 550 miles before coming down in storms, and in October 1976 hot-air pioneer Ed Yost flew the *Silver Fox*, which he had built himself, to within 700 miles of Portugal before northerly winds forced him to abandon his attempt. Inspired by a magazine account of Yost's flight, two balloonists from Albuquerque, New Mexico – Maxie Anderson and Ben Abruzzo – lifted off one year later in another Yost-built balloon, *Double Eagle*, which they had named in tribute to Charles Lindbergh. After a gruelling helter-skelter ride lasting 64 hours they ditched in a severe storm off the coast of Iceland having covered a record-breaking distance of 2,950 miles. A month later two more Americans tried in yet another Yost balloon, *Eagle*, but they also crashed in storm conditions after a mere 220 miles. Having got so close to their goal, Anderson and Abruzzo vowed to try again and by the following summer they were ready to go, this time with a third crewman, hang-glider pilot Larry Newman who, if all went to plan, would be released in his hang-glider over Europe. But the Brits were out to beat them to it.

The Scotsman Don Cameron had already made a name for himself as a balloon-constructor, and having long considered the problem of extended balloon flight he too took his inspiration from Pilâtre de Rozier's combination gas and hot-air balloon of 1784. Cameron's design featured an ice cream cone profile, with the ball of ice cream represented by the helium-filled gas cell and the cone by the hot-air section heated by small propane burners situated just above the capsule. This configuration allowed the hot-air to warm the helium – either to prevent it cooling at night to stop the balloon sinking, or in order to ascend during the day. If the pilots needed to make the balloon descend they could also release some helium from the gas cell. As a tribute to the first aeronaut and originator of the concept Cameron christened this configuration the 'Rozière' – a name that has since stuck to all balloons of this type.

To tackle the Atlantic Cameron had courted the sponsorship of the domestic appliance manufacturer Zanussi through Alan Noble, a former journalist, marketing man and balloonist, who took on the role of Flight Director for this project and who would later become a prime mover in the global race. As his co-pilot Cameron chose army major and fellow balloonist Christopher Davey, and on 26 July 1978 the two Britons beat their American rivals into the air when *Zanussi* launched from St John's, Newfoundland, on course for Europe. At first all went well, then on the second day the bottom of the internal inner helium cell membrane split with a sound like a pistol shot. Despite their initial alarm, the two men discovered that the outer main envelope remained intact without losing the precious helium, and they managed to control the balloon enough to limp on towards their goal. But by the fifth day aloft *Zanussi* had become marooned in gentle winds in the Bay of Biscay only 108 miles from the coast of France, and with thunderstorms threatening to erupt around them the exhausted and demoralized duo splashed down. Having actually flown further than Alcock and Brown did on their crossing, the two balloonists were appropriately dubbed by the British press the 'unlucky devils'.

And as if to prove it, just two weeks later on 11 August 1978, the *Double Eagle II* was on its way and after 35 hours the Americans touched down in a wheatfield near Miserey in Normandy. Abruzzo, Anderson and Newman had travelled over 3,000 miles in a flight that had pushed their helium balloon to its limits, forcing them to jettison all loose equipment, including

Newman's hang-glider, to maintain altitude on the last stretch over the British Isles to France. Like Lindbergh before them they were fêted as heroes and that night at the American Embassy in Paris the three men drew lots to decide who would sleep in Lindbergh's bed. Newman won, but he spent most of the night on the floor because the famous bed felt too soft after so many nights of sleeping aboard the balloon.

This transatlantic crossing was made possible by successfully identifying the low-level meteorological situation over the Atlantic and riding with it. With that realization, other successful crossings followed. In 1984 the American Joe Kittinger, famed for his 102,800-foot parachute jump, became the first to do the Atlantic crossing solo when he flew the *Rosie O'Grady* helium balloon all the way to Italy. Two years later the Dutch balloonist Henk Brink became the first European to make the crossing on his second attempt. Together with his wife Evelien in a Cameron Rozière, the flying Dutchman landed within sight of his home near IJmuiden in Holland.

No longer an insurmountable barrier, the Atlantic had instead become the sports ground of the balloonist and soon endurance and distance records were falling like ninepins under the Rozière's dominance. Such was the confidence in this system that in September 1992 a batch of five identical Cameron Rozières set off from Bangor, Maine, to race with the wind to Europe in the Transatlantic Challenge, sponsored by the car giant Chrysler and masterminded by Alan Noble. These were relatively small balloons with a volume of just 77,000 cubic feet and the two-man crews rode in small unpressurized capsules for a relatively low-level crossing. Two of the teams didn't make it – the Germans were forced to ditch in mid-Atlantic and the Dutch team did so just off the Scilly Isles. That left three others including the winning team who had been the first to make landfall, the 'Belgians' – although it comprised just one Belgian, balloonist Wim Verstraeten, his inexperienced co-pilot being from Switzerland. Bertrand Piccard, a charismatic young man with chiselled features and a high forehead

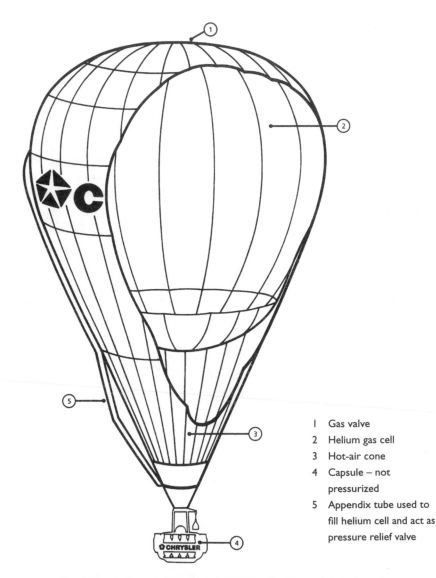

1 Gas valve
2 Helium gas cell
3 Hot-air cone
4 Capsule – not
   pressurized
5 Appendix tube used to
   fill helium cell and act as
   pressure relief valve

The Rozière balloon devised for the 1992 Chrysler Transatlantic Balloon Race provided
a blueprint for a new generation of combination balloons with hot-air
(in the lower cone area) warming the gas in the upper sphere.
See page 90 for a cutaway of the capsule
(*Cameron Balloons*)

above piercing blue eyes, had earned his wings as a champion hang-glider flier first and foremost, but he was also the grandson of the famous stratospheric balloonist Auguste Piccard and son of undersea explorer Jacques Piccard. Clearly a man with a destiny to fulfil, Piccard hit it off with Verstraeten from the start and together they made a good team. So not surprisingly after their success in the Transatlantic Challenge their thoughts readily turned to an even greater challenge.

'Back in Europe, people asked us what we planned to do next,' recounts Piccard. 'Almost as a joke we said we were going to fly round the world.' It was a joke they shared on a visit to King Baudouin of Belgium – just as Piccard's grandfather had talked to Baudouin's elder brother King Leopold in the 1930s about his plans to fly a balloon to the stratosphere. Afterwards the two young men turned to each other and they knew at that moment that they had no option but to chase this fantastic dream. But they were not alone.

Part two

GOING GLOBAL

'The way the public sees it is this. If we don't leave, we are idiots.
If we do leave but don't succeed in our mission we are incompe-
tent. But if we do succeed it's because anyone could have done it.'

Bertrand Piccard, 1999

7 THE SPIRIT OF JULES VERNE

A circumnavigation is defined by the FAI as a non-stop flight that begins and ends at the same line of longitude, although not necessarily at the same latitude, and covers a minimum distance corresponding to two-thirds of the largest circle around the Earth, the circumference at the Equator, which equates to roughly 16,600 miles or 26,700 kilometres. This latter stipulation is to prevent any cunning balloonist flying a small circle near the Poles and claiming the record. At the very minimum the balloon must fly below the 60° northern latitude or above the 60° southern latitude, or their equivalent allowing for the Earth's tilt, if it is to achieve a sufficient distance.

So what does it take to fly a balloon around the world – a journey from 'A to A' that relies on the vagaries of the air currents, that might last anything from two to three weeks or more and all without refuelling? Much of the answer lies in getting the four 'Ms' right – Man (or woman of course), Machine, Meteorology and Money. Without any one of the first three you won't succeed, and without the fourth it will always be a lot harder. But perhaps a fifth M, a Measure of good fortune, is needed to bring all these factors together at the right time.

The lure of the global balloon challenge attracted a wide variety of contenders from the millionaire adventurers to the simply adventurous. United by a common vision, most of them knew the very real dangers that they faced and while some were among the most experienced balloonists in the world, some had never been

near a balloon before the start of the adventure. And yes, by the
conclusion of this story the flight crews will have been exclusively
male, although there were certainly some women teams looking
for backers and no doubt their time will come.

Undoubtedly the proving ground for long-distance ballooning
had been the Atlantic ocean, and although the first crossing had
been by conventional helium balloon, *Double Eagle II*, in 1978,
the Rozières had come to dominate the scene. By the culmination
of the Chrysler Transatlantic Race in 1992 a total of seven
Rozières, all of them constructed by Cameron Balloons in Bristol,
England, had successfully crossed the pond. The only other types
of balloons ever to make an Atlantic crossing, even now, were the
helium balloons of the first and second crossing and a single later
flight by hot-air. So it was no surprise that the majority of the
global teams would choose the Rozière for their attempts. But one
balloonist was determined that the Rozières wouldn't have it
entirely their own way.

   In 1987 Per Lindstrand, a former Swedish Air Force pilot who
had turned his skills to manufacturing and flying balloons,
teamed up with the high-profile British millionaire adventurer
Richard Branson. Having recently claimed back the blue riband
for Britain with the fastest crossing of the Atlantic by boat,
Branson was intrigued by Lindstrand's scheme to take on the
crossing with a hot-air balloon for the first time by flying in the
fast jetstream winds at around 30,000 feet. The two men
launched from Maine on 2 July 1987 riding in a pressurized aluminium capsule in order to survive at such heights, suspended
beneath the massive *Virgin Atlantic Flyer* hot-air balloon. The
result was a high-speed crossing of just 31 hours and 40 minutes,
about half the time of any previous lower altitude attempt, which
ended in high drama when they bumped into the mainland of
Ireland before splashing down in the Irish Sea. Lindstrand
jumped from the capsule, Branson didn't. The lightened balloon

then shot back up into the clouds with Branson the sole occupant before it gradually drifted back for a second splashdown. A helicopter came for Branson who immediately said to his rescuers: 'Where's Per?' They found him still in the water a few miles back, attempting to swim for his life and the Irish coast in little more than his underpants. Undeterred, in 1991 the two teamed up again to complete the oceanic double with a successful flight across the Pacific in an even bigger hot-air balloon, finally landing on a frozen lake in Canada despite accidentally jettisoning a third of their fuel on the way. Although they were not the first across the Pacific ocean – that honour had gone to Ben Abruzzo's *Double Eagle V* gas balloon team ten years earlier – Lindstrand's and Branson's two transoceanic flights were especially significant in the lead-up to the global race in proving that it was possible to fly a manned balloon in the jetstream.

Originally identified by the Japanese balloon bombers and by the USAF's atomic fallout studies in the Second World War, the jetstream is the balloonist's fast lane and represents the most likely key to a successful round-the-world flight. These bands of wind encircle the globe at around 30,000 feet at speeds of up to 200 mph. Caused, as explained in Chapter 5, by air movements from the cold polar regions squeezing against warmer air spreading outwards from the tropics, they generally move from west to east because of the effect of the Earth's rotation. They also tend to be highly seasonal because the movement of the polar air depends upon the reduced influence of the Sun caused by the tilt of the Earth's axis and hence they are strongest in the northern hemisphere from around mid-November to mid-March and in the southern hemisphere during its winter months.

While it is perfectly feasible to attempt a circumnavigation at lower altitudes than those where the jetstream occurs, such a flight will inevitably be slower and take place entirely within the 'ordinary' weather systems – a risky and unpredictable business; whereas, in theory at least, the jetstream fliers riding in a pressurized capsule will be above the worst of the weather. But high-altitude flight isn't all

plain sailing as the jetstreams behave more like a constantly chang-
ing river system than a conveyor belt, with their own currents and
tributaries which sometimes go off in the wrong direction or lead
to dead ends. Only consummate skill and a certain amount of luck
on the part of the meteorologists, predicting events on the other side
of the world up to two weeks ahead, will enable a balloon team to
navigate those aerial waters.

Although the cost of the round-the-world balloon attempts
made in the 1990s varied enormously, launching any project on
this sort of scale wasn't going to be cheap. Balloon-builder Don
Cameron estimates that each attempt might have cost anything up
to two million pounds. 'There are a lot of parts to this including
building the balloon, managing the flight itself and the logistics of
moving the equipment and so many people about the world to
where they are needed.' Understandably it therefore required the
involvement of high-profile companies such as Virgin or Cable &
Wireless, and the lesser known Breitling, to underwrite such an
undertaking. The 'shoestring' projects were financed either
through private money or, in one case, by the pilot remortgaging
everything he owned.

Before the main surge of global activity in the 1990s there were
several earlier attempts using conventional gas balloons and a
handful of hybrid oddities, which all failed abysmally.

As early as 1964, the American journalist David Royce
announced plans for project *Gulliver* – a tall slender helium
balloon which he would fly around the world in stages. To anyone
with the slightest understanding of ballooning it was quite clear
that Royce had none whatsoever as he proposed to make the epic
flight over a twelve-month period, hopping from one location to
another and anchoring the balloon at convenient stop-off points.
'This type of tour, with its built-in welcomes, seems like the best
way to meet people the world over,' he commented. However, the
chances of successfully mooring a large helium balloon after

landing time and time again were just about zero, and the *Gulliver* concept remained on the drawing board.

Another project being floated at about this time anticipated, in theory at least, the winning global formula with unerring accuracy – nineteen years before the successful flight. *Innovation* was an all-British project sponsored by ICI. In an article published in 1980 in *Aerostat*, the journal of the British Balloon and Airship Club, then editor and coincidentally Project Director for *Innovation* Alan Noble summed it up: 'Travelling in jetstream winds at average speeds of 100 mph and up to 40,000 ft high, the crew will fly in a gondola suspended beneath the 1,000,000 cu. ft combination helium hot-air balloon.'

The four-man crew for the epic *Innovation* flight was to have been Don Cameron, balloonists Julian Nott and Peter Bohanna, and cameraman Leo Dickinson. Cameron Balloons were to build the envelope and the construction of the cylindrical two-tier aluminium capsule was in the hands of the College of Aeronautics at Cranfield. ICI even offered to supply some of the materials, but the project floundered when the company began to feel the bite of the mid-1980s recession. Suddenly it was no longer good PR to be supporting a project of this nature.

For Julian Nott the global dream wasn't so easily dismissed. Holder of several ballooning records, including the hot-air altitude record, Nott devised his own round-the-world project, *Endeavour*, conceived as another high-altitude flight but this time using what is known as a 'super-pressure' balloon – a sealed helium envelope shaped like a pumpkin and strong enough to contain any expansion of the gas. Nott, along with Australian co-pilot Spider Anderson, proposed to ride the jetstream in a lightweight pressurized circular capsule 8 feet across, constructed of Kevlar and a polyester resin by the *Endeavour* team in London.

Described by the *Evening Standard* as a '*Boys Own* bachelor hero', Nott spent much of the 1980s chasing funding. In 1984 a one-third size prototype took the two pilots 1,500 miles across Australia, although it is doubtful that the envelope did function as

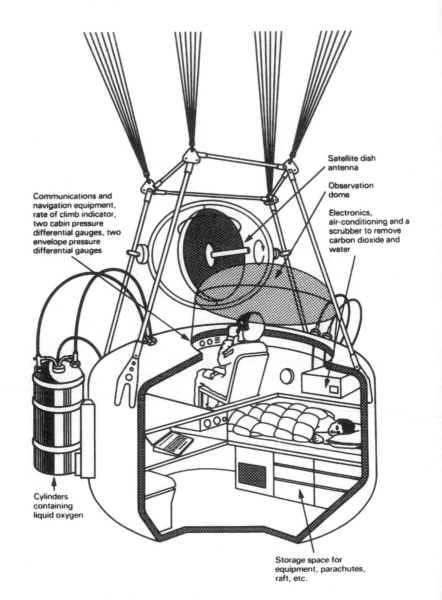

Satellite dish antenna

Observation dome

Electronics, air-conditioning and a scrubber to remove carbon dioxide and water

Communications and navigation equipment, rate of climb indicator, two cabin pressure differential gauges, two envelope pressure differential gauges

Cylinders containing liquid oxygen

Storage space for equipment, parachutes, raft, etc.

Global ballooning 1980s style. Designed by engineer John Ackroyd, this 8-foot diameter pressurized two-man capsule for Julian Nott's attempt was to be constructed of lightweight Kevlar and epoxy resin
(Julian Nott)

a super-pressure balloon on this flight; in effect it behaved as a conventional gas balloon. By 1988, when Nott appeared at a series of international press conferences to announce a launch scheduled for the following March, the project had evolved into another hot-air/hybrid design under the new title *Explorer*. But a dispute arose with the manufacturers and the envelope never left the factory.

The first of the global balloons to get airborne had actually done so several years earlier. On 11 January 1981, Maxie Anderson of the historic *Double Eagle II* Atlantic crossing, together with fellow American co-pilot Don Ida, lifted off in the appropriately named *Jules Verne* balloon from Luxor, Egypt, a location chosen to help them avoid Russian airspace. Their plan had been to fly the 408,000-cubic-foot helium-filled polythene envelope, built by Raven Industries in the USA, at around 20,000 feet to catch the lower edge of the jetstream. It was an ambitious scheme as their open gondola meant the two men would have to breathe from oxygen masks for most of the flight. Yet it was clear from the start that Anderson himself had little confidence in making a circumnavigation non-stop. 'We will complete the voyage even if forced to land a time or two.' And indeed, the leaking envelope forced them to terminate the flight in India, where they returned one year later to start the second stage, although poor weather curtailed this attempt after just 20 miles in the air. On their third attempt they launched from South Dakota and managed a respectable 1,162 miles. But in 1983 both men were killed when the release mechanism for their gas balloon envelope malfunctioned during the revived Gordon Bennett race, launching on this occasion from Paris to commemorate the 200th anniversary of the first balloon flight.

Project *SHARE* (*Southern Hemisphere Aerostat Research Expedition*) was another of many variations on a gas/hot-air hybrid and the first of these to attempt a global flight. Devised by American businessman John Petrehn who wanted to make the flight in order to raise $6.4 million for charity, the *SHARE* balloon consisted of a pair of helium balloons mounted in tandem above a conventional hot-air balloon. Petrehn and his co-pilot, Colonel Towland Smith, would ride within a spherical pressurized capsule high into the southern hemisphere jetstream. They decided to launch from Mendoza in Argentina, a site selected because of the shelter offered by the Andes Mountains and its position directly under the jetstream, but an attempt to get off in March 1988 almost came to grief when one of the army-surplus helium balloons tore during inflation. Petrehn vowed to try again, but in 1990 he died of a heart attack at the age of 55.

By the early 1990s the most prominent project on the global scene relied on an entirely different and perhaps unlikely alternative to the Rozière theme. Led by another *Double Eagle II* veteran, Larry Newman, *Earthwinds* had a most extraordinary configuration designed by Tim Lachenmeirer of Raven Industries – a helium balloon above an inverted cold-air ballast or 'anchor' balloon with a pressurized capsule linking the two, the whole affair resembling a vast hourglass. During the day air would be pumped into the lower balloon to provide extra weight and then during the cold of the night, as the helium contracted, this air ballast would be pumped out again. In the same way the quantity of air could be added to or reduced in order to change altitude as required. As a solution to the problem of replenishable ballast this scheme certainly had some merit but, as is often stated in engineering circles, if something doesn't look right then it probably isn't. And *Earthwinds* looked far from right. One of the main problems was launching the awkward double envelopes with the capsule situated in the middle between the two.

While the practicalities of this system had to be ironed out, at least the crew could expect to enjoy their share of creature comforts on the flight, for when Barron Hilton of the hotel empire signed up as main sponsor the 23-foot-long capsule pod, constructed of composite materials by Bert Rutan of *Voyager* fame, took on something of a four-star ambience. Thanks to one of

Climbing out of Reno, Nevada, on 12 January 1994 – the distinctive hour-glass configuration of *Earthwinds Hilton* with its upper helium balloon and lower cold-air anchor or ballast balloon

(*John Ackroyd*)

Hilton's interior designers the in-flight amenities included light-weight cushioned aluminium chairs, daily newspapers delivered by fax, first run movies, direct dial satellite phone, customized bed and bath and even a lavatory, all wrapped in a sound-absorbing insulation covering the walls. As I commented in an article at the time, 'Let's hope that they are actually airborne long enough to take in dinner and a good movie.' These proved to be prophetic words.

Newman's original flight companions included Vladimir Dzhanibekov, a Russian cosmonaut brought on board to aid in securing Russian overflight permissions, and none other than Richard Branson. However, by the time of the first launch attempt in 1992 Branson's place had been taken by the American balloonist Don Moses because, it was widely reported, the Virgin boss could not spare the time for training. (Incidentally, exactly the same reason was given by the Russians when they turned down Branson's bid to be the first Briton to ride in their *Soyez* spacecraft.) Nonetheless, Virgin's distinctive red logo appeared on the lower air-filled envelope, although it was never seen for long, as the renamed *Earthwinds Hilton*'s litany of disasters kicked off. In February 1992, the two envelopes were successfully inflated in the shelter of Goodyear's giant airship hangar at Akron, Ohio, but as they were moved outside they became twisted by gusty winds blowing off Lake Erie and the launch had to be abandoned.

December that same year, and wary of hangars the team had moved to the wide open flats of Nevada at Stead Airport, near Reno, with the balloon protected by a huge inflatable tent intended to be unzipped at the appropriate moment of launching. But as luck would have it, even before a launch could be attempted the tent was blown away taking the anchor balloon with it.

January 1993. This time the balloon got off the ground without incident but shortly into the flight it was unable to push up through a severe atmospheric inversion – a barrier encountered when warm air sits above a layer of colder air – and it drifted for approximately seven miles in the wrong direction before rubbing up against Mount Peterson. Roughly 15,593 miles short of a circumnavigation.

The *Earthwinds Hilton* team prepared to try again for the third time in November 1993. Moses's place was taken by Richard Abruzzo, the son of *Double Eagle II*'s Ben Abruzzo, but just moments before the crew were due to enter the capsule the restraining bolts driven into the crumbling concrete of the old disused runway gave way, sending the capsule 60 feet into the air and causing severe damage to the balloon in the ensuing pandemonium.

January 1994. Dzhanibekov had returned to Moscow by now and in his place was another American, the experienced balloonist Dave Melton. This time *Earthwinds Hilton* got away without incident but, as with many of the later global balloons, it set off in the wrong direction initially – heading southwest. Not a problem in itself as they expected to pick up the winds going eastward as they climbed higher. But instead the disappointed crew was forced to land after a valve in the anchor balloon became frozen. This was the longest flight yet with seven hours in the air and 202 miles covered from the launchsite.

December 1994 and *Earthwinds Hilton* made a final comeback with Newman and Melton joined by their former crew chief and capsule systems engineer George Saad. The launch went perfectly and the balloon flew east, but just four hours into the flight they experienced a catastrophic failure. 'As we went through 31,000 ft the balloon suddenly accelerated upwards,' recalls Melton. 'At first we didn't know what happened, but then we looked through the lower hatch and the ballast balloon was just hanging limp.' It had exploded under the internal pressure. The crew got their helium balloon under control and landed safely in Dixie Valley, Nevada, after a flight of 65 miles in the right direction. But the anchor balloon was in tatters and so was the project.

Talking of his experience with *Earthwinds Hilton* Newman would later confess, 'We had a tiger by the tail.' Reputedly seven million dollars had been spent on the project which had culminated in what was probably the most expensive trip in the entire history of ballooning. The engineering report on the final catastrophe demanded by principal sponsor Barron Hilton recommended that the *Earthwinds Hilton* team should abandon its unorthodox concept and look to the manufacturers of Rozière balloon systems as the only safe and viable solution. Hilton froze the funding and Richard Branson withdrew from the project.

8 ON THE BRINK

By the late 1980s interest in ballooning had reached new heights. A degree of economic prosperity in the countries of the western world had brought a host of newcomers to the sport of hot-air ballooning. I was one of these, having become involved in the early '80s, and by 1988 I had my own pilot's licence. For the manufacturers business had never been better and many were turning out an average of one balloon for every day of the year. All this activity naturally attracted the attention of the media and with it the commercial sponsors who were keen to have their names or products promoted in new ways – perhaps even through lending their name to a round-the-world attempt. And with the catalogue of difficulties besetting Larry Newman's *Earthwinds Hilton* project, the way was left open for the other teams.

Several new global wannabes were making their plans. Characterized by a dogged determination in their quest for fame and glory, they shared an unerring tendency to spurt spurious mumbo-jumbo about doing it all in the name of world peace and the brotherhood of man. Each new contender came equipped with a handful of glossy brochures, woolly press releases, rickety wooden mock-ups and an abundance of over-developed optimism. If it had been possible to float a balloon on the hot-air generated by sheer hype alone, then this global business would have been cracked in no time.

From his room in the Rolex offices in New York, British contender Julian Nott was still beavering away on new sponsorship deals for his big flight. He had originally announced his global intentions back in 1984 and he had become, as one elder statesman of ballooning put it, the only person to be introduced as 'the round-the-world balloonist' without actually doing it. Less kind souls were dubbing him as 'the Nott-round-the-world balloonist'. And this perhaps characterized the global flier's greatest dilemma. To kick-start a project you have to run something up the flagpole in the hope that a backer is going to salute it; you have to live the dream in order that others will believe in you.

The new batch of hopefuls certainly included some distinguished names in its ranks, most notably Richard Branson's ballooning chum, Per Lindstrand, who had been planning to make the trip ever since the duo's Atlantic and Pacific triumphs. 'My proposal is to use pure hot-air,' said Lindstrand. 'With active heat control you can do it with a gas balloon, but hot-air is more manoeuvrable, more challenging and more fun!'

Admittedly there were some advantages to using hot-air. Certainly it is possible to control a hot-air balloon very precisely and so to quickly take advantage of variations in windspeed or direction at different heights. But duration is the name of the global game and ordinary hot-air balloons are limited by the amount of propane fuel they can carry. To increase this payload the balloon's size increases to fantastic proportions, making it increasingly unwieldy on the launchfield. Gas balloons, on the other hand, can generally do much better but they are limited by the amount of ballast they can carry to compensate for the nightly cooling and contraction of the gas within the envelope. In time even Lindstrand would come to see the advantage of the combined system, the Rozière.

Unfortunately for the Swede, fun of any sort was in pretty short supply at this time. In November 1991 he had been ousted from his Oswestry-based Thunder & Colt balloon-building company in a bitter boardroom coup. And if that wasn't enough, the aftermath of the Pacific flight brought a series of legal wrangles with Virgin regarding equipment and additional costs. No wonder then that the special relationship between ballooning's most famous dynamic twosome had cooled somewhat, and that Richard Branson had linked his name, albeit briefly, to the *Earthwinds* project instead. By late 1992 Lindstrand was back on his business feet and getting his new company, Lindstrand Balloons, up and running with finance from businessman Rory McCarthy (and not Branson as widely assumed). In a typical gesture Lindstrand purchased an empty industrial building on the road leading to the Thunder & Colt factory, painted it bright yellow, and hoisted up a sign reading, 'For the best ballooning equipment in the world you need go no further.' But with so much on his plate, Lindstrand would have to bide his time when it came to seeking sponsorship for his own global ambitions.

While the cost of a balloon project, even on a global scale, might be small change in comparison with the Moon shots for example, with the notable exception of Branson there were not too many balloon-minded millionaires prepared to foot the bill. No surprise then that few of the global aspirants were turning their cutting edge concepts into cutting metal realities. Nonetheless, one project did emerge to bridge the wilderness years between the multiple downfalls of *Earthwinds Hilton* and the ascendance of Richard Branson's Virgin-reality publicity machine. Enter fifty-year-old helicopter instructor and balloonist Henk Brink, the flying Dutchman, who for a while became the man most likely to succeed in the global game.

With a wealth of ballooning experience, Brink had already cut his long-distance teeth on two transatlantic attempts, culminating in the successful 1986 crossing with the *Dutch Viking* Rozière balloon. It was therefore a natural progression for him to turn his thoughts to the bigger challenge, and in some ways he considered the practical side of a circumnavigation to be less difficult than flying the Atlantic. 'In theory once you're up into the jetstream the winds are regular and very strong. In that sense, flying around the world should be easier than crossing the Atlantic had been at a height where you had to deal with everything the weather throws at you. We aim to be above all that,' declared Brink. But there was still a lot to be learnt about riding the jetstream and at that time only the two Virgin ocean-hoppers had any first-hand experience.

Work had started on Brink's project in November 1991 and from the outset he wholeheartedly embraced the Rozière concept which had served him so well across the Atlantic. Christened *Columbus*, his global balloon resembled the *ICI Innovation* concept with a pressurized capsule slung beneath a 700,000 cubic-foot Rozière envelope. The capsule shell, a horizontal tube of stressed aluminium 5 mm thick and 15 feet long, was constructed by RDM Technology, a submarine-builder based in Rotterdam, and first saw the daylight in the spring of 1992 with the Cameron-built Rozière envelope following shortly after. At one end of the capsule was the cockpit area equipped with the very latest avionics and electronics for navigation and communications – including GPS (Global Positioning System), Omega, HF, UHF, VHF and Satcom – all installed by the Dutch aircraft company and major sponsor Fokker. In flight the crew could keep in touch via radio, telephone or fax, and in addition an array of mini-cameras were to beam back live pictures via satellite to Holland Television. The remainder of the capsule space served as living quarters with a single pull-out bed, a toilet, microwave oven, storage lockers for food and the safety equipment including the parachutes and emergency inflatable dinghies. Outside, the capsule was encircled by a deck structure so that the crew could access all the external equipment if required.

To satisfy his sponsors, and to ease the logistical problems, Brink elected to launch from Goffert Park in the town of Nijmegen, situated on the eastern (and supposedly less windy) side of Holland – not the best location from which to access the jetstream. The Dutch National Aviation Authority was working on his behalf arranging international air traffic clearances for the proposed route. 'We have only three no-go areas,' Brink told me. 'Yugoslavia, Iraq and Afghanistan. As long as we steer clear of them, we don't anticipate problems.'

Confidently announcing a launch date for the winter of 1992/3, Henk Brink appeared to have all the vital ingredients in place and he certainly enjoyed an enviable lead way ahead of any competitor. Unfortunately while the technology had more or less come together, the funding was becoming increasingly elusive. 'Because I'd managed to get a large group of sponsors together for the transatlantic attempts, I didn't anticipate any difficulties with this,' Brink ruefully admitted. 'If I'd known what it was going to be like I probably wouldn't have undertaken it.' He had discovered the importance of the fourth 'M'; a project such as this is driven by the flow of money, at least £1.5 million of it. And with the Dutch economy in recession, once the initial sponsorship money had dried up work on the balloon slowed to a virtual halt until the spring of 1994. Already the years were starting to tick by.

In the summer of 1994 the capsule of the *Holland Flyer*, as it had become known, was transported across the North Sea to Per Lindstrand's facilities at Oswestry, England, for an intensive five week period fitting-out the burners, fuel tanks, propane system, pressurization engines, cabin air control systems and generators; all using systems patterned after Lindstrand's Atlantic/Pacific hot-air balloons. (The only principal difference being with the four burners which were scaled down in output for their new Rozière role in warming the helium.) Propane for the burners was carried in six bulbous tanks suspended around the capsule, and these would also supply fuel for the generators and pressurization system. As with an airliner a number of inter-coolers and selector valves would provide temperature control for shirt-sleeve comfort for the crew on their voyage. 'We also installed the hyperbaric toilet,' mused Lindstrand. 'An item of significant importance for a long flight.'

Then it was back to the Fokker hangar at Schipol Airport, Amsterdam, where yet another entirely bizarre new title for the

Holland Flyer project was announced – *Folicard 700*. Henk Brink was quick to defend this name, explaining that it was a combination of the first two letters of each of the four main suppliers – Fokker, Lindstrand, Cameron and RDM. (Despite his earnest explanation I still wondered if it was some sort of joke.) Once covered with a thick layer of insulating polystyrene foam and painted silver, the high-tech capsule no longer resembled the clean lines of the original artist's impression and looked as much a mishmash of disparate elements as the new project name itself. Somehow it was all indicative of an enterprise that had gone ever so slightly off the rails. Yet underneath this skin the engineering remained sound enough and it was an upbeat Henk Brink who once more predicted a launch in the coming winter period . . .

'Everything is coming together now,' he told me when we met at the Bristol International Balloon Fiesta in August 1994. 'And now after four years' work the flight window opens this winter.' In his customary olive-green flying suit the Dutchman certainly looked the part of a global conqueror, and speaking with quiet confidence he outlined the intended route from his less than ideally situated launch site. 'A north-westerly wind should take me towards Turkey, and from there on I should pick up the subtropical jetstream towards India at around 28,000 to 40,000 ft. In theory the flight will last between five and ten days.'

Although Brink spoke in terms of only himself, he would in fact be accompanied on the flight by Lieutenant-Colonel Willem Hageman, an *F-16* pilot with the Dutch Air Force, who had been with Brink and his wife on their successful transatlantic flight. To recruit a third crew member Brink had come up with a dubious new method of selection – a competition run by the Dutch *Telegraaf* newspaper which was won by ex-military pilot Wout Bakker, emerging victorious after 1,400 applicants had been whittled down by a series of psychological tests, a survival course and proof of the ability to fly a balloon. Curiously though, Brink appeared to play down the role of the pilots by suggesting in an interview that flying a balloon was not that difficult: 'Given enough bananas I could teach a monkey to fly one.' Maybe his words were taken out of context, but it was going to take more than bananas to get the *Columbus, Holland Flyer, Folicard* into the air.

As 1994 drew to its inevitable close and the winter jetstream season arrived, the only good news for the Dutch team was the final and almost catastrophic failure of the *Earthwinds Hilton* on New Year's Eve. 'I admire Larry Newman's tenacity to keep trying,' commented Brink. 'But there comes a moment when he must say this is the wrong concept. Their design can only fly on the drawing board.' However, the bad news was that fresh global contenders were announcing their intentions all the time and even more were sure to be waiting in the wings. Brink had to take advantage of this breathing space before it vanished completely and he confidently promised, 'This year I'll kick it into the air.' And true to his word for once, in September 1995 the *Folicard* went flying. Not quite around-the-world, however – it flew instead to America, packed in a freight container the size of a minibus.

Renamed yet again – now it was the *UNICEF Flyer* in support of the United Nations' charity for children – Henk Brink had taken his four-year-old balloon envelope all the way to the Kennedy Space Center in Florida for a test inflation. Normally these are undertaken by partially filling an envelope with cold air in some suitably large building – a disused airship hangar, a sports hall or a shipyard for example, and then inspecting it from the inside to locate any pin-prick holes or leaks. But Brink went the whole expensive hog of inflating his balloon with helium in the massive Vehicle Assembly Building – originally built by Nasa to assemble the *Apollo Saturn V* rockets and now used to mate the *Space Shuttle Orbiters* to their fuel tanks and boosters. Brink was concerned that the envelope, designed to be flown just the once, might have already exceeded its shelf life and he wanted to be sure that the glued seams were still in a good condition. Accordingly balloon-builder Don Cameron was on hand as it assumed its full 210-foot height in the VAB's central transfer isle. And there it stood, perfectly gas tight, for a full 30 hours while Brink and his team generally 'kicked the tyres', inspecting the envelope and testing the control lines and valves. Once again 'Captain Brink', as the local media dubbed him, happily predicted a launch for the coming winter season.

Back in Holland the team continued to tinker with the capsule and refine the safety equipment, and in the autumn of 1995 Per Lindstrand made the trip to Schipol to inspect his own handiwork. 'Henk is ready to fly tomorrow if need be,' he confirmed. Yet the balloon never left the hangar and it was clear that the downward spiral of problems was finally catching up with Brink. Matters came to a head at Christmas when crewman Wout Bakker stormed out after a quarrel over the safety of the capsule. 'Dutch dream evaporates,' proclaimed the Dutch newspapers, and efforts to find a replacement from the KLM airline came to nothing, leaving Brink and Hageman on their own. As winter stretched into the start of 1996, any lead that Henk Brink had previously enjoyed had all but gone. Aviation's last great challenge was becoming a real race by this time and, in addition to such existing high-profile candidates as Newman, Nott and Lindstrand, an unknown dark horse was about to enter the running.

9 DARK HORSE

Saturday 20 August 1994, UK

It was very early on a Saturday morning when I was awakened by the ringing of the bedside phone. Most ballooning adventures begin that way and so I knew better than to be annoyed. Alan Noble of Cameron Balloons was on the line: 'There's an American flying across the Atlantic and it looks like he may come down somewhere near you, just to the south of Birmingham. I have to stay here at the Control Centre in Bristol, so would you go and find him when he lands?'

Of course I would. Alan knew me well enough as a fellow balloonist and in particular in my capacity as editor of *Aerostat* to know that I would not miss the opportunity to lend a hand. So far all the Atlantic balloonists had ended their flights on the continent and it would be great to form a welcoming party for the very first transatlantic balloon to land in Britain. 'His name's Fossett,' Alan added. 'Steve Fossett.'

As the morning wore on the regular bulletins from Camerons revealed that Mr Fossett's balloon was passing just to the north of Birmingham and would overshoot the UK entirely. In fact he and his co-pilot, fellow-American Tim Cole, went on to make a perfect stand-up landing in northern Germany, within 2.5 miles of their originally declared destination near Hamburg. Not bad for an Atlantic crossing and, for Steve Fossett, not bad for his first Rozière balloon flight. In many ways this Atlantic flight had been a curious business as it came almost two years after the Chrysler Transatlantic Race and at a time when the rest of the ballooning world had turned its back on ocean-hopping and was already concentrating on the bigger goal of a circumnavigation. It was also a flight totally devoid of publicity and, unless you were a balloonist, one that passed unnoticed. No records were broken, no newspaper columns filled – just two Americans in an unsponsored plain white balloon tackling what was once ballooning's greatest challenge and making it into what they termed 'good sport'. Surely there had to be more to it than that?

A couple of weeks later I interviewed Steve Fossett in Bristol when he was visiting Cameron Balloons to work on his next adventure. At this point I had never seen a photograph of the guy – a few weeks earlier I hadn't even known he existed – yet when I arranged to meet in the hotel foyer it never crossed my mind to wonder how I might recognize him. I figured that anyone who goes on a balloon flight across the Atlantic for the hell of it is sure to stand out in a crowd. The set of his jaw perhaps, the steely intensity of his eyes, his sheer charisma . . . But as I scanned the crowded foyer I soon realized my mistake and a little sheepishly I sidled up to the reception desk and asked them to put out a call for the elusive Mr Fossett. A man sitting just across from the desk overheard my request, put aside his newspaper and introduced himself with a firm handshake.

Warm, polite, likable, and entirely unremarkable in appearance, Steve Fossett is a fiftyish businessman with thinning grey hair, of barely average height and stocky physique. In many of the articles about Fossett, one word crops up time and time again, 'nondescript'. But impressions can be deceptive. The story goes that a couple of years later Richard Branson turned up at one of Fossett's launches. He bounced up to a guy wearing a team jacket as the balloon was being readied. 'Steve's going to have a great flight!' he told the man, who for a while listened politely and then, with just

American Steve Fossett in his Cameron-built capsule. Just 7 feet long and 4.5 feet wide,
it would serve him on both his Atlantic and solo transpacific flights and he reused it for
all four of his solo global attempts
(*Cameron Balloons*)

the hint of a wry smile, introduced himself before climbing aboard the balloon.

Why – my first question to Steve Fossett came straight to the point – why, as a newcomer to ballooning, had he decided to tackle a transatlantic crossing?

'I spend a lot of my time on adventure sports and really go after them in a rather serious manner,' he told me. And that sentence summed up the man and his philosophy. His genial manner and modesty belie the extent of his long list of achievements. As well as being an accomplished sailor – he describes this as his favourite activity and he has sailed the Atlantic single-handedly as well as accumulated eight sailing world records – he has conquered the tallest mountain on six of the seven continents (only Everest has defeated him so far), driven in the Le Mans twenty-four-hour race and the Paris-Dhaka rally, completed the Iditarod dog-sled race across Alaska, swum the English Channel and the Dardanelles (both ways) and generally got stuck-in to whatever physically arduous activities took his fancy. As an extremely successful stock-options investor he could afford to pay his way even in global ballooning without getting bogged down in seeking sponsorship deals.

'I started working on this Atlantic flight about three years ago,' he told me, 'so when the 1992 Chrysler transatlantic race got going I was kicking myself for not having got involved earlier so I could have participated. I did some research and decided that the Cameron Rozière was the proven system for the crossing. The Atlantic has been done before, so it's not like I was trying to do something totally new. It remained for me just to do a very good job of it.' And that is precisely what he did.

Fossett's only previous experience of ballooning had been a few hot-air balloon trips – hardly an adequate preparation for flying across the world's second greatest ocean. Final preparations had begun in earnest in the winter of 1993, and by then he had already invited experienced gas balloonist Tim Cole (a fellow Colorado resident) to join him as co-pilot and 'minder' on the flight. Cole introduced Fossett to another American balloonist, Bruce Comstock, who would assist with many of his future flights, and also to Dennis Brown who acted as launchmaster. Weatherman for the project was Bob Rice, a veteran of many Atlantic projects. It would be his job to predict suitable surface conditions for the launch combined with the right winds over the Atlantic, skilfully anticipating conditions over a two- or three-day period to thread the balloon all the way to Europe. So it was a small but highly experienced team that had launched the balloon from St John's, Newfoundland, on 17 August 1994.

The flight went extraordinarily smoothly. It was as if Fossett really does have a magic touch: 'It was very relaxing, although there is considerable pressure on an Atlantic crossing – with the Control Centre requiring position and status reports twice every hour. Every two hours I would send a report to Bob Rice in Boston, and then there were the three-hourly reports for the Atlantic Air Traffic Service. A few aircraft pilots called us up after hearing these, and so what with getting weather fax information and so on we didn't have a whole lot of time sitting around doing nothing.'

Conditions in the cramped unpressurized capsule were far from comfortable for Fossett and Cole shoehorned into a space just 7 feet long by 4.5 feet wide. For about half of their waking hours, and all the time when they slept, they breathed oxygen through small nose masks. It was warm enough during the day, but at night they had to bundle up against the cold. As for the toilet facilities, a bucket had to suffice. But then anything else wouldn't have been the 'Fossett way' of doing things. However, during the seventy-five-hour flight he did discover that a two-man crew has some advantages. 'There was no problem getting sleep – we chose to have about three to four hours a day and we could have had more if needed, but we were both comfortable with that.' The word 'comfortable' kept cropping up in our conversation and it was as if he was trying to play down the very real discomfort and dangers they faced. This is a recurring contradiction with Steve Fossett. He

1	Envelope connection points	12	Storage
2	Twin burners	13	Bunk
3	Anti-vibration mount for generator	14	Batteries
4	Generator	15	Navigation aids
5	Power supply	16	Communications system
6	Emergency strobe light	17	VHF aerial
7	HF aerial connection	18	Satellite aerial
8	Liquid oxygen, 2 x 40 litres	19	Hatch lock
9	Propane tanks, 2 x 40 litres	20	Observation dome
10	Propane tanks, 8 x 80 litres	21	Burner supports
11	Flooding keels to keep the capsule upright in water	22	Fuel lines

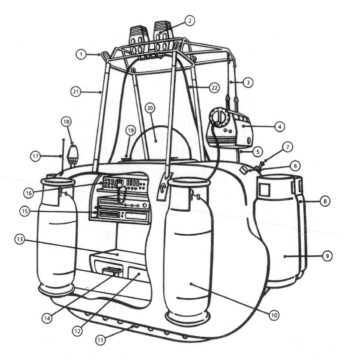

The 'Atlantic-class' capsule originally developed for the Chrysler Transatlantic Race. An unpressurized no-frills box 7 feet long and 4.5 feet across which, with just a few minor modifications including additional fuel tanks, would be Steve Fossett's home-from-home during his global flights

(*Cameron Balloons*)

methodically accumulates the sort of achievements most adventurers would be happy to manage once in a lifetime, and then plays them down.

'The trip went very smoothly. When people ask what went wrong I tell them about the first morning: I was awakened by a sudden jarring of the balloon and I was out of my sleeping bag in a matter of seconds checking to see what had happened . . .' Like other Atlantic balloonists before them, the two pilots had been rudely awakened by a passing *Concorde*'s sonic boom!

He summed up the flight: 'We hadn't set out to break any records. The one thing we were able to show is that transatlantic ballooning no longer needs to be an endeavour of desperate circumstances and grave danger. It can now be undertaken as a sport if proper preparations are made.' But Steve Fossett was clearly interested in more than just the sport, and before we parted I asked him about his future plans. He said his next goal would probably be the Pacific. He remained a little more coy about harbouring any global ambitions.

Friday 17 February 1995, Seoul, South Korea

Six months to the day after taking on the Atlantic, Fossett launched on his flight across the Pacific Ocean – solo. The man was hungry for some ballooning records and no one had ever achieved this before.

The Pacific is as big as all the other great oceans put together. Conventional projections of the globe seldom do it justice by focusing on the Atlantic and surrounding continents, literally marginalizing the Pacific, but seen from space it occupies almost one entire side of the planet. And it is a treacherous ocean; while the Atlantic is crisscrossed with shipping traffic, there are vast areas of the Pacific – especially in the southern waters – where a ditched balloon pilot might be stranded days or even weeks before rescue. A helicopter's range is too limited, and while other aircraft might get to the spot, they couldn't do a pick-up. You would just have to sit it out and wait for a ship.

The first successful manned crossing of the Pacific had been accomplished in 1981 by American Ben Abruzzo's team with the helium balloon *Double Eagle V*, in often stormy conditions. Attempting a solo crossing in 1991, the Japanese balloonist Fumio Niwa had paid the ultimate price when he ditched just 300 miles into a solo attempt. Despite a safe splashdown it took 22 hours for the rescue services to reach him, by which time he was dead.

True to form, Steve Fossett took the Pacific in his stride. He was using his existing Atlantic gondola, but this time had decided to invest in a larger Rozière envelope, increasing the volume from the previous 77,000 cubic feet up to 150,000 cubic feet. Although not particularly large by later global standards it was big enough to carry the additional fuel needed to get the job done. Seoul was chosen as the launch site, a tactical decision designed to snatch the existing world distance record from the *Double Eagle V* team who had launched from Nagashima in Japan, several hundred miles nearer to America. Fossett's Flight Director, Alan Noble, had chosen the shelter of the vast Olympic stadium as the launch site and Fossett was to select sports stadiums to launch all his subsequent solo global attempts. To supervise the launch American ballooning expert Bruce Comstock was joined by the experienced gas balloonist Nick Saum, and by sheer coincidence the British balloonist and engineer Andy Elson was also in Seoul at the time, and he was warmly welcomed aboard by the small launch team.

As the balloon rose out of the oval stadium and into the smog-laden atmosphere of Seoul there was some consternation among those on the ground as it started to drift the wrong way. Images of *Earthwinds Hilton* quickly came to mind, but Fossett took the balloon higher and the westward movement stopped and at approximately 10,000 feet he drifted back over the stadium and started the epic journey of 5,000 miles eastwards.

*

When flying over large stretches of water by balloon it is as if time itself becomes suspended. Only the clouds and the weather, the passing of the sun and the cycle of day and night give any impression of movement. The predicament of the lone aeronaut is a solitary one confined in that fragile cocoon, floating in an ethereal world over neither one continent nor the other. It is a curious paradox to be a tiny jewelled speck in the vast three-dimensional ocean of the heavens on the one hand, and in a claustrophobic's worst nightmare on the other. Surrounded by propane cylinders, there were no side windows on the tiny capsule – a bubble hatch in the roof was the only way in and it provided the only view out, and even that was misted up for most of the time. As you look upwards into the belly of a balloon, the tapered sides of the envelope create an impression of viewing it as if through a fish-eye lens and the one solid object in your field of view almost becomes an irrelevance. It is easy to imagine that you and the capsule are the only things that exist. You are riding on Ali Baba's magic carpet and except when the balloon changes level there isn't the slightest hint of a breeze. Only the tell-tale countdown of flickering numbers on the Global Positioning System (GPS), which works from signals provided by US military satellites, dispels the illusion of being entirely stationary; the waves of the sea move in the same direction as the balloon and offer no fixed points from which to measure any headway. At least over land you have the patchwork of shapes and colours sliding past.

Fossett's Control Centre, once again situated at Cameron Balloons in Bristol, operated around the clock, but in truth there was little for Noble and his team to do as the flight remained remarkably uneventful except for a few minor problems. Shortly before reaching Japan first one capsule heater and then the other stopped working, and this could be serious as the in-flight temperatures drop to below $-30°C$ at night. Suspicion fell on the late decision to use an ethane/methane gas mixture to pressurize the liquid propane fuel tanks. (It was the start of a long run of bad luck with heaters which would dog Steve Fossett on many of his flights, but he is made of sterner stuff and wrapped up in his several layers of thermal clothing, a little cold wasn't going to stop him.) The auto ignition system to one burner was also faulty, which was known about before the launch, but there just hadn't been enough time to rectify the problem.

Despite these glitches things were generally running like clockwork and, thanks to the Comstock autopilot, Fossett even grabbed some brief snatches of sleep during the 103-hour flight. Per Lindstrand once described him as 'an android'. That may be the impression his feats of endurance create, but he is only human at the end of the day and Alan Noble may be nearer the mark: 'He is a man with enormous reserves and he is one of the most focused people I have ever met. He is like Richard Branson in that respect – although very unlike him in others – and when he puts his mind to something, money and discomfort are no object.'

However, one obstacle was lying in wait as the balloon approached the coast of America – a swirling thumbprint of isobars on the weather charts indicated that a deep depression was winding itself up in the Bay of Alaska; the balloon had started to turn towards the north-east and was heading straight towards it. With the forecasters predicting thick cloud and severe icing for the remainder of the flight, Fossett climbed to 20,000 feet and with deteriorating conditions all around he managed to fly along a 'hole' in the weather, reporting no problems all the way to the coast of Canada. Afterwards Alan Noble commented, 'I found myself wondering whether successful people like Steve Fossett and Richard Branson make their own luck, or whether they are born under a fortunate star.'

One facet of Fossett's character that has little in common with Branson's is his natural introversion. He is a man of few spare words. 'Have crossed the coast at Vancouver island' was the terse message received at the Control Centre announcing the first successful solo crossing of the Pacific by balloon. (Data communications via satellite were so good and so concise that the only voice conversation Fossett had with any of his support team was a brief chat on VHF radio with Nick Saum as his aircraft chased the balloon near the end of the flight.)

At the Control Centre Don Cameron had drawn a thick line on the map running from Southampton Island in Hudson Bay up to a small place called Astoria on the west coast of the USA. This indicated the great circle distance Steve Fossett needed to cross in order to claim a new world distance record, but as the balloon approached this artificial finish line a scare about his electrical power reserves forced Fossett to shut down the satellite communications system and an eerie silence descended on the Control Centre. Now the American was really going it on his own.

The balloon was still heading east at high speed when it was sighted 45 miles to the west of Calgary. The distance record was broken but with darkness descending and poor conditions forecasted for the following morning, Fossett vented helium to bring the balloon down in a muddy field near the hamlet of Mendham, in western Canada.

Gathering up his balloon envelope, he greeted the reporters who flocked to the landing site brimming with the satisfaction of a job well done. A solo flight of 5,439 miles – measured as a great circle around the globe from the start to finish point – had put the unknown newcomer firmly on the ballooning honours board; he had flown more than a quarter of the way round the world and had set a distance record that would be the envy of many later global contenders. It is one, however, that is disputed by Per Lindstrand who claims that the Virgin Pacific crossing with an irregular track of 6,761 miles travelled across the Earth's surface constituted a greater distance. Strictly speaking the great circle is the correct measurement for the record books.

Anyway, Steve Fossett had put himself and his equipment to the test and had come through it with flying colours; now he was ready to tackle the big one. He wasn't the only one, however, with global ambitions – in Britain another millionaire adventurer was about to reenter the arena.

10 THE ULTIMATE ADVENTURE

Early 1995, UK

'Richard has agreed to do it.'

It was early on a Saturday morning. Another phone call, another adventure – and from the musical lilt of the Swedish accent I immediately recognized the voice of Per Lindstrand. And that was it. He didn't say any more and he didn't need to. Ballooning's dynamic duo was back in harness.

But hadn't Richard Branson promised his family that he wouldn't do this sort of thing again? The Virgin boss laughed this off, claiming that the decision had been taken only under duress. 'It was my father. He tricked me really. They gave me a celebratory dinner for the transpacific crossing and got me in a corner with the whole family and wouldn't let me out until I promised.' His wife, Joan, however, was not impressed by the prospect of his going ballooning again.

But Per Lindstrand was. When I called in at his Shropshire factory a few weeks later it was a hive of activity, and he showed me around with the unabashed glee of a child with a new toy. Behind a desk awash with papers, he abruptly stopped mid-sentence to give another message or instruction to his assistant and then picked up on our conversation once more. 'What's the point in doing these projects if you can't have a little fun?' He asked me if I wanted to go for a quick spin and, naively thinking that maybe he had a new car, I naturally said yes. In playful mood he led me round to the back of the factory where a Hughes *500* helicopter stood waiting. This was Lindstrand in his element, once again about to become the focus of worldwide attention. He was going to fly a balloon round the world.

The quick spin entailed some stomach-churning aerobatics around the Shropshire hills and then it was over to Lindstrand's Factory No.2 where work on the global balloon was concentrated. Until now Lindstrand had proposed making a global attempt with a solely hot-air balloon, but he was abandoning that concept in favour of his own Rozière design. I was curious to know why. 'The Atlantic and Pacific oceans were both crossed by gas first and then there was a ten-year gap before the hot-air technology caught up. The reason partly why I first wanted to do the global flight with hot-air is that it is more controllable, but it is also more difficult and more of a challenge. A hot-air flight is a sprint where you can maximize every single angle of flight. You can nail it into the jet-stream, and you can go up or down – in essence you are flying it all the time. The Rozière, on the other hand, doesn't have that manoeuvrability and lacks some of the options. But my Rozière will be unlike any other.'

Given that no balloon had ever remained airborne for longer than six days at that time, it was vital that he came up with a design that would be both fuel-efficient and maximize the heating effects of the Rozière's hot-air component to achieve the necessary flight duration. Using computer-aided design he claimed to have explored every conceivable configuration in fine detail, carefully analysing and balancing stresses against weight and efficiency. Lindstrand's concept was a massive 900,000-cubic-foot balloon – a fat exclamation mark 170 feet high with a smooth domed top – constructed of a high-tenacity nylon fabric coated with a polyure-thane compound to create a gas-proof barrier. Instead of the more traditional gluing to join the seams he would use the latest thermal welding techniques to ensure maximum strength and gas retention.

Inside the factory Lindstrand showed me the wooden mock-up of the business end of the balloon, the pressurized capsule that

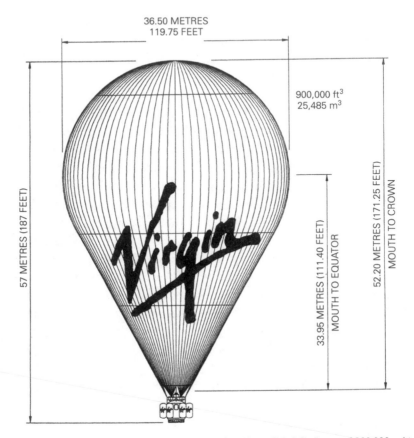

36.50 METRES
119.75 FEET

900,000 ft³
25,485 m³

57 METRES (187 FEET)

33.95 METRES (111.40 FEET)
MOUTH TO EQUATOR

52.20 METRES (171.25 FEET)
MOUTH TO CROWN

Per Lindstrand's 1995 design for the first *Virgin Global Challenger* of 900,000 cubic feet.
A smooth ice cream cone profile without the top 'tent' that characterized the
Cameron-built balloons
(*Lindstrand Balloons*)

would be the home of the three-man crew for two to three weeks. At first sight it was a bigger two-tier version of the Atlantic and Pacific models; a vertical tube, 10.8 feet high and 9.5 feet in diameter. The real one would be constructed of aluminium with six immense fuel cylinders, each containing 1,650 lb of liquid propane, strapped around its circumference. 'Why change an existing successful formula?' said Lindstrand as he led the way up some

steps and in through a small square hatchway into the upper com-
partment. The empty shell already felt claustrophobic; the real
thing would be packed from floor to ceiling with controls, avionics, supplies and a crew of three. Standing upright was only possible at the centre of the top deck, with your head poking up into
the plastic dome which provided all-round visibility of the burners
and the envelope above. Also situated on the roof of the capsule
would be two engine units running on the same propane as the
burners. These were to be the heart and lungs of the capsule,
driving compressors that converted the thin outside air at high
altitude into a breathable density for the crew and also powering
two generators to feed the on-board batteries. The only alternative
would be to carry compressed air in cylinders and to obtain
electricity from solar panels or rely on bigger on-board batteries.

Back inside, two circular trapdoors in the floor led down to the
even more cramped lower level which was divided by several bulk-
heads into spaces for storage, a single bed (to be shared) and even
a toilet. Lindstrand had endured the indignity of a 'lucky bucket'
on previous flights and he didn't intend spending such a long time
locked in this tin-can without some proper plumbing. In some
ways this global capsule was unique in that if you needed to get
away from it all, you could take yourself off to another area ('room'
is too generous a term) and even slam the door behind you. Even
so, getting on with your companions was going to be an important consideration, as Lindstrand explained: 'The longer the flight
the greater the basic psychological factors of being in a confined
space for such a long period with two other human beings. Nasa
experts have told me there is a period of around twenty-four days
that people can endure before they start going up the wall.'

To consummate their reunion Branson and Lindstrand held a
press conference in July 1995 at Greenwich, London, the symbolic
zero meridian which, they hoped, would be the launchsite for their
global attempt in the coming winter. Sound-bites and photo-ops

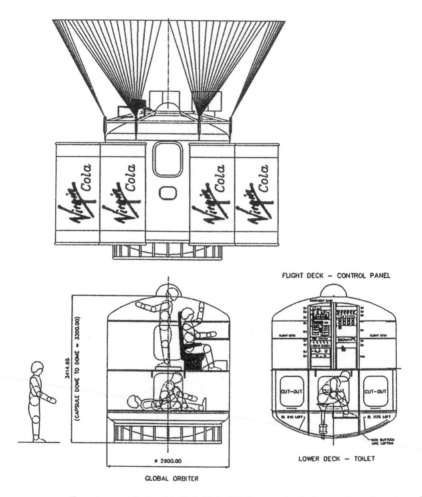

FLIGHT DECK — CONTROL PANEL

LOWER DECK — TOILET

GLOBAL ORBITER

Two-tier capsule for the *Virgin Global Challenger* – basically an enlarged version of the
earlier Atlantic/Pacific design – to accommodate the three-man crew, with a single
sleeping space and even a toilet within the confines of the lower level
(*Lindstrand Balloons*)

came thick and fast and for the Virgin boss there was much
jumping into the air clinging onto toy balloons. He was at the
height of his popularity and suddenly, as if for the very first time,
the whole world became aware that a round-the-world balloon

race even existed. Basking in the warm glow of the flashguns, Branson had brought it into the public eye and made it the realm of the millionaire adventurer.

To heighten the drama the identity of the third crew member was not disclosed at the press conference and speculation was rife. Branson jokingly suggested taking the television *Baywatch* beauty Pamela Anderson along as she had just lent her name and outline to his new 'Pammy' Virgin Cola bottle. (Branson had recently appeared in an episode of the programme water-skiing behind one of his airships.) But the joke doing the rounds was on him. The crew was to consist of Lindstrand, Branson and Lindstrand's dog, Charley. Lindstrand would fly the balloon, Branson would feed the dog, and the dog would bite Branson if he touched any of the controls! It was a cruel dig.

Branson was unabashed in his enthusiasm for the mixing of commerce with adventure and wanted to promote his Virgin brand name whenever and wherever he possibly could, as he was at the height of his 'cola-war' with Coke. 'We'll be flying the Virgin name on the balloon and hopefully countries that don't know about Virgin now will do so by the end of the trip.' But even though the Virgin logo would have prominence, Branson claimed that he was planning to spend very little on the project and that most of the expense would be covered through donated equipment and sponsorship. 'It shouldn't cost us anything,' he told the reporters. And it was not an empty boast, for when he had completed his successful Blue Riband run across the Atlantic in 1986, he had sold the *Virgin Challenger* speedboat to a wealthy Arab the very next day. But large global balloons, intended for single use only, are not so saleable, and before long the project was starting to edge over the original budget of £1.5 million. The third crew member, whoever he or she might be, had better bring some additional funding with them.

It turned out that he was right under their noses all along – thirty-five-year-old businessman and all-round action-man, Rory McCarthy who had helped Lindstrand to start his balloon company three years previously. Built of the same sort of Wright-stuff as Branson, McCarthy holds the world altitude records for hang-gliding and for a civilian sky-dive – on both occasions dropping from a balloon piloted by Per Lindstrand. And when he wasn't jumping out of things he would get his kicks flying his own fighter-jet.

Now the two were three.

Despite the impression created by the newspapers, the Virgin team was not alone in thinking globally. Spurred on by the demise of *Earthwinds Hilton*, some new ideas were being brought to bear on the problem. The *Odyssey* team, headed by American balloonist and television journalist Bob Martin, proposed encircling the Earth at ultra high-altitudes around 124,000 feet – right at the edge of space – but with financial backing proving elusive they were unlikely to pose much of a threat for some time. Another hopeful was the American Dick Rutan. Unlike the others at least he could claim to have made a non-stop global flight already, for in December 1986, together with co-pilot Jeana Yeager, he had piloted the *Voyager* aircraft non-stop and unrefuelled around the world in just over nine days. Regardless of his total lack of lighter-than-air experience, Rutan now wanted to tackle the flight with a balloon to be known as *Aeolus 1*. His brother Bert (short for Elbert), the famous aircraft designer and builder renowned for his unorthodox back-to-front canard aircraft featuring a large wing and the propeller at the back, had designed a spherical pressurized capsule to be constructed of lightweight composite materials. This, Dick Rutan proposed, would be carried beneath a Cameron-built Rozière, but in the autumn of 1995 he was still working on finding sponsorship for the project. Henk Brink, on the other hand, had a balloon and he was ready and waiting; although waiting for what exactly wasn't clear.

Pressure was mounting for the Virgin team. Probably the greatest threat was Steve Fossett, who was gearing up for a solo challenge

November 1995: Now we are three – Rory McCarthy, Richard Branson and Per Lindstrand make their first official appearance as the crew of the *Virgin Global Challenger* (*Marcus Edwards*)

– reusing his trusty old unpressurized capsule for a relatively low-level attempt skimming along the bottom edge of the jetstream. The Virgin balloon was barely off the drawing board and they would have to work to a breakneck schedule to get it completed, the equipment installed and the pilots properly trained by the end of the year. Then in November, right in the midst of all this frantic activity, the unfinished capsule was whisked away from the technicians for a second press conference in London. *Apollo 11* astronaut Buzz Aldrin was on hand this time, and so too was global rival Henk Brink who appeared from the crowd to wish the Virgin team good luck. Branson immediately seized upon the opportunity to give his presence the right spin and invited Brink to join him on the podium. The Dutchman also wrote a good luck message on the Virgin capsule (soon to be obliterated by a layer of insulation foam), but vowed that he would be the first around the world. 'I am ready to go as soon as the weather is right.' Rory McCarthy was also present at the press conference but he seemed a reluctant world conqueror, tending to keep in the background and eschewing the limelight.

Running weeks behind schedule, and already way over budget, Lindstrand's people worked flat out over Christmas 1995 so that the envelope could be completed and checked over. Nerves were becoming frayed and the chronic lack of time for training seemed to concern McCarthy more than his team-mates – especially Branson who had stated, 'Flying a balloon isn't that tricky a thing to do. The place to learn is on the flight itself.' But McCarthy was worried about what would happen in an emergency. 'Sky-diving at 35,000 feet is fraught with risk. The temperature at that altitude is −70°C and you very quickly attain speeds of 300 mph. You can't hop and pop; chances are you will be hit immediately by the capsule. You have to sky-dive away from it as quickly as possible, and I think that is why I am here. I can take Richard with me. I know I can.' Maybe he was right to be concerned about Branson and parachuting. For on his first taste of parachute training, Branson had almost killed himself when he tugged the wrong handle and sent the main chute tumbling off without him. Only his two instructors had saved him by operating the reserve chute. Lesser men might have taken this as an omen.

There was no denying that a circumnavigation would be a difficult and a dangerous task. Virgin's Project Director, Mike Kendrick, was only being realistic when he gave the chances of a success that coming winter as just ten per cent, while Per Lindstrand suggested odds at fifty-fifty. Even Steve Fossett admitted that the odds were against any of the teams making it.

11 VIRGIN TERRITORY

Autumn, 1995

For the global hopefuls the autumn of 1995 was a time to contemplate the possibilities that lay ahead as the winter jetstream season drew closer – the unfolding of a great adventure and maybe, just maybe, the sort of fame that money can't buy. To be there, alongside such figures as the Wright brothers, Lindbergh or Armstrong – true immortality. For the pilots the build-up and the media attention was a heady cocktail of mounting excitement and not a little fear. So the engineers and the technicians worked harder than ever while the PR people continued to exchange hype in this period of the phoney war.

With so much effort being expended in the scramble to get the hardware ready in time, and with so little time to spare full-stop, scant regard was being paid to the political minefield that lay ahead for the global fliers. This had never really been a problem for the long-distance ocean-hopping balloonists who, by definition, tackled the intercontinental divides by flying from one friendly nation to another. Most transatlantic crossings had started from the USA or Canada and ended up in western Europe or occasionally in northern Africa. Even the three successful Pacific crossings had launched from either Japan or, in Steve Fossett's case, South Korea, and had flown to the North American mainland.

All simple enough, but any latter-day Phileas Fogg riding the northern hemisphere jetstream was faced with the prospect of crossing up to 30 or more different countries. And while the southern hemisphere offered a route with fewer countries to be overflown, it entailed flying over large and inhospitable expanses of water for 80 per cent of the time. That left the global balloonists with a choice between the devil or the deep blue sea.

A nation's airspace, any nation's, is defined by the ICAO (International Civil Aviation Organization) as extending vertically to an altitude of 66,000 feet – about twelve miles. The air or what little there is of it above this benchmark is considered to be 'space' in political terms, and whatever goes on there doesn't really matter as nobody can stop you at that sort of height. (Hence spacecraft of the various nations orbit the Earth wherever it suits them regardless of earthbound boundaries.) Unfortunately, what this meant for the global balloonists – with the single exception of the ultra-high altitude *Odyssey* project, brainchild of the American balloonist and TV reporter Bob Martin – was that by riding at between 20,000 and 35,000 feet they would head into these vertical extensions of national territory one after the other. And until the flight itself they couldn't even predict with any degree of certainty which countries they would overfly. Choosing the right launchsite could be the key to a successful attempt.

Steeped in a sense of history and dissected by the symbolic zero meridian, at first sight Greenwich, London, was an absolutely superb location from which to begin such an endeavour. It oozed just the sort of theatricality that Richard Branson wanted for his Virgin attempt. Counting off the degrees as the great balloon began its eastwards drift – television news pictures and commentaries drawing comparisons with Sir Francis Drake and Sir Walter Raleigh setting off on their epic voyages. Great stuff! Unfortunately, the trouble with Greenwich was that it did not offer much prospect of good weather for a winter launch and it was a long way north of the nearest jetstream. Per Lindstrand took to the skies aboard a Virgin helicopter to search out and evaluate alternative locations within the UK. In Holland Henk Brink was

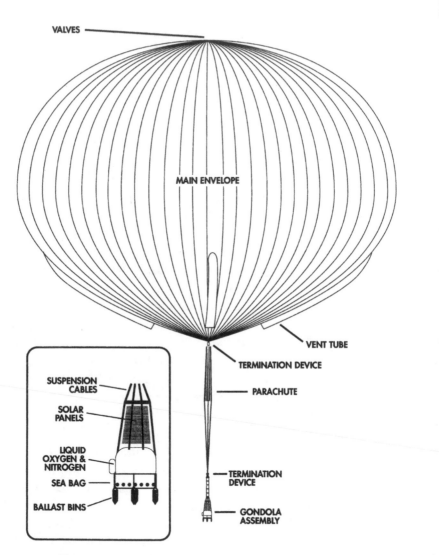

VALVES

MAIN ENVELOPE

VENT TUBE

TERMINATION DEVICE

PARACHUTE

SUSPENSION CABLES

SOLAR PANELS

LIQUID OXYGEN & NITROGEN

SEA BAG

BALLAST BINS

TERMINATION DEVICE

GONDOLA ASSEMBLY

The massive 40,000,000-cubic-foot *Odyssey*, designed to float at ultra-high altitudes of around 124,000 feet

(*Odyssey*)

facing a similar dilemma with his decision to launch from his home country – all very patriotic but not so practical – whereas on the other side of the Atlantic Steve Fossett was making preparations to use another sports stadium. He at least would have a transatlantic crossing during which he could manoeuvre his balloon into the optimum position to tackle Europe and perhaps catch the right winds.

For Virgin it was their Project Manager, David Partridge, who came up with the solution of Marrakesh in Morocco, ideally situated directly under the jetstream passing over northern Africa. Sheltered by the Atlas Mountains, this site theoretically also offered reliable launch conditions over the winter period. And the Moroccans were certainly keen to have the event there, offering the use of their facilities at the military airbase situated alongside the main airport. Maybe not as convenient as London or the Home Counties of England perhaps, this relocation also involved further expense for a project that was already way over its £1.5 million budget. Mike Kendrick estimated that the move would cost in excess of £100,000, but undeterred, Branson was quick to approve the plan and the Virgin team headed south.

While Morocco may be well situated to catch the jetstream, it is also directly upwind of some political hot-spots; notably Algeria – then in the throes of a vicious civil war – and beyond that Libya, Iran and Iraq. Further ahead lay the giants of the former Soviet countries and the great unknown territory of China. But as Richard Branson had explained at the London press launch back in August, 'A balloon has no real choice in the route it takes, so we have to get permission from about ninety-seven countries to be able to cross them.' True enough, but his next words demonstrated a cavalier attitude to sovereign airspace. 'If we miss one out, we are just going to have to radio in and say we have no choice.' Even for Richard Branson it would take a lot more than a winning smile and friends in high places to untie some of the political knots lying in wait. And just a few weeks later, events in Belarus would give food for thought to all the global contenders.

Tuesday 12 September 1995, Belarus

Balloonists Alan Fraenckel, a TWA pilot based at JFK airport, and John Stuart-Jervis, a former air ferry pilot in the US Virgin Islands, were three days into the prestigious 1995 Gordon Bennett gas balloon race which had launched from Wil near Zurich. Their balloon, registered D-CARIBBEAN and representing the US Virgin Islands, had set off on 9 September along with fourteen others, and it had flown through Germany and then Poland before reaching the Belarussian border. Because this was likely to be the first race possibly to reach Russian airspace since the end of the Second World War the organizers had prepared the way by previously contacting each of the Baltic states, as well as Belarus and the Ukraine, to request permissions to overfly these areas and approval had been obtained from each government.

Three balloons, including the Fraenckel/Stuart-Jarvis balloon, reached the Belarussian border and all three had radioed their positions to Minsk but, according to the race organizers, they had received a stream of Russian in reply even though English is the accepted language of international aviation. As the balloonists knew that permissions had been already obtained by the organizers, they maintained their eastward drift and continued to report their positions to Minsk at regular intervals.

At 11.54 am local time, the young pilot of a *Mi-24* helicopter gunship had the sights of his cannon trained on an intruder into Belarussian airspace. An almost featureless gas balloon was drifting over a remote forest area and edging ever closer to a sensitive military site. He had never encountered anything like this before because hot-air ballooning and most other airsports are strictly forbidden in his country. The last time the West had sent balloons over Russia had been in the pre-satellite days of the early Cold War years when aerial reconnaissance of this vast territory was undertaken by hordes of unmanned balloons loaded with sophisticated surveillance equipment. Now, more than thirty years later, here was another foreign balloon barging in.

It had been detected as a radar blip entering Belarussian airspace a little over two hours earlier. Two military helicopters were dispatched from the airbase south-west of Minsk and, according to the Belarussians, one circled the balloon for 25 minutes trying to establish radio contact. After firing warning shots the helicopter pilot was convinced that the balloon was unmanned and orders were issued by Major-General Kostenko, the commander of the 'anti-aircraft defence', to bring it down. The pilot opened fire! Twenty rounds ripped into the balloon, sending it plummeting out of the sky and killing its two occupants when it smashed into the ground.

The Belarussians would later claim that the information about the race and the clearances into their airspace had not been passed on to the military authorities. Initially they also suggested that the two pilots hadn't responded to the helicopter's warning shots because they might have been unconscious after a steep climb. Admittedly the balloon had been airborne for over 60 hours and the radio batteries may have become weak, but it is hard to believe that the two balloonists could have misunderstood such a clear warning . . . if it had ever been issued at all.

Of the other two American-crewed balloons over Belarussia, one was also confronted by a helicopter gunship and the balloonists unfurled flags before instigating an emergency landing near the city of Grodno. Detained by the police, they were each fined $30 for not having the correct papers, prompting a US State Department spokesman to comment after the incident, 'We had expected an apology, instead we got a bill.' The third balloon landed safely in Belarussia, without incident, because of the deteriorating weather conditions.

The wave of anger and outrage sparked by this shooting was widespread and vociferous. The governing body of ballooning, the FAI, declared, 'It was a deliberate act, not a tragic mistake.' And it produced evidence refuting suggestions that the pilots might have been unconscious and also pointed out that they were both highly experienced. The American authorities denounced Belarus's

actions as 'outrageous . . . and absolutely indefensible'. Alan Noble
was even blunter: 'It's murder.'

Demands were immediately made for an official inquiry and
the Belarussian President, Alexander Lukashenko, was inundated
with protests from all over the world. Under enormous pressure
his officials begrudgingly offered an apology and instigated an
investigation headed by the Deputy Prime Minister, but it did
little to allay the fears of the balloonists. The FAI's official report
would not be published until July the following year, but mean-
time it appeared that the two men were either the unlucky victims
of a tragic and stupid error caused by the lack of communication
between civil and military centres – symptomatic of the widespread incompetence that had plagued the former Soviet Union
since its disintegration – or that a young helicopter pilot simply
vented his feelings at their expense. Neither eventuality offered
any comfort to the global teams.

Following the incident an anxious Steve Fossett called Alan
Noble – his reply was short and to the point: 'It's still as dangerous as it always was Steve.' Ironically though, it is amid the gun
culture of the USA that balloons and airships are most frequently
fired at, apparently just for the hell of it. Three months after the
Belarus incident a gas balloon competing in the America's
Challenge was forced to land after a gunshot tore a hole in the
envelope.

Richard Branson considered inviting a Russian crewman on
board the *Virgin Global Challenger* or alternatively chartering a
Russian air force helicopter to fly ahead of the balloon and talk to
all military centres. 'Unfortunately there is no other way of guar-
anteeing a safe passage,' Per Lindstrand commented. He was also
concerned about protecting the equipment should the balloon
land in Russia. Former cosmonaut and Branson's co-member on
the original *Earthwinds Hilton* team, Vladimir Dzhanibekov came
to Virgin's London office for a crisis briefing and he suggested that
the stricken balloon had been heading straight for a highly sensitive nuclear rocket site – apparently so secret that the West didn't

The Gemini astronauts captured this graphic image of cloud caught in a fast jetstream passing west to east over Egypt [*Nasa*]

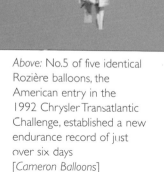

Above: No.5 of five identical Rozière balloons, the American entry in the 1992 Chrysler Transatlantic Challenge, established a new endurance record of just over six days [*Cameron Balloons*]

Too late to enter the 1992 race, Steve Fossett (right) cut his transatlantic teeth in a similar balloon with co-pilot Tim Coles in 1995 [*Carsten Neff*]

Right: Richard Branson and Per Lindstrand shared an anxious roller-coaster jet-stream ride across the Pacific in 1991 [*Lindstrand Balloons*]

Main picture: The unorthodox *Earthwinds Hilton* flew for seven hours and 200 miles in the wrong direction on its fourth global attempt in January 1994.
Top: Larry Newman, Richard Abruzzo and Dave Melton in the *Earthwinds* capsule [*John Ackroyd*]
Centre: Rivals Richard Branson and Henk Brink meet at a Virgin press conference [*Marcus Edwards*]

In January 1997 the *Virgin Global Challenger* launched from Marrakesh. On board were Richard Branson, Per Lindstrand and last-minute substitute Alex Ritchie who saved the day when the balloon became caught in powerful air currents over the Atlas Mountains. They landed in the Algerian desert the following morning [*Lindstrand Balloons*]

Winter 1997/98 was the
time when everything
seemed to go wrong.

Right: The *Virgin Global
Challenger* envelope broke
its restraints and went flying
on its own [*Chas Breton*]
Top: Dick Rutan's *Global Hilton*
went pop [*Tania Cornelison*]
Centre: The *Breitling Orbiter 2*
capsule fell back to earth at
Château d'Oex when the
suspension cables came free
[*Chas Breton*]

For solo challenger Steve Fossett life inside his cramped unpressurized capsule was far from comfortable. But anything else wouldn't have been the Fossett way [Steve Fossett]

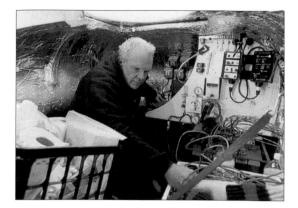

The Breitling Orbiter 2 at the beginning of its flight in January 1998 [Breitling] and in Myanmar after flying for 148 hours [Phil Dunnington]

31 January 1998, 4,000 feet above the Adriatic Sea. With the bubble hatch of the Breitling Orbiter 2 capsule leaking it was up to the designer Andy Elson to clamber outside to fix it in flight [Breitling]

After the crew of the *Ico Global Challenger* stormed into Chinese airspace in December 1998 the bamboo curtain closed tight [*Lindstrand Balloons*]

Unconcerned was balloonist/spaceman John Wallington who planned to fly the ultra-high *Re/Max* balloon from Alice Springs, Australia in January 1999 [*Grant Turner*]

Only the British! Andy Elson, complete with umbrella, standing on the kerosene tanks during *Cable & Wireless*'s low and slow detour to curve around China, 22 February 1999 [*Allsport*]

The evening before the launch – Bertrand Piccard and Brian Jones discuss their prospects for success with a journalist [*John Christopher*]

1 March 1999 – *Breitling Orbiter 3* launches from Château d'Oex, Switzerland [*Chas Breton*]

Above: Brian Jones enjoys the comforts of high-rise living *Breitling Orbiter 3* style.
Top right: During the first EVA Bertrand Piccard demonstrates his device to clean the outside of the portholes in flight
Right: A celebratory picture taken with a remote control camera, 21 March 1999
Below: Ice from the envelope cascades onto the capsule and the Egyptian desert below
[*Bertrand Piccard and Brian Jones*]

know it was there. Branson remained worried, but undeterred he told his people, 'If the absolute worst comes to the worst we are just going to decide to take the risk and go off air for a couple of hours.' His statement was greeted with silence and some extremely nervous smiles around the table. It was only a month since a Virgin Atlantic airliner en route to Hong Kong had been intercepted by fighters and forced to land at Moscow.

Before the Belarus shooting some of the global teams had not taken the political aspect seriously enough, and while this was an extreme case the reality for the mainly British and US teams was that the northern hemisphere jetstream route was fraught with such difficulties. 'During a recent briefing from the Foreign Office we were told that Afghanistan carries an even worse threat than Russia and that no British airlines should cross its airspace,' said Lindstrand. 'Various fundamentalist groups are now in possession of heat-seeking missiles and they are likely to take potshots.'

And what about China? For too long the West has taken the misguided view that China is just another Third World country. They are wrong. China is its own world and it has little enthusiasm for foreign balloonists wandering into its airspace. It is a massive, almost insurmountable obstacle to global balloonists. The Chinese authorities remained politely enigmatic in response to requests from Branson and others for permission to overfly. They weren't saying 'No', but then they weren't exactly saying 'Yes' either.

12 AN ILL WIND

Steve Fossett's *Solo Challenger* was being readied for an imminent launch, but was he just trying to wrong-foot the competition? That morning I got another of those phone calls; this time it was Dave Partridge at the Virgin office. Dave was an old friend, years previously he had given me one of my first balloon flights and as I had recently begun flying hot-air balloons on a professional basis for the Virgin Balloon Flights company he had also become a colleague. He explained that Richard Branson was in a panic at the news about Fossett and they had to hurry to get the *Virgin Global Challenger* into the air. Vital supplies, mostly vacuum-sealed food packages which couldn't be taken by unpressurized airfreight in case they burst, needed to be taken to Morocco by road . . . in just three days. Could I help?

That evening I was heading east on the M4 motorway. An incongruous start to the 2,500-mile journey to Marrakesh, but by the next morning the motorways were French and as another day gave way to the next they in turn were replaced by Spanish ones. I was driving a van packed with the pilots' food supplies and other equipment with two Virgin Land Rovers following in convoy. To make sure that we didn't miss the boat to northern Africa we drove through the second night as the familiar names of Spanish holiday resorts disappeared in the rear mirror one by one. Then as our little band came round one hillside we were greeted by a fantastic sight, the towering rock of Gibraltar silhouetted against the red and purple mottled sunset. It looked like a lit-up Christmas tree. But it was very late, we were dog-tired, and that night we grabbed a few hours of sleep in the van before the morning ferry departed. That was when the fun began.

Our first taste of Moroccan authority was at the dockside in Tangier – a blend of Italian comic opera and car boot sale – and the officials didn't quite know what to do with us. The poor locals got the full treatment with every item in their tightly packed vehicles turfed out onto the concrete for inspection; clothing, old bicycles, old balding car tyres and old balding Moroccans. Instead we were treated to a steady succession of uniforms, each a different colour and each apparently outranking the previous one judging by the acreage of their epaulets. Each 'uniform' shook its head, sucked on its stubby pencil and on tiny slips of paper scribbled down every minute detail of the vehicles, our documents and the contents of the van. They poked at the special food packs, each sealed and labelled 'Branson, Day 2, Meal 3' for example or 'McCarthy, Day 21, Meal 1'. For the umpteenth time someone was shaking his head and telling me that we could not bring foodstuffs into the country and for the umpteenth time, in pidgin English, broken French and the full repertoire of sign language, I tried to explain what we were doing and that the Virgin team was in Morocco as guests of the King. That last bit usually did the trick, and sure enough, after several hours of this multilingual debate we were packed off to the local police station.

Chaotic, crowded, with rubble strewn everywhere and water running through the streets, at first sight Tangier looked like a war zone. In places the roads became impassable as we encountered huge craters or an unfinished concrete bridge that went nowhere. At the police station we were assigned three police motorcyclists who would escort us all the way to Marrakesh. Suitably enthused by their important mission, the bikers took the lead for the final

400-mile sprint complete with flashing lights and wailing sirens. This was terrific fun – although I was not quite sure why the escorts had to force all the oncoming traffic off the road. (Well, I do know really, they were having fun too.) With only the occasional stop to sip some warm sickly-sweet green tea, we carried on into our third night on the road. In one large town the police bikes went ahead at each junction to stop the traffic and allow us to race through the red lights at full throttle.

Nearing Marrakesh our progress was impeded by a series of police road blocks at roughly fifteen-mile intervals. At each one we went through the whole rigmarole all over again and even the police escort, by that time reduced to a lone non-flashing, non-wailing bike, had to go through a similar process. By the time we finally entered the city it was 3.00 am, the streets were deserted and we headed straight to the hotel for the first proper sleep in days.

It was late on the morning of Saturday 13 January by the time I surfaced to find that the rest of the Virgin team were already at the airport a couple of miles away. The Moroccans had kindly cleared one of the wide low-roofed aircraft hangars and they had even hosed it down ready for the balloonists. Consequently deep puddles of water were everywhere, as were huddles of khaki-clad soldiers whose job-description obviously included marvelling at the folly of the foreigners but did not mention mopping up. They were there to help unload the envelope once the hangar was dried out and a clean ground sheet covered the floor. Shoes, watches and other sharp objects were removed and even zips on pockets were taped up for the delicate task of unravelling the unwieldy snake of white and silver fabric. About forty of the soldiers and every member of the balloon team joined the human centipede as it struggled under the load. Lighter-than-air? I don't think I have ever tried to lift anything quite so heavy in my life. Eventually the envelope was unfolded – it was massive and filled the entire hangar.

I was surprised to see that as well as checking over the acres of fabric some of Lindstrand's people got on their hands and knees

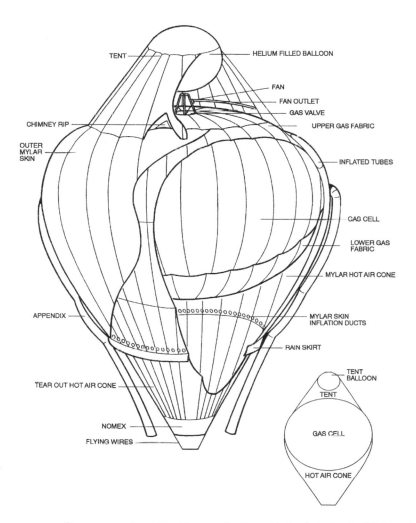

TENT — HELIUM FILLED BALLOON

FAN

FAN OUTLET

GAS VALVE

CHIMNEY RIP — UPPER GAS FABRIC

OUTER MYLAR SKIN

INFLATED TUBES

GAS CELL

LOWER GAS FABRIC

MYLAR HOT AIR CONE

APPENDIX — MYLAR SKIN INFLATION DUCTS

RAIN SKIRT

TEAR OUT HOT AIR CONE —

NOMEX —

FLYING WIRES —

TENT BALLOON

TENT

GAS CELL

HOT AIR CONE

The anatomy of a modern Cameron Rozière, with the distinctive 'tent' balloon sitting at the top of the main helium cell to protect the valve from icing
(Breitling)

and started work painting on the various sponsors' logos. Outside it was a similar story as engineers and electricians crawled over the capsule. It dawned on me that this baby wasn't ready to fly and that our rush across Europe had been somewhat premature.

Monday 15 January 1996, South Dakota

Steve Fossett, the 51-year-old American, launched in the *Solo Challenger* from the Stratobowl in Rapid City, South Dakota. His envelope for the venture was yet another Cameron Rozière, this time with a volume of 200,000 cubic feet, making it only about one-fifth the size of Virgin's, and it was the first to feature a novel new protuberance on the top. To protect the vulnerable gas valve from the risk of freezing Alan Noble had devised a tent to float above the crown of the balloon – held upright by a smaller, 20,000-cubic-foot, helium balloon – which would give the new generation of Cameron Rozières their distinctive cocktail-shaker outline. The envelope also featured improved insulation around the equator where a double skin formed air baffles like a quilted jacket.

Fossett's first global attempt went badly right from the start. During inflation it was noticed that some of the outer layer of fabric, the silvery Mylar, was tearing in places when handled. This fragile material, about the same thickness as a potato crisp packet, was delaminating from the main fabric where it was stretched over the air-filled baffles. While the envelope's ability to contain the helium gas had not been compromised, the tears in the reflective Mylar would have a detrimental effect on the heat insulation. The launch went ahead despite this obvious set-back and for the first 48 hours all proceeded more or less according to plan with the United States obligingly slipping past underneath at a respectable 50 knots. But as his flight progressed Fossett's balloon entered thick cloud, drastically reducing the electrical output of the solar panels which charged the batteries in daylight in order to provide enough power for the nights. No problem, he thought, start the small propane-powered generator. Big problem, he decided, when the generator stalled every time the electrical load cut in. He probably wasn't setting the throttle correctly, but nobody could be sure as the generator ended up in the drink.

*

Solo Challenger exited the eastern seaboard near Norfolk, Virginia. This was much more to the north than anticipated and the balloon's track was slowly turning further northwards despite the best estimates of his weather team. Something, an unexpected weather phenomenon, was bouncing the balloon off its intended course to Europe and during the night Fossett's problems escalated in quick succession. Sounding like the crackling of static electricity, the Mylar fabric around the envelope's equator continued splitting under pressure from the swelling envelope and this dramatically reduced the efficiency of the balloon, and because of the continued cloud cover the solar panels were not doing their job and any residual battery power was fading fast. Fossett also had a problem with one of the burners, which was later put down to low fuel pressure caused by an incorrect propane/ethane mix in the tanks.

Flight Director Alan Noble sent Fossett a message suggesting that he consider a landing as he was clearly caught in the grip of a low-pressure weather system with reports coming in of snow in the area. At first light the Control Centre really started to worry when an automatic Inmarsat satellite position signal didn't come through on schedule. Thirty minutes later the next report also failed to arrive, and then on the hour there was still no signal. 'I advised ATC (Air Traffic Control) and the US and Canadian Coast Guards that we were in what is known as "a period of uncertainty"', said Noble, but added that it might simply be a 'communications difficulty.'

At least Fossett hadn't activated his self-powered EPIRB (Emergency Position Identification Radio Beacon) which gave his team some comfort. But this was soon shattered when the US Coast Guard reported that they had picked up a satellite signal from the EPIRB giving the balloon's position as 60 miles within US territorial waters. A helicopter and jet were scrambled. A little later the Canadian Coast Guard reported that they had the beacon's signal, but at a position many miles further north in their waters. Accordingly the Canadians launched a *Hercules* aircraft and diverted a surface vessel to look for the balloonist. 'There then followed the longest hour I can remember,' recalls Noble.

The Canadians were the first to have something new to report. They had located the balloon's solar panel and a propane tank cover in the sea and they were convinced that Fossett had ditched. 'I suggested that he might be cleaning up for a landing,' Noble says. 'It was only a guess, but it gave some hope.' And he was proved right. A little later the *Solo Challenger* emerged out of dense cloud above the entrance to the harbour of St John, New Brunswick. Fossett had been flying at low level for several hours, throwing out all unwanted equipment to be ready for a landing beside a frozen lake further inland. By the time the television crews reached the scene he was visibly humiliated by his predicament. The balloon's silver outer skin was in tatters and Steve Fossett is not a man accustomed to failure. 'I am very disappointed and embarrassed that I didn't do better on this.'

Although the problem with the Mylar fabric delaminating and tearing, and to a lesser extent the other minor technical glitches, had undoubtedly put paid to any prospects of a global flight by reducing the balloon's anticipated flight duration, Steve Fossett's main undoing had been the weather. It was a salutary lesson that even with the most sophisticated weather-monitoring equipment and computer forecasting techniques, the forces of nature were not entirely predictable. At this early stage in the global game the main players were climbing a steep learning curve.

Monday 15 January 1996, Marrakesh

In Morocco the main posse of reporters and cameramen had arrived on the day of Fossett's launch. I was assigned to show them around the airfield and undoubtedly they were disappointed by what they saw. The capsule and envelope were still being worked on and Richard Branson was not due to arrive until later that evening.

In fact it was nearly midnight when we all gathered in the hotel foyer to await Branson and his entourage. There was a definite buzz in the air and a real sense of impending 'greatness'. Normally relaxed people assumed a stiffer pose with hands clasped in front of their genitals in true royalty-receiving style. A small Moroccan band appeared and trays of the ubiquitous green tea were laid out in anticipation. Excitement mounted as the bright stars of the television cameras weaved their way into the building and moments later there was the man himself – the 'Virgin King' – haloed in the web of lights. Wearing a baggy blue jumper and looking as relaxed as ever, he beamed his toothy smile and exuded bonhomie as he greeted his family and the assembled dignitaries. A true pro, he played out his role and he did it well. Very well.

I overheard two photographers taking bets on how many days it would take them to get Branson posing on a camel. (It took only two.) Giving the media boys what they needed is a vital part of the game and the next morning the first of many regular press conferences was called. Per Lindstrand was also present but third flight crew member Rory McCarthy had yet to arrive.

'Are you scared?', the reporters asked Branson.

'I'm not. Maybe I should be. I shall save that for when it is necessary. I remember the extreme fear on the last two flights and I know that it is counter-productive to be scared. Having been through the Atlantic and Pacific flights with Per it has taken some time to decide to do it, but we have gone out of our way to ensure that, should the gas cell rupture for example, we will still have a hot-air balloon to get us down.'

'Don't forget the parachute,' Lindstrand interrupted in a loud stage whisper. Branson laughed, slightly nervously. 'We will land with the capsule – I'm not parachuting!'

On the Friday news came that Fossett had aborted his flight. That was one less rival, leaving just Henk Brink who seemed to be waiting for Virgin to launch first. Sunday and then Monday passed without the hoped-for launch conditions materializing, but they probably weren't ready to go anyway. To add to their problems a Moroccan Air Force aircraft taxied up close and its backwash blew a cloud of dust and grit right into the balloon's hangar and all over the fragile envelope. 'Any little holes could ruin the flight,' sighed Lindstrand as his team began a careful inspection and clean-up operation. 'A hole the size of my little finger could reduce our endurance by half.'

Still the promised weather failed to turn up. Rory McCarthy did, however – this time the man of many haircuts had shaved his head and he joked that it was to save weight. Buzz Aldrin was also on the scene to lend some gravitas to the situation once more and, with all the grace of a gawky teenager meeting his pop idol, I joined him for breakfast one morning. One of the first two men to walk on the Moon (he doesn't like to be referred to as the second), Aldrin is one of my childhood heroes, and I happened to have a copy of his autobiography with me. He didn't seem at all surprised by this and gladly signed the book, even though his tee-shirt advised the curious to 'Buzz off!' Over the next few days his priorities became obvious as he took every opportunity to promote a Buzz Lightyear doll from the new Disney film *Toy Story*. So much for gravitas.

As more days passed without any action the press corps became fidgety and so Branson decided to treat them to a hot-air balloon flight over the city. 'Are you scared?' he taunted them with a grin as we prepared to launch. He was in one of the big red Virgin balloons and I was at the controls of one of the others flying alongside. It all started well enough, but once above the city we were alarmed to see a vertical wall of slate grey moving in from the west, and as the balloons touched down the skies opened and the deluge began. By the time we finished packing away the sodden envelopes everyone was caked from head to toe in warm sandy-coloured mud. It was a bad omen for the Virgin boss – especially as the rain meant that the roll-out of the capsule scheduled for later that afternoon had to be cancelled. Accordingly the daily photo-calls took on a new theme, 'Rain stops play', and the three pilots obligingly jumped into the swimming pool and column inches were filled as the camera shutters chattered like machine-guns.

To fill the vacuum the rumour mill began to grind. Apparently Rory McCarthy had never intended flying as he suffered from claustrophobia . . . It kept on raining and the locals, delighted to see the sandy soil turning green, were soon referring to Richard Branson as a rain god. Delay followed delay and by late January the despondent reporters were heading home.

Lindstrand announced that if they were not off the ground by 15 February they were packing up. 'He would say that,' claimed Henk Brink. He believed that the announcement by the Virgin team was just a ruse. However, in reality Brink was more concerned about Fossett's problems with the Mylar delamination. 'If the same happened to me halfway over the Alps I don't see how I could land safely.' His envelope was over three years old by this time – it had never been designed to sit on the shelf for so long and upon inspection similar faults were evident. He wasn't the only one concerned and the Dutch aviation authorities moved in to condemn the balloon as unfit to fly. 'They have grounded me after five years of work,' he announced with a weary shrug of resignation. But a scurrilous and anonymous newsletter was doing the rounds by fax machine. Entitled *UNICEF Liar*, it parodied him as 'Fink' – the Dutch hero who never intended to fly, and even tried to suggest that he had instigated the authorities' actions.

Rumour was running out of control by this time, and on 14 February, the day before Per Lindstrand's self-imposed deadline, there was an astonishing message from Virgin denying that Lindstrand had been killed in a car accident in Marrakesh! It turned out that his Land Rover had tumbled down an embankment when he tried to avoid an oncoming car. Time and luck really had run out for the Virgin team and they called it a day for the 1995/96 winter season.

*

All that frantic effort had come to nothing, and the delay would give any new global contenders time to prepare their assaults next winter when the northern hemisphere jetstreams reestablished.

As if to prove the point, when I called in at the Cameron factory in Bristol Alan Noble showed me around one new project that was already taking shape. Behind some screens was a chipboard and fibreglass mock-up of a capsule, about 15 feet long and 7 feet in diameter and shaped like a horizontal cylinder with rounded ends. 'Of course the real thing will be made of Kevlar and carbon-fibre,' he told me, but even in its present form it certainly looked impressive.

It had been designed by the engineer Andy Elson, based on a layout devised by Noble. A balloonist himself, Elson had his own global ambitions and ideas on how to tackle the problem, ideas which he was more than happy to explore through this project. Inside the mock-up a console at the far end housed an array of satellite communication aids, computers and other controls. Moving back through the cylinder there was a food preparation area and then, on either side, simple beds situated above storage spaces. At the back, where I had entered through a bubble hatch, was the emergency equipment – the parachutes and immersion suits – which would be velcroed onto the curved walls so that the pilots could step straight into them and out through the hatch.

Two important innovations were not apparent in the mock-up. When Cameron's were asked to construct the balloon they had little experience in designing capsule pressurization systems and that, Don Cameron told me, proved to be an advantage. 'We didn't have any preconceived ideas about how the job should be done. However, it was easy to see that other global teams proposed carrying as much fuel to power the air pressurization engines as they required to warm the helium at night.' While engine-driven pressurization was the norm in most aircraft, the Cameron team preferred to take its inspiration from the space race and opted for a method of maintaining the capsule atmosphere using a controlled mixture of oxygen and nitrogen obtained from inboard

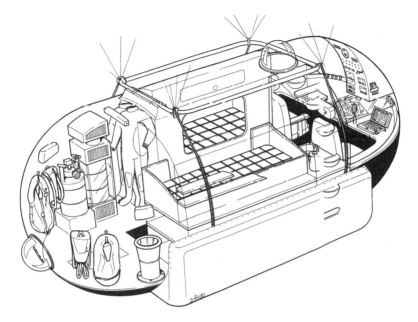

Andy Elson's design for the first *Breitling Orbiter* capsule, 15 feet long, with the kerosene
fuel contained within a large tank at its base, so that no additional propane cylinders
were required. The burners are not shown
(*Cameron Balloons*)

flasks filled with liquid gases. It was an elegant solution to the
problem of providing an air supply, one that resulted in a more
reliable system with fewer mechanical components to go wrong
and eliminated the droning background noise associated with
engine-driven systems.

'This is an enriched oxygen system,' explained Elson. 'The crew
will simply close the main hatch at an altitude of 8,000 to 10,000
feet and the equivalent pressure and mix of gases will be automatically maintained as they climb to their cruising altitude. The
carbon-lithium scrubber should keep the atmosphere reasonably
sweet.'

In another breakthrough intended to save carrying the weight
of heavy pressurized propane cylinders, Elson had devised a

revolutionary burner system that operated on kerosene – jet fuel, to be precise – to be stored in simple lightweight tanks underneath the capsule. The result was a balloon of only 450,000 cubic feet, about half the volume of the *Virgin Global Challenger*, which should require a lot less fuel for a circumnavigation. And to take further advantage of these factors there would be a crew of only two on board. I was sworn to secrecy when Noble revealed that the pilots for this attempt were to be the winners of the 1992 transatlantic race – Bertrand Piccard and Wim Verstraeten. 'And who is the sponsor?' I asked him.

'It's Breitling – the Swiss watch people.'

13 TAKING THE PLUNGE

January 1997, Marrakesh

Richard Branson and the Virgin team returned to Morocco one year later and this time it was not raining. It had been a particularly busy year for Per Lindstrand and his people, conducting several test flights with smaller balloons and constructing a new and slightly larger all-white envelope for the second *Virgin Global Challenger*. Their rivals hadn't been exactly idle either. Fossett had a replacement envelope and the Breitling team had been working against the clock to get their *Orbiter* balloon completed and on-site in Switzerland. Other teams were also lining up but neither the American *Odyssey* high-altitude attempt nor fellow American Dick Rutan had the sponsorship in place to be ready for this winter. Their turn would come later. By this time Henk Brink was out of the picture completely, even though Branson considered letting him have the original Virgin global envelope 'to make a real race of it'.

After the disappointment of the previous winter, Branson was determined to put on a good show and to get off before the other teams. Greedy for success, he was convinced that the race was in the bag this time, and incredibly the jetstream was actually shaping up nicely. Although his Met team could offer only a brief weather window for a launch, on the night of 6 January 1997 the Virgin balloon was readied for flight. At last they were going for it!

Unfortunately, the third man, Rory McCarthy, had developed

a chest infection – mild pneumonia, said the team doctor – and he was forced to stand down. In the shadow of the gently swaying balloon Branson gave his friend an affectionate hug and McCarthy was visibly disappointed to be left behind. Then, clutching a thick volume of *Mensa Puzzles* and a travelling chess set, Branson climbed into the capsule to join Lindstrand and last-minute recruit Alex Ritchie. A small energetic figure with glasses and a mop of unruly black hair, Ritchie had worked with Lindstrand as a design engineer for many years and had been closely involved in the construction of the Virgin capsule. What he might lack in flight training he more than made up for in his intimate knowledge of the balloon's systems.

It was getting late, a little past 11 am, by the time the explosive bolts released the balloon from the grip of its concrete launchpad. In the heat of the morning sun the helium was already swelling and the white balloon ascended swiftly and silently into a gin-clear sky. 'Launch was a little hairy . . . we were spewing helium,' Branson radioed back. 'Oh boy did I go up,' confirmed Lindstrand afterwards. 'I did about 1,600 feet per minute in the beginning. We had too much helium and I had to vent on take-off to get it down to a 700–800 fpm climb.'

On board the *Virgin Global Challenger* Lindstrand was at the controls while Branson monitored the camera equipment and new-boy Ritchie occupied the third seat. It was pretty crowded as the capsule was stuffed with provisions for the long flight. The side hatch remained open at first and drifting over the city of Marrakesh they had a bird's eye view of the intricate labyrinth of narrow passageways and secluded courtyards below. At 10,000 feet the air had become noticeably cooler and thinner and it was time to seal the hatch and begin pressurization. All being well it would be twenty days or more before they expected to open it again.

Sixty minutes into the flight and the fax machine spat out its first and most contentious message. 'Look at this,' groaned Lindstrand and with a face like thunder he passed the flimsy sheet to the others: 'Please be aware that the connectors on the propane fuel tanks are locked-on.' In the headlong rush to get the balloon airborne this simple but vital task had been overlooked. These connectors had to be locked-off if the crew were to release the used empty tanks to rid themselves of their unnecessary weight or, more importantly, if they needed to drop full tanks as ballast in an emergency. Lindstrand was furious. For the rest of the day his large frame was hunched over the controls and he responded only to direct questions. As a solution to their predicament Ritchie proposed that they reduce height in order to depressurize and he would climb out and release the locks manually. 'It's not a problem,' he tried to reassure the others. But the only way to bring the balloon down in the heat of the day was by valving helium and they couldn't afford to waste it so soon into the flight. Instead they must wait for the cool of the night and allow the balloon to descend as the helium contracted naturally. It would be a tricky operation avoiding the dangerous mountain winds, but it had to be done.

Locking-off the connectors was not the only item missed on the checklist – there was no loo paper on board! So they had to wait for incoming faxes before they could disappear down to the tiny toilet. For Branson, who was suffering from a dose of Moroccan tummy, the messages couldn't come in quickly enough. Another distraction presented itself at the Algerian border when they were informed that they were heading straight for a military base at Béchar. 'You are *not* . . . repeat . . . you are *not* authorized to enter this area.' Much frantic negotiating ensued and a promise that they were not carrying any powerful cameras smoothed the way with the Algerian authorities.

By 5 pm the surrounding air, and hence the helium, was beginning to cool as the sun slipped lower in the western sky. Lindstrand fired the powerful propane burners to keep the balloon at 30,000 feet but to his alarm it started to sink. He knew that something was wrong. Either helium had automatically vented from the gas cell as the rounded envelope had pushed its way upwards through the air at launch, or the heat of the day had given them a false sense of buoyancy. 'We're not supposed to be going down this fast.' Through a side window Ritchie checked on the position of the sun and it was not good news. 'It's just over the horizon – sunset won't be long.'

'Then we're going to go down,' responded Lindstrand grimly.

'Are we?' Branson sounded anxious now. 'What do we do then?'

'Panic,' said Ritchie.

'What height are we at?'

'15,000 feet.'

'Christ!'

Lindstrand continued to fire the burners but the balloon didn't respond. 'We've got to dump ballast,' he instructed the others and they struggled to release the ballast, which was supposed to be held in reserve to soften their eventual landing. For a while the balloon steadied, but then it plunged again like an out of control elevator heading for the basement. Lindstrand feared that they had been caught in huge circular air movements, known as rotors, caused by the proximity of the mountains.

Falling out of the sky at a rate of 2,000 feet every minute, time was running out fast and Lindstrand gave the order to get the hatch open. 'Dump everything!' he shouted. Freezing air rushed in as the capsule depressurized and they were already down to 12,000 feet. Gradually the fall was arrested as equipment and supplies tumbled out, but the respite was only momentary and the altimeter indicated that the relentless rush downwards had resumed. It was vital that they drop some of their fuel tanks and they had to do it now!

'Have you ever parachuted before?' Branson shouted to Ritchie over the din of the constantly ringing fax and telephones. Ritchie shook his head and Branson quickly showed him the ripcord before Ritchie clambered out of the top hatch and onto the roof of the capsule. They were at 7,000 feet, in utter darkness and still falling! If he couldn't get the connectors locked-off then they would have no choice but to jump for it.

Per Lindstrand struggled to keep the balloon airborne, but it was flying like a sack of potatoes and out of the blackness below the jagged peaks were rushing up to meet them. Ashen-faced, Richard Branson was shoving anything that wasn't bolted down out of the hatch; food, cameras, equipment, even a bag of dollars. It all had to go to stop the fall. This was a living nightmare for the man who hates parachutes. His minder Rory McCarthy was back in Marrakesh, and anyway the prospect of parachuting in the darkness into these mountains was the last thing any of them wanted to contemplate. Perched on the top of the capsule it was Alex Ritchie, the last-minute stand-in, who was now fighting for their lives.

When the powerful burners fired just feet above his head Ritchie could feel the heat penetrating his clothing and scorching the back of his neck. But at least they provided some light and wrapped in the orange glow he couldn't see beyond the task in hand to what lay below. The capsule was never designed with EVAs in mind ('Extra-Vehicular Activity' to Nasa – 'going outside' to you and me) and Ritchie had to clamber around and over the tangle of equipment and hoses. Inch by inch he reached forward between the enormous propane tanks, incongruously decorated like giant cans of soft drinks, trying to release the safety catches that held them in place. There was no time for recriminations, no time to blame himself or anyone else. The shit had well and truly hit the fan and if he wasn't successful the three-man crew of the *Virgin Global Challenger* would soon be splattered on the treacherous mountains below.

He worked quickly, his fingers deftly finding the locking mechanisms, and as he worked he shouted back to Branson, whose head was now poking up through the top hatch, 'One's off!' Then another and another. And as he fell back through the hatch, Lindstrand pushed the firing switch to the explosive guillotines which were supposed to sever the tank cables and release the first tank. If this failed they were dead men. It was already too late to bale out.

As the tanks fell away the balloon jerked to an abrupt halt and they were thrown down into their seats like rag dolls. A moment's lull and it started to climb again. But it was far from over and for most of the night they fought to control the balloon as it pogoed up and down. They might have survived the ordeal, but all three realized that their global ambitions had been thwarted. 'There was no way we could have taken on the Pacific with no inboard ballast. The flight was over,' Lindstrand later admitted. There was certainly no point in going on to China and risking not getting the balloon back out again, so instead he opted for a landing in Algeria from where it could be more easily retrieved.

At first light the *Virgin Global Challenger* came in low over the orange sand of the Algerian desert. Ritchie sat on top of the capsule to act as Lindstrand's eyes because the view from inside was obscured by the remaining fuel tanks. 'Power-lines ahead!' yelled Ritchie suddenly. But Lindstrand couldn't believe him and quickly popped his head up through the top hatch to check for himself. Incredibly, they had managed to find the only set of power-lines in the middle of this vast desert! Instantly he slammed the balloon down on the soft sand. The explosive bolts were fired and the envelope separated, floated up to 300 feet, inverted and then landed a little downwind of the capsule (a technique designed to prevent excessive dragging by the envelope upon landing, especially in water.) They had been airborne for a little over twenty hours and covered a mere 400 miles. But it was good to be alive and Richard Branson silently vowed to himself that he would never do this again. Yet at the back of his mind he knew he couldn't quit now. 'It's an irresistible challenge and it's buried too deeply inside for me to give it up.'

Sunday 12 January 1997, Château d'Oex, Switzerland

In Switzerland the Breitling team was trying not to sound too smug about Branson's misfortunes. 'There but for the grace of God . . .' was the official response to the media.

The deep sheltered valley of Château d'Oex is a spectacular location and there was a commendable homeliness to the proceedings. Large sheds normally used to house equipment for the local farming community had been taken over by the Breitling team and outside Cameron's people continued their painstaking work preparing the Rozière envelope for inflation. With a volume of 450,000 cubic feet this wasn't the biggest of the global balloons by any means, but engineer Andy Elson had great faith in his kerosene burners and he was confident that this was the winning configuration. The weathermen had given Bertrand Piccard and Wim Verstraeten the green light for a launch on 12 January. However, it was clear that like Virgin they too were rushing to be ready. 'During the night before take-off we couldn't even load our food because the capsule was full of technicians,' admitted Piccard later.

At dawn the cold shadows retreated across the valley floor to reveal the silver balloon standing erect and proudly displaying the five Olympic rings. Piccard had used all his charm and standing in Switzerland to persuade the Olympic officials to lend this endorsement in the hope that it would help to ease the Swiss-registered balloon through any political hot-spots. All activity was now centred around the bright yellow capsule – its upper half covered with a silver film to reflect the heat of the sun. As the two pilots made their final farewells Piccard's eyes filled with emotion as he hugged his wife, their three daughters and the tall distinctive figure of his father Jacques Piccard, but Verstraeten looked nervous. Once the pilots were on board, more helium was added to compensate for the additional weight and the balloon was weighed off – the operation to determine the balloon's buoyancy which was made all the more tricky by the position of the hinged solar panels jutting out from the base of the capsule. Then, in a moment full of the symbolism that typifies Piccard's approach to the round-the-world challenge, the burners were ignited from a torch which had come direct from the Olympic headquarters in Lausanne, and to rousing cheers the *Breitling Orbiter* was on its way into the bright sunlight.

There had been some argument among the team as to whether they should lift off with the top hatch open or sealed with the capsule already pressurized. The decision was taken to go off with it open in case they had to tip ballast overboard. At first the balloon climbed smoothly enough, but the decision with the hatch proved to be a wise one as they had to throw out sand ballast in order to push on up through an inversion layer. At 8,000 feet Piccard and Verstraeten had some difficulty closing the hatch and the balloon was at almost 21,000 feet before they were able to pressurize the capsule.

Thirty minutes later the two pilots became aware of a damp patch in one corner of the capsule. At first they thought it was merely some melted snow from their shoes, but the patch was spreading and when they lifted the floor panels they discovered that the capsule was awash with kerosene leaking from an inboard fuel tank. With their water supply contaminated by the fuel and its obnoxious vapours quickly filling the confined space, burning their eyes and their throats, they knew at once that the flight must be aborted. But as the balloon was still over the mountains they elected to remain airborne for a further six hours until they could ditch in the Mediterranean, just south of Marseilles. This allowed plenty of time to prepare a rescue operation and although the capsule was safely towed ashore everything in it was ruined by the salt water and the sodden envelope was beyond repair. It was a bitter disappointment and a humiliating end to their first attempt. The cause of the leak and their downfall had been a fault with a small connector clip – available in any hardware store, price 50 pence.

14 SOLO CHALLENGER

To portray Steve Fossett as some sort of underdog in this global balloon race would be misleading. After all, how can you have a millionaire underdog? No, what Fossett did was to set his own parameters for the task. He would attempt this flight in his own way – a low tech, low altitude, low profile affair. His capsule was a simple and cramped box. He would eat basic US Army survival rations, and he had a bucket for a loo. It wasn't that he couldn't afford more sophisticated equipment or a nice comfy capsule, but where was the achievement in that? The day after Breitling's fall from grace, he was back in the air for his second attempt.

Monday 13 January 1997, Missouri

It was a bone-chilling night as *Solo Spirit* lifted off from the white snow circle of the Busch football stadium in St Louis and climbed into a jet-black sky. Richard Branson had flown in to be among the well-wishers. 'It is one of the bravest things I have ever seen a man do,' he commented. 'If anyone can do it, I suspect Steve can.'

As the balloon climbed out of the shelter the breeze gave a little nudge into the base of the envelope and for Fossett this was the moment when the adrenalin kicked in – he was on his way. The floodlit glare of the stadium and the intricate spider's web of city lights were soon left behind and the balloon was making good progress drifting at 47 knots over North Carolina and towards the first obstacle, the Atlantic. The launchsite had been chosen as it gave some indication of conditions over the Atlantic while still offering an opportunity to abort the flight before the coast if anything went wrong. But this wasn't necessary and in the early hours of his first day aloft Fossett contacted the Control Centre in Chicago by fax. 'Decision is to continue across the Atlantic.' Fossett was no stranger to this ocean and a freshening wind whisked him across in an apparently effortless three days.

To keep on the right trajectory he valved helium to prevent the balloon climbing above 18,000 feet during the first day. However, this turned out to be a serious error of judgement because the loss of helium so early in the flight meant that henceforth in order to regain height he was forced to fly using the burners, almost like a hot-air balloon, and that would cost him dearly in propane. Worse still, the balloon was heading due east, and not edging up towards Europe as had been hoped, meaning that he was on a collision course with Libya and he had no permission to fly through its airspace.

Life inside the tiny unpressurized Kevlar and carbon-fibre box – 'capsule' almost seems too grand a term for something that resembled little more than a recycling bin – settled into some sort of routine. Just 7 feet long, its interior walls and curved ceiling were covered in a layer of insulation and silver foil like the inside of a cheap disco. A tangle of wires connected the instruments, controls and the bank of batteries, while all around supplies and equipment were piled high. Along one side was a narrow bench on which Fossett managed the occasional fifteen-minute cat nap, and this way he got perhaps two hours of sleep in every twenty-four. For the rest of the time he was crouched over his laptop computer, checking the instruments or operating the controls to give frequent blasts on the burner. His spartan food rations offered little in the way of distraction; MRE or 'Meals Ready to Eat' have a texture and taste similar to that of cardboard and each 'meal' was washed down with a serving of antacid tablets.

To add to his ordeal, one of the cabin heaters was playing up and at night he felt the bite of bitter cold despite wearing his dog-sled boots, thermal underwear, polar fleece and a flying suit. So any time spent with his head poking up through the open plexiglass bubble hatch was kept to a minimum to conserve what precious heat there was inside. Not that he could see much of the ocean or outside world anyway as the occasional forays out of the top hatch to change fuel tanks, or to empty the bucket, offered a view obscured by the clutter of straps and equipment all around. Fossett also kept his movements to a minimum to avoid using the oxygen mask unless really necessary. The weeks of acclimatizing in the mountains and sleeping every night in a special pressure chamber were paying off and he felt none of the ill-effects of altitude sickness. 'That's got to surprise my competitors,' he later said. It certainly did. 'The man's not human,' responded Per Lindstrand.

The Control Centre had originally anticipated a landfall much further north, perhaps at Portugal, but as thunderstorms were brewing in that area they decided to keep the balloon on its present track eastwards, going like an express train in an almost perfect straight line. Gibraltar and northern Africa slipped by like suburban stations and Fossett clocked up yet another ballooning record by becoming the first person to successfully fly the Atlantic for a second time. His team then wanted a slightly more northerly drift as Libyan airspace lay directly ahead on the present path, but the winds did not oblige. By Friday 17 January, four days into the flight, the alarm bells were ringing and the newspaper headlines were already proclaiming the worst, 'Qaddafi sends balloonist's bid for world record off course.'

That morning I got a call from Alan Noble who was just back from the Breitling launch in Switzerland. 'Fossett is over Algeria and trying to avoid Libya. I've been asked to go to the *Solo Spirit* Control Centre in Chicago today. I'll keep in touch.' Others were busy on the telephone too. Richard Branson was bringing his famous address book to bear upon the Libyan problem on Fossett's behalf in an attempt to change Colonel Qaddafi's mind. In Chicago, Fossett's team was adamant that he was not giving up. 'He's going to continue. We're still trying to get permission to fly over Libya.'

Early next morning Fossett sent a message from high above the Saharan wasteland. 'I'm flying at 23,000 feet and it's well below freezing in the capsule. I've had little sleep now for most of four days.' These were not good omens. A balloon is like an oil tanker in that it requires plenty of distance in which to turn; an early decision had to be made if Fossett was to take *Solo Spirit* lower to catch a more southerly route in time – a manoeuvre that would inevitably cost him more time and more precious propane fuel as it was. There were fears that the only way Fossett could avoid Libyan airspace was by landing in Algeria before the border, but it was not an option he wanted to contemplate in that inhospitable landscape. 'Any landing is a total loss of equipment. I would need a helicopter to get it out. There are no roads down here. I say we go for it.'

Fossett's meteorologist, Lou Billones, instructed him to bring the balloon down to 18,000 feet to pick up an albeit slower breeze, but one that would take the balloon around Libya's southern edge. With the long detour already well in hand – the balloon having passed into Niger's airspace – news finally came through that Qaddafi had relented. Fossett immediately dropped two of the depleted fuel tanks and applied some heat to the helium to take the balloon higher than ever, up to 27,800 feet, in an effort to regain speed in the faster winds. After travelling for 150 miles at this height he dropped a little lower into the bottom layer of the jetstream and moving along at a respectable 115 knots he cut across Libya's south-eastern corner and on into Egypt. But it was already too late to salvage the global attempt.

'Getting trashed by cold and short of sleep. RTW (round-the-world) is no longer feasible. Excess fuel consumption leaves us only five and a half days for a distance that would take ten days . . .

Objectives are now restated.' It was an honest assessment by the exhausted aeronaut. Project Director Bo Kemper announced that the extra fuel consumed because of this detour probably meant that the balloon would have to land in India. While it was easy to put the blame on Qaddafi, the fact of the matter was that *Solo Spirit* would never have had adequate fuel reserves to take on the Pacific as the early venting of helium over the Atlantic meant that Fossett had been using the burners too much just to maintain altitude. The consolation prize was that he had already broken his own distance record and that he might yet beat the existing ballooning endurance record which stood at just over six days. And, if that were not enough, he had just completed the very first crossing of Africa by balloon.

As *Solo Spirit* passed over the Red Sea, the Control Centre suddenly received a message that hinted at some local excitement at the Saudi-Arabian border. 'Two Saudi *F-16s* came out to look me over. It was not an intercept pattern.' Memories of Belarus were still fresh in everyone's mind and Fossett couldn't be in a more vulnerable situation than dangling in a bright yellow box beneath a huge silver balloon moving entirely at the mercy of the wind. However, once their curiosity had been satisfied the Saudi pilots peeled away and left Fossett to it.

Two days later the vast expanse of India was rolling by in slow motion and Steve Fossett was studying his charts for a suitable landing location. Two things were uppermost in his thoughts. Firstly, as his St Louis launchsite was just a fraction over 90° West, if he was to pass the symbolic global halfway mark he had to get to the corresponding longitude of 90° East – a line that passes vertically through the eastern edge of India and Bangladesh. And secondly, he desperately wanted to claim the ballooning endurance record, but he must find slower winds or otherwise he would run out of land before the next stretch of water, the Bay of Bengal. On the other hand he knew that he couldn't afford to catch any currents which might turn the balloon northwards into the treacherous Himalayan mountains and risk entering forbidden Chinese airspace beyond. So he took *Solo Spirit* down to a lower 'parking' altitude at just a few thousand feet to clock up the half-day he still needed for the record. But it was still far from plain sailing and his team advised him of a band of thunderstorms ahead of his track – they urged him to get the hell out of it, put the balloon down and forget about the record before it was too late.

Ideally Fossett would have preferred to have flown over the top of the storms, but he couldn't risk covering any more distance in the faster, higher winds and had to sit it out at low level. Few balloonists have experienced the swirling cauldron at the centre of a thunderstorm – powerful air currents which can toss their fragile craft up, down and sideways at an alarming rate. At times *Solo Spirit* was being thrown five miles high and hurtled along at nearly 130 mph, at others it dropped like a stone. 'First line of TSMs (thunderstorms) didn't kill me,' came the laconic message from the capsule. He pushed on.

Monday 20 January 1997, India

As dawn crept over the horizon the air was thick with a blanket of hazy pink, obscuring all traces of the ground just a thousand feet below. After six weary hours of dodging between the storms Steve Fossett informed the Control Centre of a new problem. 'Something blew – then there was sulphur smoke in the capsule.' It turned out to be a minor electrical fault with the equipment and the team was at pains to reassure everybody that he was in no danger.

Fossett faxed again. 'Will land as soon as possible. Lots of fields. Wind impossible in rain showers. Continued TSM danger.' But just when he thought that the endurance record was in the bag a new hurdle was thrown his way – his team realized they had miscalculated how long he needed to stay airborne in order to exceed the existing record by the required margin. If he landed now it would be too soon. Their vital message got to him with only minutes to spare, informing him that he had to stay airborne a few hours longer – easier said than done. At the edge of the thunderstorms the balloon was difficult to control. Twice the Control Centre lost contact with Fossett and for a while they were unsure of his exact position or even if he had landed. It was an anxious time and they all yearned for some much-needed sleep and a break from the never-ending stream of black coffee.

On the other side of the world Steve Fossett was bracing himself for a hard impact. He vented helium to make a landing approach, but the balloon was coming in way too fast and he struggled to pull out of the descent at 100 feet above the ground. He tried again and this time the capsule struck the ground and the whole balloon jerked back upwards to 1,000 feet. On the next attempt he bumped across a ploughed field, the envelope snagged on a tree and with a sharp crack of broken branches it shuddered to a stop. Not the most elegant of touchdowns, but at least he was in one piece.

News of the landing reached me via Alan Noble in Chicago. 'Steve landed near Sultanpur in eastern India after 9,594 miles and six days, two hours and 54 minutes. Final location 26.08° N, 81.57° E. I'm going to bed!'

Hordes of astonished villagers flocked to the scene as the envelope thrashed against the trees, tearing itself to shreds and squeezing out the last dying gasps of invisible helium. 'No one spoke English,' recalls Fossett. 'So I was afraid of getting out of the capsule for fear that they might start climbing in.' Some basic sign language soon made it clear that the locals only wanted to help and an excited crowd escorted him to the village of Nonkhar – so tiny it appears on only the largest-scale maps – from where he called his team. True to form, he didn't talk for long as there was a queue for the solitary pay phone and the millionaire from Chicago didn't have much loose change with him.

He hadn't slept or eaten properly for longer than he cared to remember, but his immediate concern was to make the equipment safe. Despite the tiredness it was a satisfied man who trudged back to the balloon. *Solo Spirit* had carried him halfway around the world in a flight that put him firmly into the record books with both the distance and endurance records.

When the global racers had started their attempts many had assumed that a single flight would speed the successful team round the world in one glorious dash. But it was beginning to look as if it would take one small step at a time to lead them to their goal. Fossett believed that his approach was right, that his experience over distance put him ahead of the other global contenders, and that he just needed to make a few improvements to complete the task. It would be the next winter season, however, before anyone could have another go.

15 BALLOONS BEHAVING BADLY

Richard Branson and Per Lindstrand had flown in to Marrakesh the previous Thursday to join engineer Alex Ritchie, who had earned himself a place as the third man in the capsule after the previous season's roller-coaster ride over the Atlas Mountains. Original crew member Rory McCarthy was also on hand to lend his support, and in a poignant role-reversal he would now act as Ritchie's backup. The Virgin team had pitched camp in Morocco right at the start of the 1997/98 jetstream season in order to avoid the last-minute panics that had plagued their previous attempts. They thought they had time to spare, but on the other side of the Atlantic solo-balloonist Steve Fossett was already on standby for an imminent launch – or was the American bluffing?

According to Lindstrand they had been looking forward to a quiet weekend of training and the chance to review Search and Rescue procedures. There was even time to fit in some parachute training and for good reason. Branson had always been reluctant to relive the horrors of his first and almost last free-fall and until now had flatly refused ever to do it again. And now Ritchie was a fully-fledged member of the flight crew it was vital that he too was thoroughly prepared. All their lives could depend on it. Ritchie had in fact acquired a taste for the adrenalin kick and was keen to do more jumps. Even Branson found himself leaping out of a Cessna after half a day of ground-school refresher and, much to everyone's relief, put in a creditable sky-dive in spite of landing awkwardly on the edge of the taxiway. The resulting grazed hand was more than enough to satisfy the media's blood lust for one day.

There was also the prospect of making a couple of hot-air balloon flights to bring Branson's balloon pilot licence up to scratch to meet the minimum requirement of five hours per year – hardly enough to equip him to fly the *Virgin Global Challenger*, but at least he would hold a current licence rather than be just a passenger on the flight. By the time they all went to bed on Saturday night everyone was in a relaxed frame of mind. After all, the jetstream had yet to form into anything worth getting excited about, and although Fossett remained a nagging worry the weather conditions over in St Louis were keeping his *Solo Spirit* firmly on the ground.

A few hours later the pilots were awakened early with the news that Fossett was declaring a 'go' for launch and they hastily assembled for an emergency summit meeting in Branson's room. He was in a blind panic at the news, but Lindstrand still thought Fossett was only toying with them. Meteorologist Martin Harris suggested that there could be a weather window opening for the Virgin team to launch from Marrakesh early on Wednesday 10 December – although he emphasized that it was a very narrow one. They had to act quickly if they were to take it.

With last year's bungled attempt in mind, Lindstrand's main concern was that the preparation and inflation time for the launch would be too condensed. But Branson pressed hard. He was a man with a vision. In October the *Thrust SSC* supersonic car driven by Andy Green had broken the sound-barrier at Black Rock, Nevada, establishing a new Land Speed Record for Britain, and Branson openly admitted that he wanted to win the global race to round off the year with an inspiring British double-act. Then in November the *Observer* had published details of a secret recommendation of Branson by the Conservative Party Leader, William Hague, as a candidate for a knighthood in the New Year's Honours. There were other time constraints pressing on Branson who needed to complete the flight before the year was out. It was vital that he was in London in January to attend an important High Court libel case against Gtech's boss Guy Snowden over their rival bids for the National Lottery.

So Branson was desperate to grab any opportunity to get ahead of his ballooning rivals, now numbering six teams. When this early weather window presented itself, it was as if the final piece of the jigsaw was slotting into place.

'We're going – I take responsibility,' he declared. And at midday on Sunday 7 December, flight status was upgraded from 'Green' to 'Yellow' for an anticipated Tuesday night inflation and a launch of the *Virgin Global Challenger* at dawn on the Wednesday morning. The weather wasn't quite so obliging, however, and by the early hours of Tuesday Martin Harris was saying that the slot for a Wednesday launch had gone and that if the balloon wasn't airborne by 1800 hours that day they would have to scrub the flight.

Lindstrand's worst fears had come true. The urgency would crank up the pressure on his launch crew inflating the massive balloon in the searing heat of the north African sun. Balloons, especially big ones, are at their most vulnerable on the ground and it is all too easy for a half-filled one to become a fully-fledged spinnaker in gusty or thermic conditions. Which is why the accepted practice is to prepare them in the cooler, calm conditions of the night and launch either during the night itself or at dawn. Lindstrand argued that it was way too risky to rush matters. But this advice was overridden by an inflated notion of invulnerability and the great impetus of the moment. The *Virgin Global Challenger* must fly from Marrakesh – that day.

By mid-morning the helium gas was screeching through the filling tubes and into the swelling hump of balloon fabric. Everything was going well enough, although the atmosphere on the launchsite was electric with tension. With several hours yet until the launch itself, Branson returned to the hotel to put some finishing touches to his will, write letters to his daughter, Holly, and his son, Sam and to do some last-minute packing. Meanwhile,

Lindstrand was deep inside the capsule – officially he was running through some final checks with Ritchie, but in fact he was doing the hoovering because no one else could be spared.

In a little while the capsule would be moved into position underneath the upright mushrooming envelope. That was the most dangerous part of the whole procedure. The suspension wires hanging from the bottom of the envelope would be unhooked from their concrete attachment points and transferred to the capsule. Once this process began, the 1,000,000 cubic feet envelope would be held in check by sixteen Kevlar ropes connected via its equator to winches on the ground. These winches would then slowly play out the ropes, allowing the balloon to assume its full height. With last year's inflation under their belts the ground team was well practised, but they never dreamt they would be doing it in the full heat of the day.

Disaster struck at approximately 11.00 am. The wind had become increasingly lively and the Virgin Project Director Mike Kendrick was voicing his concern. 'I don't like this at all,' he confided. It was already gusting 5 knots and more, and he knew that the launch was threatened if the ground wind rose above 8 knots.

Then came one gust stronger than the others. (Branson claims it was caused by the backwash from a British Airways jet taxiing on the nearby runway – another twist in the needle-match between the two airlines.) It punched into the flaccid envelope, causing it to flatten and lurch to one side, putting an intolerable strain on just a few of the ropes. One of them snapped like a gunshot. 'We're losing it!' yelled Kendrick. The engineers struggled to secure the broken rope. But it was too late. Another rope broke. Then another. And one by one, like a row of dominoes, they all gave way in quick succession. The vast envelope bellowed inwards, sucked in on itself. It dragged a winch across the ground and then, free at last, rocketed skywards, trailing helium hoses and showering the ground crew with dust and debris.

'The balloon's gone!' Per Lindstrand heard the shouts and looking up through the top hatch of the capsule he got a glimpse of what he thought was a toy balloon drifting past. 'It looked horribly familiar and my stomach churned when I realized it was ours.' He above anyone else knew how great a risk daytime inflation had been.

Kitted-up in his flying suit, Richard Branson was still in his hotel room when the phone rang. 'Richard, the project is off for a bit.' It was Kendrick, calling from the airfield. 'The balloon has gone!'

'You're not joking? You're not joking?' Branson pleaded over and over again. In disbelief, and barely resisting the urge to fling the phone against the wall, he rushed to the window to see for himself the ghastly truth. There it was – a huge silver and white jellyfish spiralling upwards into the azure sky – the *Virgin Global Challenger* was floating off . . . without him. And with it went his dream of becoming the first man to fly a balloon around the world. The global race was in full swing and it was his third time in Morocco, but so far he had made only one brief flight – and that had nearly cost him his life. Maybe his legendary luck had finally deserted him.

Still in a state of shock, Branson raced to the airfield to assess the damage for himself. It was not the first time that he had had to deal with public failure on this scale. When in 1990 his first Pacific hot-air balloon had suffered a catastrophic delamination of the envelope fabric just moments before the launch and the flight was cancelled, he had turned to a bottle of whisky for solace and the next day's headlines were not a pretty sight. Having learned his lesson the hard way, and never one to underestimate the influence of the media, he arrived at the airfield with a shrug of resignation and through gritted teeth smiled in the face of adversity and a sea of flashbulbs. With his children holding his hands he tried to be upbeat. 'Obviously we are bitterly disappointed, but we have to look on the bright side – at least we are alive to fight another day.'

Indeed it was very fortunate that nobody was killed or hurt that day in Marrakesh. The well-drilled ground crew had stuck to the golden rule of ballooning. Even when your natural response is to hang on for dear life, you must never let your feet leave the ground.

Marrakesh, December 1997. The Virgin threesome, Per Lindstrand, Richard Branson
and Alex Ritchie, commiserate after their envelope breaks fr
(Chas Breta

If one of them had held on for too long the shortest of falls could
have been fatal. To have been carried up with the balloon would
have had the same dire consequences, with hypoxia soon setting
in as it climbed higher and higher. It was also lucky that no one
was struck by the violent whiplash of the snapping ropes and the
flailing helium tubes, or hit by other loose equipment.

With the escaped envelope still visible high above them,
Branson addressed the devastated team – many of them were in
tears. 'Sorry everybody, it's a horrible disappointment. We have to
be positive. I promise that we will try again . . . only next time I
plan to be in the balloon.' And putting an arm around his son's
shoulder, he smiled. 'At least I'll be home for Christmas Sam.'

The first immediate task was to see if they could salvage the
envelope and, hopefully, the situation. Later that same afternoon
Branson's *Lear Jet* caught up with the wayward envelope drifting
high above the snowy peaks of the Atlas Mountains. At an altitude

in excess of 50,000 feet, it was much too high for the jet to make a close inspection – but even at that distance a triangular flap of fabric could be seen hanging limply from the hot-air cone. That wasn't so bad. It was the integrity of the helium cell that was the vital issue, and the fact that the envelope was flying so well indicated that it remained gas-tight.

However, the problems would really start when the envelope came back to earth. Would it still be usable after a landing in the desert, or worse still in the mountains? To complicate matters it was still heading eastwards towards neighbouring Algeria – a country that had strained diplomatic relations with Morocco. And beyond Algeria was Libya. Things could go from bad to worse. At least in that direction it was unlikely to come down on any built-up areas and so there was little risk of it causing any damage.

Keen to ensure that the balloon remained within Moroccan territory, Branson requested the help of the Moroccan Air Force to shoot it down. Bad idea. It takes more than a few bullet holes to make much difference to a balloon of this size. Anyway, it was still far out of reach. At dusk another sortie by the *Lear Jet* brought good news. The balloon was rapidly descending all by itself in the cooler air of the night and was already down to 8,000 feet. The bad news was that it was wavering over the border and, sure enough, during the night it finally came to rest 30 miles within Algeria (and to add insult to injury it had flown further than the Virgin pilots managed on their previous attempt).

Wednesday morning, 10 December, and the Virgin jet poked its nose into Algerian airspace once more so that Alex Ritchie and his team could take a closer look. They easily spotted the white balloon against the deep red of the Sahara sand and they saw that it was surrounded by a swarm of Algerian soldiers fighting to tether it to a small tree. There was genuine concern that it might float off as the heat of the day acted upon the helium – the whole pantomime could start all over again. The plane was ordered back to Morocco by the Algerian authorities, but Ritchie's team managed to capture the scene on video during a ground-hugging fly-past. At first sight the envelope appeared to be in a reasonable condition, except for a large rent that ran up the full height of the hot-air cone, slicing through the distinctive red logo.

When Richard Branson viewed the footage he felt optimistic. 'It looks in a very good state from the air and I think that if we can retrieve it we have a good chance of flying again.' Unfortunately the Algerians refused to let a Moroccan Chinook helicopter over the border to collect the envelope, and instead their soldiers man-handled it onto the back of an army truck. Being dragged across the desert was bad enough but, given the almost surgical condi-tions in which these envelopes are constructed, this rough treat-ment was the final straw.

Alex Ritchie was taking a more pragmatic view on the prospects of a quick repair job. 'It all depends on the extent of the detailed damage,' he told the reporters. 'It's going to take days to fix – that's for sure. A Saturday take-off is out of the question.' And he was right. It was Friday 12 December before he and Per Lindstrand got to examine the envelope for themselves. The news they relayed back to Mike Kendrick in Marrakesh was not good. Lindstrand was convinced that they had only one option – to build a new enve-lope from scratch. But with only six to eight weeks at most before the jetstream was expected to give out, it would be a Herculean task – perhaps an impossible one. Not surprisingly the mood within the Virgin camp was sombre as they packed up and headed for home knowing that they were leaving the field wide open for their com-petitors. Meanwhile Fossett had delayed his launch.

New Year's Eve 1997, St Louis, USA

For the first time there were two global balloons taking off on the same night, and they both happened to be solo attempts. This was Steve Fossett's third shot at a circumnavigation and he was looking forward to a flight without any nasty surprises. His launch team, working at the Busch Stadium, St Louis (his wife's home town), was still in the festive spirit and caught in the glare of the flood-lights the *Solo Spirit* resembled an oversized Christmas bauble hanging against the ebony sky.

It was time to get going. Fossett reached up and fired the twin burners which lifted the balloon clear of the stadium's circle, and it drifted out over the city. He was in confident mood – he had already flown further and for longer than any other person in the history of ballooning – and Flight Director Alan Blount described the launch as 'picture perfect'. All was going well and the prospects were looking good for the Atlantic crossing – except perhaps for the weather awaiting him in Europe.

Further south, global first-timer Kevin Uliassi was also prepar-ing to launch that night. Tall, dark-haired and handsome, thirty-three-year-old Uliassi was the all-American boy living out an American dream – it was the romantic quest of an architect who had given up everything to buy a balloon, named it after his wife *J Renee*, and was setting off to single-handedly conquer the world in the spirit of Charles Lindbergh.

As his launchsite Uliassi had selected a 300-foot-deep gravel quarry near Rockford, Illinois – a spectacular and well sheltered location with almost vertical rock faces rising on all sides, creating the illusion of a huge building with only the heavens for a roof. The image of the plain white balloon bathed in powerful lights was beamed to thousands of homes by the TV companies and the locals passed up on the usual New Year's celebrations to come and press their noses against the wire fences of the quarry. They wanted to see their boy and marvel at his 'majestic balloon', as one onlooker described it. This was the smallest of the global balloons, a standard Cameron 'Atlantic-type' *R420* Rozière with no frills. No clever tent on top to keep the icing off the helium valve and the white capsule was much like Fossett's, the basic economy model, although Uliassi had it made himself to save an extra $500 on the price Camerons had quoted.

The band of volunteers worked hard well into the bitterly cold night – it was −20°C and long icicles were draped across the surrounding walls of rock. It was their first experience of a Rozière launch and what they may have lacked in experience they made up for in sheer enthusiasm. But at times the cracks began to show. Wooden platforms had been prepared so that the fuel tanks could be presented up to the capsule in exactly the right position. The only trouble was that nobody got around to actually attaching the tanks and, as the helium flowed and the balloon became buoyant, it started rising up without their weight to hold it down. Organized chaos ensued with everyone and anyone near the capsule leaping on board to pull the balloon back to earth.

Kevin Uliassi managed to look laid-back about the proceedings and the flight ahead. 'I look forward to it as an adventure. I know I may be uncomfortable, I may be cold, I may not be as well fed as I am here on the ground, but I try to enjoy every balloon flight – even the tough ones.'

At just after 8.30 pm everything was finally ready. Uliassi's wife presented him with a huckleberry pie, a kiss and a hug. 'See you in ten days,' he called to her from the capsule. At 8.45 pm the restraining rope was cut. Caught by surprise Uliassi was jolted backwards before he realized what was happening. Instinctively he fired the burners, further heating the balloon which was already shooting skywards like a homesick angel. All around cameras were flashing and the crowds were cheering – the *J Renee* was on its way. The balloon ascended quickly, perhaps a little too quickly, but Uliassi was keen to get clear of the shelter of the quarry as swiftly as possible, and the envelope gave a little twist as it caught the upper breeze.

'The balloon initially took off with 900 lb of free lift,' Uliassi later confirmed, and he reckoned that it had climbed out at an initial speed of up to 800 fpm. This was already in excess of the manufacturer's recommended rate of ascent for this type of balloon and, as one eye-witness verified, the envelope was still flickering with the glow of the hot-air burners as it climbed. Uliassi was pushing *J Renee* hard. At 4,000 feet the ascent had slowed down, but with temperature inversions still to come he then dropped ballast and fired the burners again, this time taking the balloon all the way up to 15,000 feet. It didn't stop there and continued to rise at nearly 500 fpm before rounding out. 'I got somewhere just over 21,000 feet and knew I should be getting to my ceiling,' he recalled after the flight. As the balloon climbed, the ambient air pressure was reducing with height, causing the helium cell to swell. The ceiling was the point at which the helium could not expand any further without some of the gas spilling out through the appendix tubes hanging on either side of the envelope. (These were used to fill the helium cell initially and during the flight acted as automatic pressure relief valves as any excess gas was forced down and out through the open bottom of the tubes.) Sometimes also known as 'pressure altitude', this ceiling is the natural point at which a balloon should go no higher. When Uliassi saw that the appendix tubes were still slack he knew that something must be wrong. With the tubes not discharging properly, *J Renee* was like a dam under pressure – it was about to burst.

'I shook the rope that attaches the appendix to the capsule to see if something had tangled at the bottom,' Uliassi reported afterwards. 'There didn't appear to be anything wrong . . . I reached for my knife and that was when there was this huge explosion.' *J Renee* rocked violently with a loud thunderclap. Uliassi simply couldn't believe what had happened, but when he grabbed a torch and looked up into the gaping envelope there were shreds of fabric hanging everywhere. His balloon had burst! The whole bottom end of the helium cell was gone and what's more, he couldn't be sure of the extent of any other damage. 'I didn't know if there were tears on top or if it was going to rupture.'

Heart pumping, he fired both burners and then struggled into his parachute faster than during any practice drill. Luck, of sorts, was on his side. The outer envelope was still intact and there was only a gradual loss of the precious helium. In fact the balloon was actually climbing higher of its own accord because the previously confined gas had now expanded within the open-bottomed envelope, creating even more lift. Realizing this he immediately shut off the burners and the stricken balloon began its lonely fall out of the sky.

Radioing Air Traffic Control, Kevin Uliassi declared a 'Mayday'. They didn't believe him at first and it took two more calls to convince them of his plight. He knew he had to keep his nerve to get back down in one piece, but it was very dark and it was a very long way down. Fortunately the descent was more or less under control, but whenever the rate of fall exceeded 500 fpm the balloon started to make alarming popping and tearing noises and Uliassi would open up the burners to keep it in check.

In response to the Mayday the Indiana State Police launched a helicopter and it raced to the scene with a chase plane in hot pursuit. At 3,000 feet they located the balloon and began the tricky operation of getting Uliassi down in the darkness. The helicopter hovered about 2,000 feet ahead of *J Renee* and with a powerful searchlight the crew picked out suitable landing fields. It took them a while to appreciate that the balloon was at the mercy of the wind and couldn't turn to either side, but in constant radio contact with Uliassi they soon got the hang of it. Suddenly a string of tall power lines loomed up out of the gloom and Uliassi had to fire the burners to climb up over the wires before a good landing spot presented itself.

The first bump to earth was surprisingly gentle. Even the huckleberry pie survived intact. But the helium valve didn't open properly for some reason and the balloon bounced and fought to be back in the air. The local fire crew was on the scene by then and they chased after the dangling landing rope and managed to tie it off to their truck as the balloon dragged through the snow before draping itself over some agricultural irrigation equipment. It was all over for Kevin Uliassi, and as he struggled to gather up the balloon that had cost him so dearly, he was anxious to warn the other teams flying with similar Cameron-built balloons that something had gone terribly wrong. The appendix had not relieved the build-up of internal pressure within the gas cell, either because of an inherent problem with its design or manufacture, or possibly because Uliassi had climbed too fast. Either way, he wanted to prevent this happening again. But no one was listening.

16 BOOM OR BUST

New Year's Day 1998, over the Atlantic

Steve Fossett, meanwhile, had experienced no such problems with his balloon and was steaming along at 20,000 feet on course for the Atlantic. He knew that a good crossing was vital to set up his trajectory through Europe. This was the third flight over the ocean for the balloonist, another record, and he did it in double-quick time riding beneath a fast polar jetstream at speeds of up to 150 knots. Once again the anticipated landfall at Portugal was not shaping up too well with the balloon being drawn further and further north, away from the jetstreams and smack into some of the most devastating winter gales that the British Isles had experienced in many years. In an attempt to climb above the worst of the storms he dropped two empty fuel tanks off the coast of Wales, yet despite this the balloon was still caught in violent turbulence.

'Steve Fossett is not going to be intimidated by these weather conditions,' boasted a spokesman from the Control Centre at Washington University, St Louis, not the one taking the high-altitude roller-coaster ride.

'Everything is going well,' Fossett himself tried to reassure his team in a radio message. 'I'm convinced we're going to make it.' Once over Germany a lower track turned *Solo Spirit* almost 90° to the south-east and in the right direction for northern Africa and the jetstream winds Fossett had to ride to India and then onwards to the Pacific. On the other hand this course could also bring him directly in line for an encounter with an old adversary, Colonel Qaddafi, who had refused permission to overfly Libya last time . . . until it was too late.

Fossett's Flight Director, Alan Blount, redoubled his efforts to get clearance and eventually Tripoli relented, but for the most unlikely of reasons – through contacts in the British Scout movement. Colonel Qaddafi, a Queen's Scout, was giving assistance to Steve Fossett as a fellow 'scouter'. In spite of this change of heart, again it was too late. Fossett had already taken the drastic step of reducing height from 27,000 feet to 15,000 feet in order to catch another airstream bending up to the north and away from Libya. 'I overdid it,' he confessed later. *Solo Spirit* was now off course heading towards Bulgaria and Turkey. The damage was done.

The pictures transmitted from within the cramped capsule showed that Fossett certainly looked in good shape, huddled over his laptop computer studying the weather charts. But he knew that *Solo Spirit* was in the doldrums – caught in slow winds that were keeping him too far to the north. If he couldn't get back to the jet-streams he would not have enough fuel to tackle the Pacific and a circumnavigation was looking increasingly out of the question. As if that were not enough, yet again he was plagued by problems with the capsule's heaters, and the remote control device for one of the burners was malfunctioning. This meant he had to reach up through the open bubble-hatch to fire the problem burner and then return to the freezing capsule. Fossett may be known as a man who thrives on discomfort, but even he needed sleep and warmth and he was being deprived of both. 'It really wears on you to be sitting in an environment that cold,' he admitted during the in-flight exchange.

After struggling vainly to get back southwards, on Monday 5 January Fossett brought the balloon down to earth in a muddy field north of Krasnodar in southern Russia, to the east of the Black Sea – it was all over.

'I enjoy coming to Russia,' he said, putting on a brave face for the camera crews. Yet there was no disguising the disappointment as he struggled in the drizzle, ankle-deep in the sticky mud, to recover the equipment, all the while trying to endure the over-enthusiastic assistance of a band of local soldiers and volunteers. For once the bright spark in his tired eyes had dimmed. To put this flight into perspective, it had been the second greatest balloon voyage ever made – the first being Fossett's own 10,361-mile passage to India the previous winter. He had been airborne for five days and travelled 7,300 miles. But to Fossett it represented a failure because he expected to make improvements with every flight – the only way to break records, which was the name of his game.

Sunday 4 January 1998, New Mexico, USA

While *Solo Spirit* was still airborne, the *Hilton Global* balloon was being readied for inflation at Albuquerque, New Mexico. It had been known as *Aeolus 1* until the hotel magnate Barron Hilton had signed up as main sponsor. The American aviator Dick Rutan had originally recruited the *Earthwinds Hilton* veteran and fellow countryman Richard Abruzzo as his 'co-pilot'. In fact Rutan had virtually no practical experience in ballooning whereas Abruzzo was the son of Atlantic conqueror Ben Abruzzo and an accomplished hot-air and gas balloon pilot in his own right. When he had competed in the 1992 transatlantic race as part of the US team he had established a new duration record for a Rozière balloon. However, Abruzzo suddenly stood down, claiming family commitments – and Rutan's new partner was Dave Melton, another former *Earthwinds Hilton* pilot and an experienced hot-air and gas balloonist.

As darkness fell on that chilly evening of 4 January 1998 in New Mexico, Dick Rutan called to all the team members to gather around for what they expected to be a little pre-inflation pep talk.

And indeed he did tell them what a great team they were and what an incredible job they had done with the balloon. Then came the bombshell. After discussion with the Met team he had decided that conditions were no longer suitable for a global flight. 'Call it a wrap!' Everyone was dumbstruck – no one had any inkling of this. The immediate question was what to do with the envelope, laid out and fully prepared for inflation? Too much handling would do it no good, and the only solution was to take Rutan at his word – to 'wrap it up' in the groundsheet and leave it until he was ready to fly.

Thursday 8 January 1998, Château d'Oex

With most of the British journalists I arrived in Switzerland only to discover that the planned launch of the *Breitling Orbiter 2* was postponed until the morning of Friday 9 January. I tracked down Bertrand Piccard who explained that while the jetstream had been perfect for a fast flight all the way to Japan, their trajectory would have taken them directly to forbidden China. The new weather slot offered the Breitling team a much better track – to Egypt and from there eastwards to the Pacific, avoiding China altogether, but it would also bring the penalty of a much slower start with wind speeds estimated at a sluggish 15 knots. Undeterred, Piccard boldly suggested a 99 per cent chance of success for Breitling since *Solo Spirit* had landed by this time and both Virgin and Uliassi were out of the picture. With Bob Martin's *Odyssey* high-altitude team – now a joint American/Australian project – holding out for a southern hemisphere flight in the middle of the year, that left only the newcomer Dick Rutan to worry about.

On the Thursday morning the 650,000-cubic-foot envelope was laid out on a carpet of snow and plastic sheeting. The capsule was expected to arrive at any moment. Inside the nearby buildings the ill-fated *Breitling Orbiter 1* capsule was on display and to pass the time I looked around the small exhibition. I watched as a young child climbed the steps up one side of the yellow pod just as an elderly woman climbed the other, and they met on the top – two generations united in their curiosity.

By early afternoon the weak sun was dipping behind the mountains. As the temperature began to fall the photographers and camera crews were growing impatient, kicking their heels in the slushy snow. The capsule's arrival had been delayed. At least Piccard and fellow pilot Wim Verstraeten were on the scene – although there had been no sight of Andy Elson, who would be joining them on this attempt in the capacity of flight engineer. For days he had been working tirelessly around the clock on the capsule and his veins were probably coursing with pure caffeine by this point.

Four pm and the sense of anticipation was almost tangible. In the distance the flashing lights of the transporter marked the capsule's slow progression towards the launchsite. It was a darker colour than the previous one and with heat-reflecting foil covering its upper half it looked like a cross between a diving bell and Nasa's latest spacecraft. Following just behind it was Elson driving a pick-up containing the balloon's solar panel array. He looked dishevelled and tired, but still managed to give me a broad grin in greeting, complete with the trademark gap in his front teeth. The crowds parted as the transporter manoeuvred into position beside a crane and moments later Elson was on top of the capsule directing operations and hooking on the crane's lines. I was standing just a few feet away as the capsule was hoisted upwards, ever so gently . . . Then crunch! In one heart-rending moment it fell back onto the trailer with a sickening thud. Something was seriously wrong. The burner and load frame had completely pulled away at one end and the capsule's ladder was twisted at an awkward angle. 'They've fucked it up,' I unintentionally spurted out loud – a lone voice in the stunned silence. And that just about summed it up.

This was the first time that the capsule had been lifted with a full load of fuel on board and closer inspection revealed that one of the main suspension cables had pulled out of its connector under the strain. If the cable hadn't failed at that moment, the next time the capsule was to have been lifted would have been underneath the balloon as it took off – with the additional weight of the three-man crew! The consequences of that happening were almost too terrible to comprehend. And thank God nobody had been in its way or that it hadn't fallen from a greater height causing more significant damage – perhaps even rupturing the fuel tanks and engulfing the launchsite in a massive fireball.

Verstraeten, who had also been right beside the capsule when it fell, was visibly shaken. Piccard had been further away and he immediately rushed over to see what had happened. He couldn't believe his eyes and fighting back the tears he explained the situation to his wife Michelle and their little daughters. 'Daddy isn't going to fly around the world today.'

The Breitling team gathered for an immediate post-mortem press conference and as the world's media shuffled inside, the bearded figure of Flight Director Alan Noble sat with his head buried in his hands. It had been a bitter disappointment at the eleventh hour, but Noble hadn't completely lost his sense of humour. 'It spoils your day – it's been a good day up to now.' So what went wrong? The capsule had been lifted by crane many times before and although it was now fully laden with fuel, this simply should not have happened. Andy Elson explained, 'These are completely standard parts. For some reason, and we don't yet know why, the cable pulled out of the fittings. We obviously have to do some repairs to the capsule, but structurally it is sound . . . and we can be ready to be in the air by next week.'

In fact the cables and fittings had been installed by a specialist company – they were one of the few components on the balloon not to be fitted by the Breitling team themselves. Why they failed under loading has never been explained by the company which continues to deny liability for the incident.

Piccard remained philosophical. 'Today was a nightmare and I

hope the dream will come true in the next few weeks. There is only
one way to avoid any problems . . . it is never to try anything.'

Friday 9 January 1998, New Mexico

The same day that the Breitling capsule went off its trolley, Dick
Rutan was ready to try again with the *Hilton Global* at
Albuquerque. The distinctive spherical capsule had been on site
for several days and was now encircled by a cluster of lightweight
propane tanks which sparkled in their copper-coloured coats. As
well as the Hilton name, the capsule displayed the Pepsi logo and
the ominous legend 'Experimental'.

There was a slight delay in proceedings while they dealt with a
pressurization problem, though Bert Rutan soon had it sorted out.
Then with the 180-foot balloon towering skywards, Dick Rutan
and Dave Melton said their goodbyes and wriggled through the
tangle of ropes to enter the capsule through its single top hatch.
Shortly afterwards the restraints were cut and the *Hilton Global*
balloon jerked free. With a blast from the quadruple burners
sending it climbing swiftly into the New Mexican sky, it was going
up like a cork out of a bottle; radar later confirmed that the initial
rate of climb had accelerated to 1,500 fpm. 'Maybe we did take
off a little hot,' Rutan subsequently admitted. 'There were two
inversions we had to go through. We were going up fast and Dave
started valving off helium.'

Trailing the Stars and Stripes, the *Hilton Global* headed out over
the Sandia Mountains and was on its way. The rate of climb gradually reduced, stabilizing at 200 fpm within fifteen minutes, and
by the time the balloon approached float altitude at 27,500 feet it
had slowed to a stately 100 fpm. With the heat of the rising sun
now on the envelope the helium, which had already expanded as
the surrounding air pressure reduced with height, was fully
extended within the gas cell to the point where excess gas needed
to escape through the appendix tubes dangling on either side of

the envelope. Both pilots later reported that they noticed that the helium appeared to be constricted within the tubes and that one of them seemed to be completely obstructed. With the balloon no longer climbing and in level flight, all was quiet for about ten minutes. Then, without warning, the balloon shuddered and they heard a loud whoosh as the gas cell burst. Looking up inside the mouth of the envelope they could see that a good 50 per cent of the bottom membrane of the helium cell was in tatters. And the balloon was spinning, suggesting that helium was escaping elsewhere.

'It kept creaking and popping,' Rutan recalls. 'Then there was one really loud creak that made me determined that we were going to bail out.' He declared a Mayday as the balloon climbed to 32,000 feet on its own – just as with *J Renee* the helium which had been confined under pressure was free to expand and was generating more lift. Melton tugged on the helium valve to release some of the gas and the balloon started its slow spiral downwards.

'I think it was almost two hours later that we decided to abandon the balloon,' Rutan said later. 'So it wasn't a decision made in the heat of the moment.' They considered landing the *Hilton Global*, but the ground wind was already a steady 25 to 30 knots and gusting. To put down with the full propane tanks strapped around the capsule was a dangerous option, and dropping them off one by one might be too big a shock for the damaged envelope – not to mention the potential danger to anyone on the ground. Once the balloon was down to 9,000 feet the two pilots climbed out onto the top of the capsule and prepared to jump for their lives. Melton went first and his orange parachute opened immediately, soon to be followed by Rutan who executed a graceful free-fall before operating his chute.

In the windy conditions at ground level Melton was badly hurt, breaking his hip as he was dragged across the rough terrain, while Rutan suffered the final indignity of a bloodied face full of cactus spines. 'I was looking forward to doing a little sky-diving again,' Rutan told his rescuers. 'I thought, what the hell, it may be my last parachute jump. I might as well enjoy the sport of sky-diving.' He certainly wasn't enjoying the sport of ballooning that much. The *Hilton Global* had so far flown just 100 miles.

The crew abandoned the balloon because it seemed to them the safest thing to do. On its first contact with the ground, eleven propane tanks and two nitrogen tanks were torn free. It then flew on for a further seven hours and the US Air Force tracked it as it bumped down five times before finally coming to grief when it struck power-lines. The propane tanks duly exploded, lighting up the night sky as flames engulfed the capsule, but still the severed envelope didn't want to call it a day and it drifted on for another five miles before coming to rest.

Within the ballooning community both Rutan and Uliassi were widely criticized for their inexperience and blamed for their own downfall. However, the official report of the American NTSB (National Transport Safety Board) stated that, for several reasons, on both balloons the appendix tubes, the outlets for excess helium, were insufficient and could have been operating well below the manufacturer's own design specifications. If these appendix tubes were not discharging the excess gas then it was almost inevitable that the internal pressure within the gas cell increased to a point where something had to give, and the bottom of the cell was designed to do just that. In the case of the *Hilton Global* balloon there is clear radar evidence to prove that it was not climbing too quickly, causing the helium to expand faster than the tubes could deal with, except during the initial climb-out. The pilots were not to blame.

Rutan wishes that he had heeded Kevin Uliassi's warning. 'God, here's this guy's balloon with a major structural failure and we didn't even look into it that much. Sometimes in the press of the moment and getting going, that is something that you just don't want to hear.'

When this winter's fifth attempt went wrong it was described as 'ballooning's latest fiasco' by the media. The sky thick with Maydays, one balloon had gone off without its capsule, one capsule hadn't gone anywhere except back onto its trailer, another balloon had come down after just a couple of hours, and to cap it all, a crew had come down without its balloon!

By mid-January both Virgin and Breitling were frantically regrouping. Back in England Per Lindstrand was building a new envelope at breakneck speed and in Switzerland Andy Elson was fixing the Breitling capsule while their envelope had been returned to Cameron's factory in Bristol – officially to be checked over after being spread out on the snow at Château d'Oex – but there were also concerns that whatever had befallen the *J Renee* and *Hilton Global* balloons shouldn't happen again. To date, only Steve Fossett had managed to put in anything resembling a Global-class flight, but at least nobody had been killed . . .

Sunday 18 January 1998, Marrakesh

The global jinx struck its last and most tragic blow when Virgin's Alex Ritchie sustained grave injuries as the result of a practice parachute jump that went horribly wrong. He was using a Moroccan sports parachute and the pilot chute had failed to open properly at first. When it did eventually deploy, the jolt was so severe that his pelvis was smashed to pieces, and already too close to the ground to recover, he thudded into the concrete runway.

His known injuries included a broken leg and arm, and lung and kidney damage were also suspected. The following day he was accompanied by his old friend Per Lindstrand on a Virgin air ambulance back to London where he was admitted into the Middlesex Hospital. Ironically, Virgin's replacement envelope was leaving Manchester airport for Marrakesh that same morning. The prognosis for Ritchie was not good. For almost three months he fought bravely, in and out of intensive care, in and out of consciousness. At times there were indications of a recovery, but in the end nobody can survive a developed septicaemia. Alex Ritchie died on Easter Day 1998.

17 THE SILVER BUDDHA

January 1998, Château d'Oex

Amazingly, following the embarrassing and potentially lethal parting of the suspension cables on the capsule, only a couple of weeks later the Breitling team had dusted itself down, picked up the pieces and was ready to try again. Ironically, those cable connectors were so specialized that it had been a technician from the supplying company who had originally fitted them. 'While we took the can for that incident in a large way with the media it really wasn't our fault,' explained Brian Jones who was coordinating the Breitling effort. 'We had simply assumed that the professionals had come in, done the job and that was it. We didn't touch them.'

Jones had been brought onto the team earlier the previous year. He and Andy Elson had previously worked together in a venture that operated balloons commercially as well as undertaking pilot-training and any other projects that came along. 'With the first *Orbiter* Andy had been asked to work on the technical side, and so we set up as consultants to Camerons in an office they gave us in the workshop,' says Jones. 'But when *Orbiter 2* came along, they had to make a few changes. Andy – and I'm sure he won't mind me saying this – is a very talented person in many ways, but as an organizer he is an absolute nightmare.' And so Jones's unofficial job title became 'Andy's user-friendly interface'. 'That's what I was known as. Andy has this great habit of flying off the handle sometimes – not at technical things but at people. If he is working on something and it's not going right technically he just carries on and tries to work through it – he's quite a focused person. But if somebody says something stupid to him he goes absolutely potty. So I tended to look after him in that sense.'

The interval since the capsule's crunch had also allowed the Breitling team time to get the envelope back to Cameron's factory for some modifications to the pressure relief valves. The post-mortem into what had befallen both the Uliassi and Rutan balloons was still underway and it would be some time before the NTSB report was published, so Don Cameron remained non-committal on the subject. But he seemed to be implying that the catastrophic failure of the gas cells had been due mainly to pilot error. Whatever the cause, it was obvious that neither balloon had coped with the expansion of the helium gas – the base panel had blown out, as it was designed to do under excess pressure. The Breitling team didn't want a repeat performance.

It was 28 January, coincidentally the birthday of Piccard's grandfather, when the first launch window presented itself, combined with a strong jetstream over the Mediterranean. Not quite ideal as they would have to work their way south initially, but beggars can't be choosers in the global game. During inflation in the early hours of the morning a series of minor problems, firstly with a satellite communications antenna and then freezing on the liquid oxygen tanks, had held up the flow of helium for several hours. When the gas taps did eventually turn the envelope quickly swelled and assumed its full height, but a gusty breeze picked up and twisted the balloon, tangling some of the steel flying wires that connected the envelope to the capsule. It needed to be sorted out before inflation could be completed and so Andy Elson was hauled out of his hotel bed to come down to the launch field to deal with the problem. Consequently it was two hours after dawn, well behind schedule, by the time the balloon was finally ready and Elson, completely worn out, perched on the roof of the capsule and symbolically lit the burners from an Olympic torch to send the *Breitling Orbiter 2* on its way, slowly climbing out of the deep valley. In fact progress was so slow that three hours later it was still visible hanging over the mountains.

As the balloon reached 25,000 feet, an ominous hissing sound could be heard from the rear bubble hatch which should have been located in a groove but had been misaligned. Air was seeping out and until they devised a way to seal the hatch the capsule could not be pressurized, which meant that the crew had to breathe from oxygen masks for most of the first couple of days. To add to the problems Andy Elson developed a pounding headache – for weeks now he had been working flat out and the long hours and lack of regular sleep were finally taking their toll. Dr Piccard put his patient to bed, diagnosing that Elson was feeling the worse for wear because of sudden caffeine starvation.

The next problem presented itself the following morning – inexplicably, one-third of the kerosene fuel had been lost during the night. Two of the six tanks were empty and the source of the leak remained a complete mystery. A despondent Bertrand Piccard was silently cursing himself for allowing kerosene to be used again. 'We have completely run out of one fuel tank on the left and another one on the right,' he told the Control Centre. 'The rear hatch doesn't seal – we really have to find a solution if we want to climb higher up. Up until now we have flown at Flight Level 240 unpressurized. But we can't do that for long – we are not Steve Fossett.'

By the time Andy Elson was back in action the balloon had continued its south-east drift, travelling across France and on towards the coast of Italy. If they were to continue the flight the first priority was to see to the leaking hatch and, accepting responsibility for the problem, Elson clambered outside. 'It had been put in place on the launch field slightly out of position. That was my fault, so it was only right that I should be the one to fix it.' But he was probably the only one of the three men capable of undertaking the task and, as with Ritchie on the Virgin balloon the previous year, the inclusion of an engineer on the crew was vindicated.

Once Elson had eased himself down beside the hatch he paused from his exertions to catch his breath and for the briefest moment reflected on his situation. He was hanging in his rock-climbing harness at the blunt rounded end of the orange pod looking in at his two companions. Surely this must be what it is like to walk in space, he told himself, or perhaps to be a deep-sea diver peering into the safe cocoon of a submarine. He didn't look down, he didn't need to. He knew that all that separated him from the Adriatic Sea was 4,000 feet of air and a thin wispy layer of cloud. Getting here had been bloody hard work and he was already exhausted. His breath was laboured and despite the chill of altitude he was covered in a sheen of warm sweat. And he loved it. He adored it. This was ballooning at the edge. The fact that if he couldn't get back inside he would have to drop every one of those 4,000 feet to parachute into the sea, simply added piquancy to the situation. Adrenalin was pumping and he felt alive.

An experienced rock-climber and caver, Andy Elson had been an enthusiastic convert to the delights of ballooning. But not for him the gentler meanderings over the countryside; as with everything else in his life he relished the challenges, pushing himself and his equipment to the limit. To date the pinnacle of his high-flying career had been in 1991 when he had piloted one of a pair of balloons making the historic first flight over Mount Everest. After that he had gladly accepted the invitation to join the Breitling project, building the gondola and devising systems for sustained flight in the jetstream.

Hanging off the side of *Breitling Orbiter 2* he knew that if he couldn't fix the leaking hatch then this global attempt was over before it had really begun. With Piccard working from the inside, together they released the Plexiglass bubble. It was an opportunity for Elson to breath some fresh oxygen from a mask before he resumed his labours, then together the two men reseated the hatch which happily gave them no further problems. By the time Elson had heaved himself back in through the top hatch and into the sanctuary of the capsule, he was utterly exhausted. But now they could take the balloon up into the faster jetstream winds to pick up some much-needed speed.

The only remaining obstacles ahead were the artificial ones of national airspace. The Chinese authorities were still refusing permission for the Breitling balloon to overfly their territory and the only jetstream capable of getting them round the world would entail their doing exactly that. They could attempt to head south, go round China and pick up a jet over the Pacific, but after losing a full third of their kerosene on the first day they knew that *Breitling Orbiter 2* lacked the endurance. And as if life wasn't complicated enough, Syria lay dead ahead. After some in-flight negotiations smoothed that one over, Iraq was next. A lack of diplomatic relations between Iraq and Switzerland meant that the politicians were unable to help, but the Swiss government put the team in touch with the Red Cross in Baghdad and they agreed to pass a message on on their behalf. Meanwhile Alan Noble was trying a different tactic and he called the CNN television news people in Atlanta. 'Within minutes I was repeating the story live to a world-wide audience,' said Noble after the flight. Shortly afterwards the balloon received a call from ATC (Air Traffic Control) in Baghdad giving the necessary clearance. 'I don't know which carried the most clout with the Iraqis – the Red Cross or CNN.'

Less publicly, Noble was keeping mum about the balloon infringing the UN's no-fly zone over Iraq. In fact the balloonists didn't spot any aircraft during their crossing and they breezed on into neighbouring Iran without difficulty until the Air Traffic Controllers politely requested them to land at the next airfield for identification! Noble got back to CNN and the problem soon went away. Over Afghanistan there wasn't so much as a peep on the radio and over Pakistan normal ATC service was resumed.

As the balloon continued on its low-level track to the south-east avoiding China, the Control Centre was pulling all the plugs out, trying every diplomatic and private avenue possible to get overflight clearance from the Chinese. But to no avail. In fact the response was a deafening silence. The crew of *Breitling Orbiter 2* did their best to accept their lot and to enjoy the ride as they crossed into India on the seventh day. With the higher winds pushing northwards towards the Himalayas they were forced to hug the contours, keeping to between 1,000 and 3,000 feet above the ground. Progress was agonisingly slow, and moving along at around 30 knots the team were able to sit out on the top of the capsule enjoying the warm hazy sun and soaking in the fragrant aroma of spices which wafted up from the settlements below. Just occasionally the faint calls of excited groups of children could be heard and cupping their hands to their mouths they yelled greetings in return. On their first dawn drifting over India they saw the distinctive white onion-shaped dome of the Taj Mahal, tinted pink in the morning glow – an unforgettable and truly magical moment. But this emphatically was not what they should be doing. Theirs was a sophisticated high-altitude high-speed balloon designed to fly round-the-world, not to go on a sight-seeing cruise.

For the three aeronauts this enforced period of inactivity was an unexpected opportunity for introspection. Bertrand Piccard's temperament enabled him to accept the snail-like progression philosophically, but his thoughts ran over the failings of this attempt and he made two important resolutions for next time. Firstly, after the previous year's early bath in the Med and the fuel leakage on this flight, he was adamant that he would not fly with the kerosene system again. Designed to save weight, it had caused him nothing but problems; in future he would entrust himself to the tried and tested propane fuel. Secondly, he would not fly with a three-man crew again. Although the cabin was somewhat cramped they got on with each other well enough, but Piccard couldn't dismiss the feeling that they were carrying unnecessary weight. The problem had begun early in the project when it became clear that Wim Verstraeten could not put in sufficient time for training and familiarization with the equipment. Piccard felt morally unable to bump his partner off the crew, and the net result was that Andy Elson had to come too because he and Piccard were the only two fully familiar with flying the balloon.

If Verstraeten felt superfluous, then Elson was feeling miffed at

being officially designated as Flight Engineer and not properly recognized as one of the pilots. Anyway, he was getting irritated with
the lack of progress and didn't hesitate to voice his opinion that
they should land because the global flight was out of reach. Piccard
wondered whether he had other motives; he knew that Elson had
found a sponsor for his own attempt next year. Were the *Orbiter
2* to land too early, possibly causing Breitling to think again about
funding a third attempt, then Elson's project would have one less
rival.

With spirits slumped to their lowest ebb, it was Alan Noble who
came up with just the right morale boost for the Breitling boys.
He informed them that they had already broken Steve Fossett's
146 hours and 54 minutes endurance record for balloons set on
the flight to India in January 1997, and that the absolute endurance record for all aircraft was within their grasp. It was currently
held by another global contender, Dick Rutan, who along with
Jeana Yeager had taken just over 216 hours to encircle the Earth
non-stop in the *Voyager* aircraft in 1986. This record was something worth going on for, exactly the sort of challenge to reawaken
their enthusiasm. It also helped to soften the blow when the news
was relayed to the balloon that incredibly, at this late stage in the
game, the Chinese authorities had relented and the balloon could
enter their airspace. 'It was of course too late for Breitling and my
initial reaction was that it would have been ironic if we had been
instrumental in clearing the way for Richard Branson,' said Noble
later.

After three long days crossing India they were over the Bay of
Bengal and heading towards Myanmar, as Burma was now called.
Their leisurely progress meant that Noble and his team, including
Brian Jones who had the task of recovering and returning the
balloon, had adequate time to fly by *Falcon* jet to Rangoon. From
there they took a helicopter to meet the balloon as it made a gentle
landing in a paddy-field beside the famous road to Mandalay.
Elson greeted the team with the broad gappy grin that had so
much endeared him to the British press, and climbing aboard

Noble helped him to tug on the rip-line. But the envelope didn't want to come down and the Myanmar militia, never slow to display their marksmanship, obligingly put bullet-holes into the gas cell to speed up the deflation. It was the signal for the crowds of spectators to join in the jamboree and pandemonium ensued with the flaccid balloon succumbing to their greedy onslaught. In a moment of surreal humour part of the rigging caught on a bicycle and whisked it up into the air while its protesting owner jumped up and down to get it free. Christened by the locals the 'Silver Buddha', the balloon's envelope was torn to shreds until there was nothing left.

A sad ending for the balloon perhaps, but Piccard felt that at least they had put in a worthy performance in global terms and, through the demonstration that a balloon could stay in the air long enough to make a circumnavigation, another piece of the jigsaw had fallen into place. Ten days aloft! 233 hours 55 minutes. All they had to do now was to bring the other elements together.

A couple of days after *Breitling Orbiter 2* had landed Per Lindstrand called me. 'Of course you realize that actually there is no official overall duration record for aircraft?' Well no, I had to admit that I didn't, and I resolved to look into it.

Next day it was Alan Noble's turn. 'Do you know that there is no official duration record for aircraft?'

'Yes, of course I do.'

The FAI in its wisdom does not recognize one overall official endurance record to cover all types of aircraft (although they do when it comes to altitude or distance). A spokesman from the FAI explained that if they included all types of aircraft it would be like comparing roller-skates with Formula 1 racing cars. And anyway, while *Breitling Orbiter 2* may have flown for longer than the *Voyager* aircraft, and may hold a new absolute record for balloons, it unfortunately was still some seventy-something hours short of the record set by the US Navy blimp *Snowbird* in 1957. This airship had flown across the Atlantic from the USA to Europe, then on to Africa and back to the USA again – all without refuelling or stopping.

Back in Britain the Virgin team was working flat out collecting together every piece of fabric it could lay its hands on to complete a new envelope while Richard Branson famously fought and won his libel case against Guy Snowden of the lottery company Camelot. But lady luck didn't remain with him and the jetstreams fizzled out for the season, meaning that Virgin would have to wait until November or December 1998 to give it another try. The only other option was to attempt a riskier southern-hemisphere flight which could be undertaken in the middle of the year. But it would take a particular sort of person to tackle that route. One of a kind.

18 GOING THE DISTANCE

Friday 7 August 1998, Mendoza, Argentina

'This is the most dangerous thing I have done in my life,' admitted Steve Fossett, a man who has done more than his fair share of such things, shortly before launching from Mendoza, in the shadow of the Andes Mountains. The American was well aware of the gamble he was taking on in this his fourth global attempt. In a bid to outmanoeuvre his competitors he was taking advantage of the southern hemisphere's 'winter' jetstreams at a time when the other teams were still preparing for the northern winter. Flying almost 90 per cent of the time over water offered the advantage of more consistent conditions because there would be less variation in temperatures to cope with, and having only five countries to overfly, this route greatly reduced the risk of the sort of political complications that had screwed up his two previous attempts. Qaddafi wouldn't stop him down here! But undeniably, with vast areas of inhospitable ocean far from the reach of rescuers, this was a much more hazardous undertaking should anything go wrong.

The new *Solo Spirit* balloon (built by Cameron's once again) that climbed from yet another sports stadium was a slightly different beast from its predecessors. Fossett had increased the volume of the helium cell to 450,000 cubic feet, allowing him to double the amount of fuel carried, and he now had four burners instead of two. In addition the lower hot-air chamber had been reduced to a slender cone to minimize solar heating during the day. The balloon looked different too; the fabric was white with just the top 'tent' finished in reflective gold Mylar, the result looking less like a cocktail-shaker in profile and more like a a golf ball perched on its tee.

On 7 August 1998 Fossett's highly experienced team put in a picture-perfect launch and initial progress was good. 'The balloon is already making 26 knots,' announced Chief Meteorologist Bob Rice. 'It's perhaps a little faster than we expected.' All being well, once over the Atlantic the balloon would swing towards the tip of South Africa and then across the southern expanse of the Indian Ocean and on towards Australia and New Zealand, lining up for a long Southern Pacific crossing back to South America. Fossett looked unstoppable. But he was already experiencing a few early glitches with the equipment and he sustained minor injuries from a propane fire during the first night aloft. 'The flight, from the beginning, has been plagued by a minor problem with the pilot-light regulators on two of the four burners,' Flight Director Alan Blount explained to the press. 'Steve attempted to correct the problem by disconnecting a pilot light hose and apparently the quick-disconnect valve did not seal off the flow of fuel and Steve had a fire.' But this description of events did not quite convey the drama Fossett had experienced when the fuel line had spewed out a blowtorch of flame. As he described the incident himself, 'If I had burned through another propane hose I would have had a totally out of control fire.' And by radio he detailed his injuries: 'It burned off my left eyebrow and I have a little bit of sunburn on my face.'

With only two of the four pilot lights functioning, *Solo Spirit* continued to eat up the miles and Fossett soon reached the coast and the vast South Atlantic. 'I am not sure whether I will be able to land again before I finish the round-the-world – so this is a go!' he confidently announced. At this latitude the Atlantic is at its widest, but travelling at a respectable 40 knots by day four he was already more than halfway across. This was the twentieth anniversary of *Double Eagle II*'s historic first crossing back in 1978, a time when the Atlantic presented an almost impenetrable barrier to balloonists. Now Steve Fossett was going over for an incredible record fourth time.

Solo Spirit reached first landfall, South Africa, on the fifth day and by the following morning it was 800 miles south-east of Cape Town and flying at 24,574 feet. Fossett was the first person to attempt the Indian Ocean crossing by balloon and he did so at a point where it is 2,000 miles across, nearly as wide as the North Atlantic. The flight had already covered nearly 7,000 miles, but there was a note of caution from Bob Rice when he advised that this was a crucial decision-making time with the balloon approaching an area where the winds diverged. Get it wrong and *Solo Spirit* could be pushed too far south and swirled into the dangers of Antarctica; too far north and the balloon would enter a fair-weather zone, causing it to lose the momentum it needed to complete the journey. Fossett's team chose wisely and *Solo Spirit* remained on course and the solo aeronaut in good spirits. All was going well and with the Bruce Comstock-designed autopilot keeping the balloon at a predetermined altitude he even had a chance to get some sleep.

Early on day nine he reached Australia and had exceeded his own ballooning distance record of 10,361 miles. In a flashback to the days of astronaut John Glenn's first orbital flight in 1962, the Aussies were planning a nationwide reception for the impending flyover. They would wave thousands of white towels at the balloon if it was a daytime crossing, or flash their car headlights if it was after dark. Already he was more than halfway towards a circumnavigation, and back at the Control Centre in Washington University, St Louis, celebrations were underway. Yet it wasn't all plain sailing, for they had calculated that Fossett's oxygen tanks might be depleted in the next four or five days and he still had to cross the Pacific and then climb over the high Andes before getting back to Argentina. 'We are worried about the oxygen,' admitted Blount. 'We are questioning whether the gauges are correct.' If the oxygen ran out Fossett would be forced to lose altitude and the subsequent reduction in speed could cost too much time in the delicate equation of fuel against duration.

As the balloon passed over the coastal town of Geraldton, about 250 miles north of Perth, it was making good speed at around 130 knots at 29,000 feet. Rice now called for a drop in altitude to 8,000 feet to improve the trajectory and conserve some of the precious oxygen. 'It is looking right now that at least we have a chance.' When Fossett took the balloon down to 20,000 feet it slowed down to only 50 knots. But some good news came later in the day when concerns about the oxygen were abated after revised calculations indicated a supply of at least six to ten days, and so the balloon was returned to 29,000 feet and it continued its faster drift over south-central Australia. 'We're now confident we'll make a run to South America,' announced Blount. *Solo Spirit* was expected to leave Australia on Sunday afternoon and Met man Bob Rice described the last twenty-four hours as being a 'dream run'. However, as the balloon approached the eastern coast there were thunderstorms building over the mountains and Fossett needed to climb 1,000 feet over the top of one of the storms. It was a portent of things to come and Rice warned him that the balloon was approaching some intense thunderstorms over the Coral Sea which were virtually impossible to avoid.

Sunday 16 August 1998, the Coral Sea

When Fossett's regular position signals failed to come in during the night the Control Centre team became increasingly concerned. And confirming that a satellite positioned over the Pacific had not picked up any signal from the balloonist's emergency beacon, they began to fear the worst. 'If he's in his raft, we should have got a signal from him. If he had to bail out due to failure of the envelope then he will be much more difficult to find.'

A *C-130* rescue aircraft from the Australian Coast Guard was dispatched to the Coral Sea where they believed he had gone down during the night – 500 miles off the eastern Australian coast and a long long way from any help. But it would take five hours for the aircraft to reach the area and it was not equipped for a water landing even when it did get there. Suddenly there was a signal from the Emergency Personal Identification Radio Beacon – nobody could be sure if it had been activated manually by Fossett or automatically by immersion in the water. The anxious *Solo Spirit* team didn't know whether to celebrate or cry. They could only speculate as to what might have happened and it was not until the aircraft picked up a signal from the stricken balloonist that they knew he was still alive. Two hours after dawn a French rescue aircraft, flying from New Caledonia, spotted him bobbing in his tiny life raft which was still attached to the remains of the capsule. They dropped a larger raft and supplies to Fossett who would have to wait another four hours until the nearest boat, the ketch *Atlanta* – being sailed by the Australian Laurie Piper who was nearing the end of his own solo voyage around the world – arrived on the scene. Fortunately, surface conditions were good and the boat had no difficulty in finding Fossett who was fast asleep in the raft after being adrift for sixteen hours.

Suffering only a little bruising from his ordeal, a bedraggled and shaken Steve Fossett declared, 'This was a sobering experience . . . the closest I have come in my life to being killed. I'm not sure I should keep going every year and take this risk. It was maybe too much of an adventure.' A little later he was transferred to the Australian ship *Endeavour* and back in dock, at Townsville, Steve Fossett faced the world's press. After expressing his profuse gratitude to his rescuers he gave a dramatic account of his long lonely fall into the sea:

I was at an altitude above the thunderstorm line, clearing the tops of the thunderstorm. But I suspect there was some inter-action with the tops of the thunderstorm and the jetstream where I was flying and I started a descent. At first the descent was at 500 fpm, but then I reversed it by turning on the burners and climbing back up. But then I was already under the influence of the thunderstorm and started a descent of 1,500 ft per minute. I used the burners more and I flew back up at an extreme rate of 1,500 fpm, and I believe at that point the balloon ruptured. So I started a descent and I don't know how fast this was because my variometer has a maximum rate on it of 2,500 fpm and it was pegged at 2,500 for my entire descent from 29,000 ft to the surface.

As I was going through the thunderstorm the balloon was just being thrown from one side to another, it was visibly tearing and there were tremendous amounts of hail – the hail would just come in huge sheets and cover me. In order to slow this descent I turned on the burners full blast, and then I had some auxiliary high power burners which I also turned on. And still I was descending at this rate and the balloon was being buffeted very heavily back and forth. The burners were melting the edge of the balloon and it was dripping polyester on me and ropes were burning, and meanwhile there were sheets of hail in the middle of the thunderstorm, sweeping over me.

At that point I actually said out loud, 'I'm going to die', because I couldn't arrest the descent rate. When I got down to the final 2,000 ft of the descent I cut away a large number of the tanks to lighten the load of the balloon. Then I lay down on the bench inside my capsule to take the impact on my back. But it was still reading over 2,500 fpm when I hit the water. I believe that I was briefly knocked unconscious . . .

When he came to, Steve Fossett found that the capsule was inverted and filling with icy water. It was also on fire – the blazing propane tanks were burning through from the outside and filling it with noxious resin fumes. The tiny yellow cocoon that had protected him on so many flights from the worst that the elements could deliver had become a deadly cage. He couldn't remember the moment of impact, but suddenly he was in a fight for his life in the darkness – scrambling to find his way through a swirling tangle of equipment and supplies to locate the small bubble hatch which was his only way out. Up and down had no meaning in the tumbling capsule which was still taking in water, and caught in the violent storm the envelope was dragging and twisting it in the churning waves.

'I took two things with me,' recalls Fossett, 'my small life raft and the EPIRB. I swam out of the bottom of the capsule, and tried to stay with the balloon after that.' A strong swimmer, he emerged gasping for air in the pitchblack of night with only the flickering light of the dying flames to guide him. 'It was quite a storm, and the balloon came down on top of me when I was in the raft . . . I was being suffocated by the fumes and this heavy balloon on top of me. The balloon was blowing around, and I lost contact with it and just floated in my life raft that night.'

Unquestionably it had been an incredible flight – Fossett had flown 15,200 miles, setting a new absolute distance record for balloons that covered almost two-thirds of the distance for a round-the-world flight. There was no doubt in anybody's mind that it took a very brave man to attempt such an undertaking solo. But was it possible, just possible perhaps, that Steve Fossett – the human dynamo – had succumbed to exhaustion and after nine monotonous days aloft had fallen asleep, only to be awakened when the balloon hit the water? It was a startling suggestion and one that he vociferously denied.

He preferred to speak about his chances of success.

We took this on with the full expectation of being successful this time, and now I didn't make it, it is very frustrating. I have made the four longest flights in the history of ballooning now, this one being the longest. I had enough fuel to finish the round-the-world flight. We estimated approximately four to five days to reach Argentina. In fact, I was going to run out of oxygen, probably during the last one to two days. But I was climatized pretty well, so I believe I would have been able to finish the flight flying at an altitude of approximately 22,000 ft. This is a disappointment all the way round. Then you just have to be thankful for what you have. I realized, forget about the disappointment of the mission failing, it's time to worry about surviving. '

And as for his next move:

I'm not in a position to compete against the other teams which will be flying this December and January. It leaves an open field for the competitors. I think we are getting very close to success in this endeavour, so I think there's a good chance that one of them will succeed this year. In fact I spoke to Richard Branson yesterday. He called me to say how happy he was that I had survived. And I pointed out that this is very dangerous and that I wasn't really sure that we should be attempting it.

Concluding the press conference he told the gathered media pack, 'It's a fascinating project and I think whoever succeeds will also earn themselves a place in aviation history.' But what Steve Fossett didn't tell them was that Richard Branson had actually phoned to offer him Alex Ritchie's place aboard the Virgin balloon. And when Cameron Balloons confirmed that they could not build a replacement for *Solo Spirit* in time for the coming northern hemisphere season, Fossett swallowed his pride and accepted Branson's proposal – the solo challenger would become a team player and he would be back in the air before the year was out.

19 THE GARDEN PARTY

28 June 1998

Steve Fossett wasn't the only jetstream jockey to change horses in 1998, a year of frantic behind-the-scenes activity resulting in at least one new global team straining at the bit.

On the sort of blustery yet sunny day that passes for summer in these parts, I travelled to the Wiltshire home of balloonists Jacques Soukup and Kirk Thomas, and to one of the most surreal global events I have ever attended. Set in the grounds of the sixteenth-century Laycock Manor, it was more like an English summer tea-party, complete with a blessing by the local vicar, than the announcement of the latest high-tech round-the-world balloon challenge. But my fellow guests sipping the champagne and enjoying the chamber music were high-calibre globallers: Don Cameron was there, as well as Alan Noble, Kevin Uliassi, Andy Elson and, representing the Breitling connection, Brian Jones and newcomer Tony Brown, a Flight Engineer on *Concorde*.

With much aplomb the newest global conquerors, the *Spirit of Peace* pilots, were announced: the Anglo-American Jacques Soukup, a former Jesuit priest and a leading light in the international ballooning scene, the well-known British balloonist Crispin Williams, and the American Mark Sullivan, a member of the original *Odyssey* line-up and an accomplished gas balloonist. Their balloon would be another Cameron-built Rozière, basically a clone of the Breitling balloon, to be financed with funds from

New boys on the global block: Crispin Williams, Jacques Soukup and Mark Sullivan, at a
very English country garden party, 28 June 1998
(*Ute Feierabend*)

Thomas's aunt, Martha S. Weeks, an Episcopalian priest – and apparently to be flown around the world in 'the spirit of peace'. Construction of the capsule was already well in hand under the supervision of Brian Jones, who was also coordinating the *Breitling Orbiter 3* project.

By this time Andy Elson, who had constructed the capsules for the first two Breitling balloons and had flown as engineer with Piccard and Verstraeten on *Breitling Orbiter 2*, had left the team. He was now up to his elbows with his own project backed by the British businessman James Manclarke, an exponent of elephant polo among other things and as unlikely a jet-streamer as you could ever meet. Inspired by Richard Branson's headline-grabbing antics, Manclarke had decided to claim a bit of the action for himself. Despite never having even flown in a balloon he arrived at Cameron's factory one morning to announce, 'I'm going to fly around the world. What are you going to do about it?'

Accordingly Manclarke had been introduced to Elson who was working on the Breitling capsule, and even though the two of them were chalk and cheese they soon became immersed in conversation and a deal was struck. Manclarke would provide the funding and, if possible, a sponsor, and Elson would build a new metal capsule of his own design – the result being a slightly squatter cylinder than Breitling's in appearance. They would also fly with a Cameron-built Rozière envelope although Elson was still firmly committed to using kerosene fuel for the burners. Life support would be via a system of oxygen and nitrogen supplied from inboard canisters similar to that in the Breitling capsule.

Newcomers to ballooning often assume that it is easy, when it's not, and James Manclarke soon came to realize that he had bitten off more than he could chew. He withdrew from the flight crew and Elson recruited a new partner and co-pilot, his old ballooning friend Colin Prescot – an archetypical old-Etonian with a penchant for extreme ballooning. And through Prescot's advertising balloon operating company, Flying Pictures, came a high-profile sponsor in the form of telecommunications giant Cable & Wireless, which already had an established global pedigree after sponsoring a successful assault on the record for ocean-going ships under power.

Bertrand Piccard, meanwhile, had been true to his word and the third *Breitling Orbiter* would fly with propane fuel and a crew of just two. But who was to be Piccard's partner? Wim Verstraeten was too busy with his own ballooning operations in Belgium and he couldn't spare the time to train properly for another global attempt, so the Breitling team had to look elsewhere. Alan Noble suggested fellow-Brit Tony Brown who combined the skills of an experienced balloonist with his professional role with *Concorde*.

British Airways were happy enough to release him from his duties – especially if there was a chance he might beat their old adversary Richard Branson – and before long the new Breitling capsule was posing in the shadow of *Concorde*'s famous droop-snoop for the new line-up of Piccard and Brown to be photographed.

A back-up pilot was also needed in case of illness or injury before the flight. Publicly Wim Verstraeten was named, but the obvious thing was for Project Manager Brian Jones to slip into the slot. He had originally been brought onto the team by Andy Elson to coordinate the work on *Breitling Orbiter 2*, and when Elson left he continued in this role.

'This was a very sensible solution to the back-up problem,' Jones says. 'Firstly, I'm a balloon pilot. And secondly, while I may not be an engineer I have been around the systems long enough to know how they work better than either Bertrand or Tony. It wasn't planned. We were just so focused on the project that we said, here's the problem, here's the solution.' And with that Jones went back to work on the capsule. The unassuming fifty-two-year-old from a sleepy village in Wiltshire could not have anticipated the momentous chain of events that had been put in motion.

Kevin Uliassi had little to say at the garden party about his mishap on New Year's Eve and only confirmed that he had a 'good deal' on a replacement envelope from Cameron's and that he would be trying again in the coming winter.

By this time Dick Rutan had turned his back on the Rozière concept entirely and instead he was proposing a southern-hemisphere attempt with cluster balloons – bundles of smaller helium balloons. These balloons have had a chequered history, marred by the almost mythical exploits of the 'lawn-chair' flyer Larry Walters who in 1982 went aloft under a huge bunch of weather balloons armed only with an airgun to pop them one at a time to get back down again. (In 1997 Walters was honoured with the tongue-in-cheek Darwin Award for 'outstanding contributions to natural selection through self-sacrifice' – awarded posthumously as he had taken his own life by then.) However, time was against Rutan and funding still had to be completed for his newly named *World Quest* project.

One figure conspicuous by his absence at the garden party was Richard Branson, but he also had a little summer surprise up his sleeve. Virgin would no longer be the main sponsor for his next attempt, and when he unveiled the new envelope it was emblazoned with the logo of another international telecommunications company, ICO. Though ironically Branson's name had become so irrevocably linked to the global challenge that market research later confirmed that most people still thought of the *ICO Global Challenger* as the Virgin balloon.

There was also some speculation at the garden party that made the gathered northern-hemisphere flyers more than a little nervous. It concerned an impending launch for the ultra-high-altitude project originally known as *Odyssey*. With new backers this had become a joint American-Australian venture and it was reported that their equipment was being prepared for an attempt from Australia, possibly in the next few months.

August 1998, North Atlantic

And then just one week after Fossett's attempt failed so dramatically, a rogue unmanned balloon decided to demonstrate to its human counterparts the folly of their ways. Launched from Canada on 23 August, the balloon's scientific payload was supposed to monitor the ozone layer before a controlled self-destruct, but the balloon had other ideas and went walkabout in the busy transatlantic airways. Fighters were launched to bring it down, but 1,000 rounds of ammo failed to do the job and international air traffic had to be diverted around the rogue aerostat. Having successfully made its way across the Atlantic it then found a new lease of life and continued eastward into Norway's airspace, then

Russia's, until it eventually drifted northwards to meet its end among the ice-packs. It had successfully travelled in the jetstream at 30,000 feet for over a week, and after the mixed fortunes of the global contenders earlier in the year its exploits must have made a few egos smart.

20 A CHINA CRISIS

December 1998

As 1998 drew to its close there was a real sense that one of the balloon teams might soon accomplish a global flight. After all, the last twelve months had seen *Breitling Orbiter 2*'s marathon ten-day flight from Switzerland to Myanmar and Fossett's sprint from Argentina all the way to the Coral Sea – approximately 230° of the Earth's 360° or nearly two-thirds of the way round. If someone could bring together these two elements of duration and distance, and combine them with a little kindness from the weather gods, it could be all over by Christmas.

For many the Branson/Lindstrand/Fossett trio looked like the front runners at this stage of the race. Take one aluminium tin can about the size of a small caravan, pack it to the gunwales with sophisticated electronics, equipment and supplies, shoehorn in three of the most famous aeronauts you can find and then dangle the whole thing underneath a 200-foot-tall balloon resembling a plump exclamation mark bloated with 1,100,000 cubic feet of helium gas, and you have in essence the *ICO Global Challenger*.

Branson and Lindstrand were, of course, old friends with the background of flying the Atlantic and Pacific behind them and when combined with Fossett's easy-going temperament the three-some were comfortable with each other's company and level of expertise. And following a flawless launch, this time, the balloon climbed above Marrakesh on Friday 18 December with the whole

Virgin team in an optimistic frame of mind. If sheer effort alone counted for anything, then the global crown must be in the bag. There was, however, one ticklish problem – they had overflight permissions from some 90 different countries, but not from Iraq, Iran, Russia or North Korea – although none of these was directly in their predicted flight path at the time of the launch. As for China, permission had been granted to overfly south of the 26th parallel, and the Virgin people had received an informal verbal indication that should the balloon stray further north it would be allowed through.

After a leisurely climb-out, Lindstrand took the balloon to a float altitude of 29,000 feet where it tracked slightly south at first before turning on to 110° at 60 knots by nightfall. By the following morning they were doing a healthy 90 knots due east over Algeria when suddenly their sight-seeing was interrupted with a message from the Libyans denying overflight permission – despite having given written consent before the balloon's departure. At first Branson and Lindstrand considered running through Libya without permission, a thought that horrified Fossett. Then Richard Branson pulled out his address book and dialled King Hussein of Jordan who was not available; next he tried President Nelson Mandela who was asleep at the time and could not be disturbed. Then, with just two hour's travel time to the Libyan border, he faxed a letter direct to Colonel Qaddafi pleading for permission. It did the trick and they pushed on. 'The Libyan desert had a slight orange colour to it,' Per Lindstrand recalls. 'It was the most beautiful I have ever seen. No sign of life or other air traffic.'

Speeding up to 120 knots they were heading directly for Cyprus as they entered their second night, and over the Mediterranean they were treated to a spectacular light and sound show of thunderstorms. A Virgin chase plane had caught up with them by this time and it flew a little ahead, but the crew reported that there were no storms directly in the balloon's path.

Next they were faced with the delicate task of threading the balloon through the eye of a needle – a twenty-seven-mile gap between Russia and Iran. A balloon is swept along by the wind, and it is only possible to steer it by taking advantage of any variation in wind at different altitudes, but fortunately on this occasion the gods were kind to the ICO balloonists. 'We saw Iran,' confirmed Lindstrand afterwards. 'And we saw Russia, but we didn't enter their airspace. That's how close we came.' Once through the gap they climbed a little; the *ICO Global Challenger* drifted towards Turkey and by the morning they were above Armenia. The countries were beginning to whiz by: next came Azerbaijan with a superb view of the Caucasus mountain chain indicating the southern Russian border and, after the respite of the Caspian Sea, Turkmenistan and Kazakstan, the harsh and sparsely populated landscapes blending each country into the next. Then it was briefly back over Turkmenistan and by nightfall Uzbekistan followed by Tadzhikistan. As Lindstrand summed it up in a fax sent direct to me from the capsule via the Inmarsat-C satellite transceiver, 'The geography here is stunning and something unique. But not a place to land a balloon.'

They were to fly over Afghanistan and follow the Himalayan chain deep into China. 'We tried to get more right to pick up the jetstream sitting over India', explained Lindstrand later. 'We came close to both K2 and Everest and it was as if the Himalayan chain, rather than push us out over the Indian plain as we had hoped, sucked in the balloon.' On the fourth night they were approaching Nepal and increasingly tracking left and to the north. In a few hours they would enter Tibet, a part of China and then China itself.

Suddenly Project Director Mike Kendrick radioed Richard Branson that China was refusing them permission to go on and that they should land immediately, Branson's reply was unequivocal. 'Where the fuck are we supposed to land?' And he had a point. With the balloon loaded with several tons of propane, and the most hostile terrain in the world poking up through the darkness below, they had no choice but to maintain a safe altitude.

Frantic negotiations were underway, but the ICO team had painted itself into a corner and there was no way out except to push on through Chinese airspace. The air traffic controllers were insisting that the balloon should land at Lhasa airport which was not far from their present track. But the pilots were not acclimatized to the high mountain altitude and they could easily have died once out of their protective capsule. It was never an option. Out came the famous address book once again and this time Branson called Downing Street, asking Tony Blair to send a personal message to the Chinese authorities. Thanks to this intervention, and the efforts of the British ambassador in Beijing, by the end of day five they had permission to continue, albeit granted reluctantly.

Day became night and then day again and after passing over the Great Wall and endless miles of rugged terrain they began to appreciate just how big China is. And at speeds as low as 42 knots at times they were also travelling much more slowly than Lindstrand had hoped. By midnight on day six the balloon had edged out over the Yellow Sea and then on towards North Korea, which let them through with its best wishes, and over South Korea a US Air Force AWACS plane took them under its wing to ensure a safe passage. By Christmas Eve they were over Japan and with meteorologist Bob Rice predicting a safe passage all the way to Europe in another four to five days, and over half their fuel reserves remaining, they had cause to feel confident.

Day eight, over the International Dateline and a second Christmas Eve for the ICO pilots. They were now travelling at a respectable 150 knots when they noticed that the balloon was beginning to turn slightly to the right, southwards. After a while the speed had dropped to 90 knots and their heading was 140°, a few hours later 50 knots and eventually 20 knots. Bob Rice informed them that a trough of low pressure was building in the eastern Pacific, and he was concerned that its influence was slowing them down or, even worse, might deflect them to the south. The next fax from Lindstrand revealed his concern. 'The next couple of hours will be critical if we are going to make it. Since we have enough fuel for a complete circumnavigation, it would be sad if we got stuck in a merry-go-round in the mid-Pacific.' Accordingly a US Coast Guard *C-130* scouted 200 miles ahead of the balloon and confirmed that prospects did indeed look bad.

Lindstrand went to bed at midnight. 'Steve took over, we agreed to stay at 20,000 feet for the night as that produced the best track, and we would see what Bob would say in the morning.' But by the time he woke up it was all done and dusted. During the night Mike Kendrick had talked through the situation with Branson who didn't want to spend the next week going nowhere fast. Glum-faced Branson and Fossett informed Lindstrand that they had just been instructed by the Control Centre to ditch off Hawaii as the wind had turned. (In fact for the last few hours they had been going backwards.) The rescue helicopters were already on their way to meet them.

In retrospect Lindstrand says, 'We probably didn't lose the flight at the trough, but over China where we should have travelled at twice the speed we did. This caused us to arrive at the trough more than a day later than forecast.'

They prepared the capsule for a sea ditching, donned their immersion suits and descended towards the waves. Through lack of local knowledge they opted for the eastern side of Hawaii where the seas are much rougher than on the west. Lindstrand brought the balloon down gently with one eye on the radar altimeter and the other on the GPS hoping for a decrease in forward speed. The normal method of ditching calls for envelope release on touch-down, but the safety pins jammed on the release bolts and as they splashed into the 9-foot swell the envelope dragged the capsule through each cascading ridge of water. After five minutes of venting helium the balloon settled a little and Fossett, followed by Branson, clambered out of the top hatch and on to the sloping roof of the capsule. As Lindstrand joined them he surveyed the scene. Upwind was the billowing mass of the dying envelope, to his left two US Coast Guard helicopters were flying in close formation and a Coast Guard cutter was trailing a mile behind. Despite the disappointment of ditching, Lindstrand was enjoying himself. He had flown halfway round-the-world and before he jumped into the warm Pacific water, he thought to himself, 'It doesn't get any better than this!'

His northern-hemisphere competitors – Bertrand Piccard and Brian Jones of the *Breitling Orbiter 3*, Jacques Soukup, Crispin Williams and Mark Sullivan of *Spirit of Peace*, Andy Elson and Colin Prescot of *Cable & Wireless* and solo globaller Kevin Uliassi – were probably thinking exactly the same thing. Having watched the *ICO Global Challenger* team snatch defeat from the jaws of victory they were still in with a chance. Better still, Branson and Co. had lost their capsule and equipment – even that address book was now lying under 6,000 feet of salt water. What a Christmas present! However, while the ICO team might be out of the picture, their headlong rush through Chinese airspace had sparked a diplomatic crisis that resulted in the other British registered balloons being refused permission to enter Chinese airspace. But for one global team the closing of the bamboo curtain presented no problem at all and on the other side of the world they were waiting to launch.

December 1998/January 1999, Alice Springs, Australia

Team Re/Max was a high-altitude, high-risk gamble which first saw the light of day under the project title *Odyssey*. American balloonist and television reporter Bob Martin says the idea came to him like the clichéd cartoon light-bulb going ping above his head. His plan was to fly a balloon at the limits of the Earth's atmosphere where fast and reliable winds would carry it round-the-world in sixteen to eighteen days. The *Odyssey* balloon had been constructed by Raven Industries of South Dakota, to the same specifications as Nasa's scientific balloons, and its scale was almost

Formerly *Odyssey*, renamed *Team Re/Max*, this ultra-high-altitude attempt features a pressurized space capsule for the crew. Solar panels shade its top, water and oxygen tanks are strapped to the side and sand ballast bins can be seen at its base

(Team Re/Max)

beyond comprehension. Filled with 170,000 cubic feet of helium at ground level, it would expand to a staggering 40,000,000 cubic feet by cruise altitude – roughly forty times bigger than Branson's balloon – and fly a westerly route following the Tropic of Capricorn at between 80,000 and 130,000 feet. (By comparison *Concorde* cruises at 60,000 feet as it zaps across the Atlantic.)

This scheme was not without some merit. Flying at such dizzy heights, the balloon would be well above the man-made obstacles of airspace and high above the effects of the weather. On the down side, so to speak, concerns were expressed by some experts about the reliability of the gossamer-thin envelope which looked and felt like nothing more than plastic food wrap and when fully extended would be virtually transparent. Apart from getting it off the ground the greatest challenge might be landing such a beast safely – balancing the release of helium gas and ballast without cratering it into the Australian desert. And if the crew didn't land in their capsule the record would be invalid.

After the initial press launch back in 1994, complete with an all-singing, all-dancing media pack, plywood mockup of the capsule, artist's impressions and even a range of promotional merchandise, Martin had struggled to raise sufficient backing. Then both of his original co-pilots, Mark Sullivan, who later reemerged on the *Spirit of Peace* team, and Troy Bradley quit the project, causing him to seek sponsorship and new co-pilots further afield. Australia beckoned as an apparently ideal launch location and the Australian balloonist John Wallington, the first to cross Australia by balloon, joined the team and a new major sponsor was signed up in the shape of the bookselling company Dymock. Martin then approached the American billionaire businessman Dave Liniger for the final piece of funding needed to realize his dream. Liniger's Re/Max franchise network of real estate agents had earned him a vast fortune, and appropriately enough the business is promoted via the biggest fleet of hot-air balloons in the world. A keen balloonist himself, four times Liniger turned Martin down as he worked on his own global game plan including a possibly solo attempt, but by the mid-1990s and fearing that he might already have missed the boat, Liniger relented. He would become the third member of the flight crew and his financial backing ensured that the *Dymock Flyer* was renamed *Team Re/Max*.

The balloon had arrived at Alice Springs on Christmas Eve. This remote location is the home to the Alice Springs Balloon Launching Station, a joint research facility that routinely launches vast high-altitude balloons to carry scientific packages into the stratosphere. These people are the real experts in this field and the Director of the Station, Professor Ravi Sood, was singularly unimpressed by what he saw unfolding. For a start he couldn't understand why *Team Re/Max* had come to Alice Springs at the height of the Australian summer. It might be a good time for the high-altitude winds but they couldn't have chosen a worse possible time for launch conditions as it was known to be a period of frequent thunderstorms.

Lindstrand was concerned that the team could get themselves killed, as these extremely fragile research balloons have a fail rate at launch of between five and ten per cent. And what if anything should go wrong at 130,000 feet? The crew would be way beyond any help and far too high to parachute back safely. Liniger readily dismissed such criticism as 'very narrow-minded'. He pointed out that unmanned balloons had repeatedly made such high-altitude circumnavigations. 'The precedent does exist, the problem with this approach is that it is much more high-tech than any of the lower atmosphere attempts and has far more problems inherent in it.'

Launching such a vast balloon is extremely difficult. The capsule is suspended in front of a large crane with the envelope trailing behind on a flat-bed truck. As a bubble of helium lifts the envelope into a towering sausage the truck has to stay underneath it, keeping track with any breeze, until the capsule can be released. These balloons are so large and so delicate that the operation cannot be carried out in wind speeds above 5 knots; launch opportunities for *Team Re/Max* would be few and far between.

On 27 December the first launch was cancelled because the team was simply not ready. They were still working on the capsule – a squat cylinder just 8 feet across and 7 feet high – which would be all that protected them from the virtual vacuum at the edge of space. Outside temperatures could drop to −25°C during the day even though the sun's rays would scorch the capsule's exterior. 'If one of the windows broke you would have an explosive decompression,' Bob Martin explained. 'At 130,000 feet without your spacesuit it would be instantaneously fatal.' At zero feet with the capsule sitting in its shed, one of the circular windows cracked under the intense heat of a photographer's lighting during a photo session. Hastily the toughened glass was changed for even tougher polycarbonate.

Two days later another launch had to be cancelled because of the winds that battered Alice Springs. And so it went on. Unbelievably, on 2 January the capsule was actually calculated to be 1,100 lb overweight. One of the life support systems had to be sacrificed to make way for more lead ballast – to be released as the balloon punched up through the troposphere, a band of extreme cold at around 60,000 feet. Get rid of a life support system and with it goes the man whose life it was intended to support. The mission was coming apart at the seams, and next day Bob Martin made an emotional announcement that he was the one who would not be going where no man has gone before. 'It was an honest error. But we needed one guy off and as the guy who came up with this crazy idea it was my responsibility to make sure it was done properly.' That left just the two newcomers to the project, Dave Liniger and John Wallington, as flight crew.

The ground team made the adjustments to the capsule and announced their intention to launch a couple of days later, but once again wind conditions forced another stand-down. Cracks in the team were showing and infighting had openly erupted since Martin had stepped down as the third pilot. In effect there were three teams now: the 'Bob Squad' as it was known, supporting the project originator Bob Martin; Liniger, the major financial backer, and his extensive entourage – which the Bob Squad accused of hijacking the project; and finally, home-grown balloonist John Wallington who was piggy-in-the-middle and did his best to avoid public comment on the goings-on.

Bad weather stopped play for three more days. Then, on 11 January, it was all systems go and the two-man crew was all suited up by the time the plug was pulled because of an approaching storm showing up on the satellite pictures. 'I feel like the bride left at the altar,' confided a despondent Liniger, a chubby spaceman slumped in one corner of the tin hut. He was sweating buckets in the sweltering heat, looking for all the world like a dejected Michelin man who had sprung a leak; 'all dressed up and nowhere to go'.

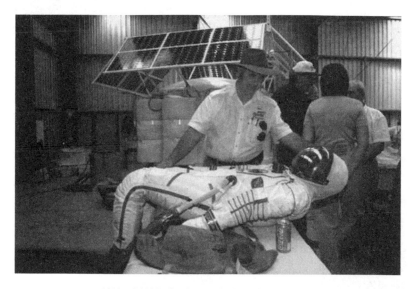

13 April 1999 – back into the box. Another day at Alice Springs and another
cancellation for *Team Re/Max*
(*Grant Turner*)

Next day another launch was abandoned because of rain in the
vicinity – any moisture on the envelope could cause icing capable
of ripping the fragile polythene as it climbed through the atmosphere. To entertain the balloonists, black thunderclouds gathered
on the horizon and flashes of lightning danced across the sky in a
typical display of Alice Springs summer weather.

The unlucky 13th of January. The space-suited pilots were
inside the capsule when it finally left the ground – lifted by a huge
rusting crane. Unbelievably, preparations took so long that by the
time everything was ready the launch weather window had closed,
leaving the crew sitting it out on the dusty launchpad. The crane
trundled back into the garage and the pilots went back to their
hotels. On the following day the high altitude winds were too
strong for a safe climb-out. Launch cancelled. It was 'Groundhog
Day' all over again.

Finally, on 15 January, after five weeks in the windy heat of the

Australian desert, many years of planning and more than $8 million spent, an emotional Dave Liniger announced to the media that *Team Re/Max* was being aborted. 'It appears we have a craft that is far too sensitive to weather conditions,' admitted John Wallington. 'That's part of what we'll redesign . . . and we are eager to return next year,' he announced, much to the delight of the hoteliers and bar-keepers who had never experienced such a welcome boost to the local economy. Further distancing himself from the debacle, Liniger explained that he had come into the project after the capsule had been completed and that he had had little say in its construction – the final act in a bizarre comedy of errors. It was left to the Australian *Daily Telegraph* to sum it up as 'the funniest show on Earth'.

21 ANOTHER WAY

They say that it isn't over until the fat lady sings, but by mid-February 1999 the prospects for the four remaining teams did not look good. Time was running out. In past years the northern hemisphere jetstream season had closed at the end of February and already this year had produced no suitable winds since the end of January. With an expected duration of two to three weeks for a global flight, the middle of the month looked increasingly like the cut-off point for any launch decisions.

The *ICO Global Challenger*'s sally through China's airspace hadn't helped matters, and while Per Lindstrand began work on a replacement balloon the other teams were left trying to unravel this Chinese puzzle. Beijing's stance had more to do with air traffic difficulties than any concerns over aerial espionage – after all, hundreds of satellites crisscross the entire surface of the planet on a daily basis. 'To be precise,' Alan Noble told me, 'the Chinese have said please don't fly until we have analysed the ICO flight. Apparently eleven aircraft were diverted.' But as he freely admitted himself, 'It's easy to criticize – there but for the grace of God . . . ICO just happened to get there first.'

In January the Chinese authorities had issued a questionnaire to the remaining teams asking about their intentions, but there was no indication of when a decision would come from Beijing. By the beginning of February there was still no response.

For the Breitling team the last few months had brought some dramatic internal changes. New boy Tony Brown had pulled out, leaving the stand-in, Brian Jones, in the hot seat. As a *Concorde* Flight Engineer, Brown had expected to do things by the book, but when preparing a global balloon for a circumnavigation whole chapters – if not the entire book – tend to be discarded. There is no shake-down crew – you have to get in, switch on the ignition and fly. Brown had come into the Breitling project late in the day and while trying to make his own mark he had inadvertently been creating tensions between himself and Bertrand Piccard. As a psychiatrist Piccard sensed the problems and began to push, bringing matters to a head over dinner one night in November. The disagreements quickly escalated into arguments and by the next morning Piccard's mind was made up; he would not be flying with Brown. After a long discussion the two men went to seek out Brian Jones in the workshop. 'You're on Brian,' they told him. And with that the three of them shook hands. 'And that was it,' says Jones. 'Grown-up people making a joint decision.'

On the other side of the Atlantic, Jacques Soukup and his Anglo-American team were also sitting it out, anxiously watching several ideal launch slots come and go. Officially they continued to toe the line: 'Out of respect for the People's Republic of China, the *Spirit of Peace* is temporarily holding for another window and a reinstatement of overflight permission before launching.' And solo-flier Kevin Uliassi echoed these sentiments. All very politically correct, but there was no denying the mounting sense of frustration. Then on 12 February Soukup rang me to say that he was calling it off for the time being. Like some of the others he was turning his attention to a southern hemisphere attempt in the summer, confident that no northern hemisphere fliers would get off at this late stage. That left just two teams undeclared; Breitling and newcomers Cable & Wireless.

And the fat lady, bless her, was clearing her throat.

Colin Prescot and Andy Elson on board the *Cable & Wireless* balloon on 17 February
1999, complete with lucky fluffy dice
(*Chas Breton*)

Wednesday 17 February 1999, Almería, Spain

Eclipsed by the glare of publicity surrounding Richard Branson's activities, the British duo Andy Elson and Colin Prescot had been largely ignored by the media, despite their high-profile sponsor Cable & Wireless. They decided to go for it with a new game-plan in place. They would fly the balloon low and slow for the first part of the trip in order to manoeuvre to the south and around China, to pick up the jetstream eventually over the Pacific. It was a long shot, viewed by some as a bold attempt to sidestep the problem and by others as a cynical display designed to give the sponsors a run for their money. But Andy Elson was convinced that this plan was viable because he calculated that the restricted height ceiling at the beginning of the flight – to keep beneath the faster winds straight to China – meant that they could take an extra three tons of kerosene. Accordingly he had devised a method of carrying nine barrels of fuel piggyback on either side of the capsule, enabling them to stay airborne for possibly a whole month if they had to. Anyway, they would give it their best shot.

On 17 February the silver and gold *Cable & Wireless* balloon made a perfect lift-off from the shelter of the seventeenth tee of the golf course at La Envia, near Almería in southern Spain. The familiar outline of yet another Cameron Rozière ascended into brilliant sunshine before it slowly drifted south-westwards as planned, backwards in global terms. By midnight the balloon was situated over Morocco and had begun a slow curving turn to the east, and on the second day *Cable & Wireless* was approaching the Western Sahara at 18,000 feet. 'It should reach the subtropical jet-stream at around midday,' said Flight Director Ian Ashpole of Flying Pictures. 'At which point they will gain altitude to approximately 24,000 feet from the natural heat of the sun and their speed will increase dramatically.'

Inside the squat 16-foot-long aluminium capsule, built by Elson himself, the two men were getting accustomed to their new environment, settling into shift patterns and snatching spells of two to three hours of sleep. Given the balloon's sluggish progress they had plenty of time for essential maintenance and Andy made repairs to a leaking hatch (from the inside on this occasion). Meanwhile, messages of good luck were pouring in from fellow balloonists, including the ICO team, and from Breitling who hoped to launch later in the week!

The Breitling team had one ace up its sleeve, however. As their balloon was Swiss-registered as HB-BRA – Piccard called it his 'wonder bra' – they had obtained permission from the Chinese to pass through its southern airspace on the provision that they stayed south of the 26th parallel. 'We worked incredibly hard with the Chinese,' explained Brian Jones after the flight. 'Both of us toing and froing to the Chinese Embassy, and constantly on the phone and fax to the Swiss diplomats in Beijing. But eventually it paid off. This was because we were constantly negotiating and because Bertrand and Alan Noble had gone to China the previous year and had met with the officials. I honestly think that this is why they were on our side and they were looking for an excuse to let us go.' Even so, they still had no option but to wait for weather conditions which would carry them south of the Himalayas, and suddenly Switzerland wasn't such a sensible place to start from. 'We developed this scenario that if we had to go down to Africa and loop around to find the jetstream down there, we would do a low slow flight and therefore we took an extra four tanks of propane,' said Jones.

To formalize their agreement with the Chinese, Piccard and Jones travelled to the embassy in Bern and signed a promise to say that if there was any risk of them going over the 26th North they would land. 'We signed it in front of the TV cameras – so we had no option – in that scenario there was no question, we would have landed,' Jones confirmed.

They were under other pressures too. While Breitling had told them that it would still support them if they decided to shelve the project and try again next winter, there would be no money for an *Orbiter 4*. Accordingly, Piccard and Jones were adamant that they would not launch unless there was a good chance of success. This would be their one and only shot.

For Andy Elson and Colin Prescot, life, or more specifically northern Africa, was passing them by at a leisurely pace on their fourth day aloft. 'It's warm and pleasant,' Prescot e-mailed the Central Control. 'We hardly touched a control all day, settling at 8,000 feet with the hatch open and some welcome fresh air. We spent an hour outside refuelling from the piggybacked barrels of kerosene and taking pictures. At lunchtime we ate our last piece of fresh food – avocado.' Plates were the only equipment they had forgotten to take with them. After the fresh food supply had run out they resorted to a variety of soups and dried pasta or muesli mixed with water in whatever plastic containers they could muster.

As they worked on the outside of the capsule the two pilots

managed to produce a black umbrella to shade them from the harsh sunshine. Only the British! A little later Prescot faxed his impressions via the Inmarsat: 'It is amazing to think that in a few hours time we will have been flying for five days. On the other hand the launch seems just a distant blur. On the first night my memory is of watching the lights of Marrakesh go by directly underneath. Since soon after that we have seen no sign of a road, house or even a camel. Just interminable sand to every horizon. When I was at school I learned that Timbuctoo was the most remote place on earth. Well, we passed twenty miles to the north of it yesterday.'

Since launching from La Envia they had barely moved a single degree to the east, but this was all part of the strategy; they always knew that the first leg of their journey had to be a very long one if they were to have any chance of avoiding China. After travelling at only 15 knots at times, on the sixth day they climbed to 24,000 feet and picked up some speed at last, although life on board remained relaxed. 'The boy genius has thought of everything,' reported Prescot while Elson slept. 'My bed is comfortable and we both manage to get some sleep. Right now the whole capsule shakes with snoring. Quite reassuring really. We do not eat much because we are using little energy.' The next morning the balloon skimmed just south of the Libyan border, passing it by about 2,500 feet, although permission to overfly had been obtained. At 1400 GMT they crossed the Nile and they were on course for Jeddah in Saudi Arabia, 'surfing' the jet between 22,000 and 27,000 feet and travelling at around 50 knots over the relentless desert.

On day eleven the *Cable & Wireless* balloon smashed the existing ballooning endurance record set by Elson himself and his companions aboard the *Breitling Orbiter 2* the previous year. Elson and Prescot had travelled for over 235 hours and were some 5,900 miles from their launchsite. After a brief moment of celebration it was back to the job in hand to get the balloon through India and then on to the south of Rangoon to meet an airflow which should take it round southern China. 'Low and slow' was becoming the team mantra.

Bertrand Piccard, ready to take on the world with *Breitling Orbiter 3*
(*Breitling*)

For the pilots there was another reason to celebrate after they successfully completed an on-board repair job reinstating voice communications after two days without the satellite phone. In true *Apollo 13* style the solution came after Technical Director Anthony McQuiggan set up a dummy capsule with the satellite phone suppliers. Together they identified the fault and searched around the capsule for something on-board to replace the faulty parts. The answer came in the form of a lavatory light and instructions were relayed to the pilots by fax and they completed the repair. Unfortunately the cabin heaters, which had broken down on the third day, couldn't be fixed. But as Prescot recounts, 'It was never going to be a luxury cruise and we coped. There were some occasions when it was so cold that I would hop around in my Arctic sleeping bag to keep warm.'

Then on 1 March some news from Switzerland: *Breitling Orbiter 3* was launching. The race was on!

Monday 1 March 1999, Château d'Oex

I had returned to Château d'Oex the previous day and after a rest-
less night had gone to the launchsite a little before dawn. A crowd
was already gathering around the slender envelope of *Breitling
Orbiter 3* which was standing upright looking like a silvery flame.
As the sky began to colour from the east, last-minute preparations
were well in hand and the two pilots could be seen making final
checks and saying their goodbyes. Among the crowd to see them
off was the distinctive tall figure of Jacques Piccard, Bertrand's
father and the man who had descended to the deepest part of the
Pacific Ocean. And by chance it was Bertrand Piccard's forty-first
birthday, so a successful launch would be the icing on the cake.

By the time the sun's first warmth reached the valley floor they
were ready to go at last. It had started to get noisy, a final top-up
of helium was shrieking through the white filling tubes (to compensate for the pilots' additional weight) and a swarm of helicopters buzzed around overhead. Piccard was hidden deep inside the
capsule while Brian Jones squatted on top, but he was having to
hold on tight as the balloon was being buffeted by a freshening
breeze flowing down the valley. The capsule lifted and bumped.
The Mylar fabric swayed and crackled, and the propane tanks
clanked loudly against the fluorescent red capsule as it pulled one
way and then the other against the restraints. To make matters
worse a horrible groaning sound was emanating from beneath the
capsule as the polystyrene cushioning scraped across the snow.

'Cut the damn rope,' urged Jones, but his words were lost in the
din. The capsule was taking a pounding now and there was a real
risk of some serious damage to the equipment. From his perch
sitting among the equipment on the roof of the capsule, Jones had
visions of everything going pear-shaped. 'I was thinking of the
flight in terms of hours at that stage instead of days, and what
would happen if we got airborne and had to land again before
we got out of the Alps.' Worse still, if one of the propane tanks
ruptured then the whole launchsite could have been engulfed in

flames. 'I saw this propane tank sticking out, caught on one of the ropes, and fortunately I didn't see it smash against the side. This was just a complete nightmare.'

At 9.05 am (0805 GMT) Alan Noble severed the final restraining rope and as the *Breitling Orbiter 3* lifted into the air the reverent hush of the crowd was replaced by cheers. For a moment the balloon seemed to dip down towards the journalists' enclosure, and then it pulled up into the sunlight above our heads and began to climb steadily, turning back up the valley and over the hill-top church of Château d'Oex. The launchsite fell quiet once more.

'We went up like a rocket,' Brian Jones commented later. 'They had put too much helium in and I thought we had blown it after the other two balloons had burst by going up too fast.' But the rate of climb quickly steadied and Piccard, who was monitoring the instruments, instructed Jones to get a bag of sand off as they encountered the first of several inversion layers. 'I was still on the top,' confirms Jones. 'I was the one with the view, except of course that the skirt came within eighteen inches of the load frame, so you had to squat down to look out. The first thing I had to do was to cut the straps which held the really thick polystyrene blocks which were underneath. I looked over, the knife in my hand, and I thought there's no way I can cut these off – they're going to hit somebody – so they stayed on for the flight (and possibly saved disaster on landing). One of our pieces of luck.' He then lowered the rack of square solar panels below the capsule and took care of a few minor jobs before scrambling back inside as they approached 6,000 feet. Once the hatch was down they clamped it and started pressurization and there was beautiful silence in the capsule – the previous year there had been a whistle. 'Absolutely brilliant,' recalls Jones. 'Thank god we got one thing right.'

As the silver jewel of the Breitling balloon slowly climbed above the craggy mountain tops to an altitude of 21,000 feet, *Cable & Wireless* had already been airborne for ten days. With two balloons now in the air the media compared the new race with Aesop's 'tortoise and the hare' – inevitably *Cable & Wireless* was cast as the 'low and slow' tortoise – but then it was the tortoise which had won in the fable. Certainly the *Cable & Wireless* team felt they had an advantage with their kerosene fuel system which theoretically offered a much greater endurance than the smaller Breitling balloon could expect. But in reality it was more like a case of the 'tortoise and the tortoise' at this stage, and as Piccard observed after their first night aloft, 'We have no way of catching up.'

By 3 March the *Cable & Wireless* balloon had been flying for exactly two weeks and had covered over 9,000 miles. Their Met team remained confident that they were still on course for a jet-stream, currently over Japan, which would whisk them across the Pacific in a further three to four days. Yet it was far from plain sailing for the two British pilots and as they neared Myanmar they were subjected to a terrifying 90 minutes on the edge of severe thunderstorm activity. Conditions were so violent that large rents were torn in the outer skin of the Mylar fabric. Indeed, Elson described it as the worst two hours of his life and after their ordeal they both brushed their teeth to wash the sour taste of fear out of their mouths. But at least by the following day they had the consolation of putting the major stumbling-block of China behind them as the balloon eased within 30 miles of Hainan Dao island in the South China Seas – the most southern point of China's territory. Laos and Vietnam had refused overflight permission initially, despite having issued written authorization beforehand, but the ground team soon smoothed the way through, and breathing a massive sigh of relief Elson and Prescot were in high spirits.

For Bertrand Piccard and Brian Jones their slow start had also given them time to settle into their new mobile home. Jones in particular was very tired for the first couple of days. 'I had done a lot of travelling back to England, I hadn't slept much the night before the launch and the months of accumulated stress were catching up,' he later told me. 'Bertrand felt better than I did and so I would go to bed for an hour and a half and then wake up.' (The two men shared the free bunk in turns as their survival gear was laid out in readiness on the other one.) Jones also suffered from headaches until they established some sort of routine. 'We had this system where we tried to do eight-hour shifts each – sleep for eight hours, come on duty for eight hours and then have eight hours together. Initially the time together came from lunchtime to around sunset.' However, once the balloon was heading eastwards the shortening of the days caused this period to roll back and sometimes it became difficult for the two men to work out which day it was. They found one solution was to measure the thickness of the stubble sprouting on their chins.

After passing through a humid front on the third day they reported to the Control Centre that thick ice had collected on the capsule and that long icicles were hanging from the envelope. 'We can actually see nine-foot-long stalactites, some of them touching the propane tanks,' Piccard told them. 'It's a wonderful sight.' It may have been, but they needed to bring the *Orbiter* lower in order to thaw the ice and relieve the balloon of the unnecessary burden. This wasn't their only problem; early in the afternoon the Control Centre received an alarming fax from the Swiss Embassy in Beijing, stating that permission to overfly had been valid only until the end of February, although after some frantic phone calls the Chinese authorities kindly agreed immediately to extend the authorization. 'We're both very relaxed and very happy,' said Jones as they began to turn eastwards.

During that night they allowed the balloon to descend naturally as it cooled and at first light they eagerly clambered out for their first EVA like two schoolboys playing truant. The ice had thickened considerably and Piccard gleefully hacked it off with a fireman's axe. For the first time in thousands of years it was raining ice on the Sahara desert.

The balloon's curving course to the east was proving slightly slower and further south than anticipated, although the latter would help the meteorologists guide it to India and along the Chinese tightrope. Met men for the project were Pierre Eckert, an expert in routing ocean-going yachts, and Luc Trullemans of the Royal Institute of Meteorology in Brussels, a veteran of the Chrysler Transatlantic Race. These two were the master magicians, casting their spells to weave the *Orbiter* along a gossamer-thin thread of wind encircling the globe. They must use the weather, deciding when to hold back and when to push ahead, in a slow unfolding game, gradually building advantage upon advantage. And while good fortune must certainly play its part, it was the skilful use of whatever the weather gods bestowed that would be the real key to success.

At last the balloon passed the Zero Meridian and spirits were high. 'We really have the impression that we have started the round-the-world flight,' exclaimed Piccard. On 5 March the balloon was over Libya and heading south-eastwards towards the Egyptian pyramids where Brian Jones hoped they might land at the end of their journey, and for the first time the *Orbiter* was encountering the jetstream which swept it along at a more respectable 90 knots. The next morning they deliberately went back down to 10,400 feet and only 27 knots, under orders from the Met boys to lose a little speed in an attempt to divert around an angry red mark on their maps – a forbidden military zone in the Yemen. It also helped to melt more of their accumulated ice burden.

With both balloons making slow but steady progress I left Switzerland and travelled back to England where I took the opportunity to visit Per Lindstrand's factory in Oswestry to see how work was progressing on the replacement *Virgin/ICO* capsule. Lindstrand was in confident mood, convinced that the jetstream would not hold together for his two airborne rivals. And with a distinct impression of déjà vu I followed him into the workshop where the bare metal cylinder of the embryonic capsule was standing. He posed for a few photographs and as an act of defiance to the fates pulled out a giant marker-pen and scrawled across the pristine aluminium: 'I promise not to sink this one in Tahiti.' But he did so with a nervous grin.

Monday 7 March, the Sea of Japan

Struggling to stay on course for the diverging jetstream across the Pacific, and caught in ever-slowing winds north of Taiwan, the *Cable & Wireless* team had begun to doubt that they could still complete a circumnavigation. The balloon had become trapped between layers of cloud and rain as it approached the southern tip of Japan. Elson and Prescot tried to climb above the clouds and the weather, but the wind pushed them too far east and heavy falls of sleet and snow caused a massive build-up of ice on the envelope, and the heavy balloon began to fall. The thick cloud cover also meant that the solar cells were being robbed of vital sunlight and were not functioning properly. Elson had held such faith in these solar panels that they weren't carrying any back-up batteries; all his electrical eggs were in the one basket. Deprived of power, they were unable to pump the kerosene to the burners – their balloon was dying.

At 0200 GMT the authorities were notified of their intentions and two hours later they ditched 76 miles off the Japanese coast. 'We fought our way down through tremendous wind and snow-storms. Andy did a brilliant job,' recalled Colin Prescot afterwards. 'We got it down very gently, which was a relief as it could have been nasty.' The two men were in the water for fifteen minutes before being scooped up by a waiting helicopter of the Japan Self-Defence Force. The forlorn balloon was left adrift, wallowing in the choppy water with its delicate metallic outer covering split like an over-ripe tomato from the effects of the storms. Their efforts to protect the capsule by sealing the heavy dome were to no avail and it was abandoned to the grey drizzly expanse of the ocean as water rushed in through the open hatch.

Back on dry land, looking like twins with their greying stubble, the two pilots were asked what they most needed. Elson replied instantly, 'After eighteen days – a shower!' They had set a fantastic new endurance record and they had made the headlines on just about every front page around the world, but their global quest was over. 'Obviously we are sad,' Prescot told the gathered reporters. 'But we have pushed back new barriers in balloon flight and have nothing to be ashamed of.'

'I don't think we have failed,' added Elson with unintended irony. 'We have just found another way that doesn't work.'

22 FULL CIRCLE

Sunday 7 March 1999

Twilight. Low on the western horizon the last vestiges of pink were slipping beneath outcrops of undulating cloud, creating the illusion that they were distant continents and that the sky itself was a vast ocean, and with a final flourish of glowing embers the sun slid from view. After seven days aloft for the crew of the *Breitling Orbiter 3* this was their domain. During the night Bertrand Piccard had gathered his thoughts as far below the land gave way to the shadowy darkness of the Arabian Sea. 'Brian is sleeping and I try to sum up my first impressions of this flight . . . Over the ocean after six days of flying over the desert, I would rather have to write "deserts" since each sunrise revealed another mixture of sand and rocks, designs and shapes, shapes and colours. Boundless spaces without human track . . .'

Within the confines of the capsule the passage of time and days began to blur. Throughout the flight they were running on GMT but this had no correlation with the hours of light or darkness outside. As Brian Jones explained later, 'It became really difficult to know whether it was morning or evening. So Bertrand made up a piece of paper that said "AM" and "PM" and we would slide this bit of paper backwards and forwards across our Breitling analogue clock so that we would know what time it was in GMT.' Morning or evening, they were kept very busy throughout the flight. Early on alarms had kept going off on the burner control panel. The burners had safety systems built in to ensure that if neat propane was shooting through without igniting the gas flow would shut down, or if they were burning vapour they would also shut down and set off an alarm.

'These things were starting to go a bit haywire and so we turned them off and there was a lot of playing around to make them behave,' recalls Jones. But by India the problem with the pilot lights had become progressively worse. 'From a good flame we were getting an increasingly smaller one due to the amount of moisture up there. We also had standard pilot lights on our heating system and so this got progressively worse throughout the flight while the balloon was getting higher. The whole thing was a vicious circle and towards the end it was very uncomfortable, but there was nothing we could do about it.'

The burners were also equipped with a timer that set a pause time between the burns and their duration. 'We set up the auto pilot to burn before the residual flame went out and with all that liquid in the hoses it took maybe six to seven seconds to burn out. This way we would burn again before the flame disappeared so that we could do without that pilot light.' But if the gas failed to ignite, the method of lighting it was to hit two sparker buttons on the burner control panel which was situated in the middle of the capsule above the bunks. 'So you would be sitting at the controls at the front with a headset on, which had only a 4-foot lead, and the burner would go out and you would have to leap out of the seat, hit the sparker button, and try to reignite the burner before too much propane had gone up into the envelope. If you failed to do it, there was this big 'Wumph!' as the neat propane ignited – the whole balloon would shake and ice would come pouring on top of the capsule with an almighty noise which would wake the other person up. Looking back on it it was funny, but at the time it wasn't funny at all. Particularly in heavy air traffic areas.'

Monday 8 March, India

On arrival in Indian airspace on 8 March the pilots had an unexpected fright when ATC in Bombay couldn't find the balloon's identification number and denied permission to overfly! Fortunately after a few faxes and phone conversations with ATC in Geneva, where the Swiss Controllers were helping with clearances, the matter was quickly resolved. On the next day, around noon, they passed close to Sultanpur (the site of Fossett's Indian landing in 1997), and then flew on north of Calcutta and into Bangladesh, giving the pilots some spectacular views of the Himalayas. When they approached Myanmar (former Burma), Brian Jones called up ATC at Rangoon who responded by asking for his departure and landing points. 'HB-BRA, departed from Switzerland, intention to land somewhere in Africa,' replied Jones who was unable to pinpoint their final destination any more accurately. The Controller was somewhat perplexed by this; 'If you're going from Switzerland to Africa, what the hell are you doing in Myanmar?'

That night, at 2120 GMT, the *Breitling Orbiter 3* crossed the border into southern China's airspace. It was going to require a lot of careful manoeuvring and not a little good luck to keep them within the narrow air corridor permitted by the Chinese, and Piccard and Jones were only too aware of their promise to land the balloon if it strayed into prohibited airspace. Just in case they had forgotten, the first message from the Chinese ATC was unequivocal; 'HB-BRA, remember, it is forbidden to fly north of 26 degrees.' This was the make or break time for the entire flight with barely a handful of miles separating success from total failure. Flying just above the cloud-tops to keep to their track, they were walking a wire – heading straight down the line. Incredibly, the balloon maintained its heading due east for the next 1,300 miles – the only part of their long round-the-world journey when this happened – and it was a key piece of good fortune.

Thursday 11 March, the Pacific Ocean

At 1330 GMT the balloon exited Chinese airspace at exactly the same latitude as it had entered, at 25.9° N. But Piccard and Jones didn't have time to celebrate as they were more anxious about crossing the Pacific – 8,000 miles of water, the equivalent of the distance they had already flown from Switzerland. Unfortunately the balloon was on a more southerly track than anticipated, taking it towards Hawaii instead of over Japan and the central Pacific. Trusting themselves to the Met men once more, the two pilots had to allow the balloon to be carried south towards the equator, and they would have to sit it out for three or four days waiting for the new jetstream to form. It was a route that would cost them more time and more of their precious supply of propane, although they estimated that they should still reach Mexico in another six days. At this stage they had exhausted only ten of their 32 propane cylinders, which should give them a possible further fifteen days of flight if all went well. Even so, they couldn't afford any delays and as Jones admitted at the time, 'What frightens us most about crossing the Pacific is bad weather in an area where rescue will be long and difficult.'

As *Breitling Orbiter 3* commenced its slow trek across the ocean, it had beaten the endurance record of its predecessor *Orbiter 2* which had flown for nearly ten days. The balloon was now very close to the Tropic of Cancer and its speed had dwindled to around 40 knots, but things were still running to plan as they had to slow down in order to catch the right jetstream which was still forming over the Pacific. They were faced with two options: a Polar jetstream which would carry them over the USA (with all its air traffic restrictions) or a subtropical one towards Mexico and the Caribbean Islands.

Remarkably, after so many days cooped up in their little pod, the two pilots were getting on perfectly well. 'Bertrand and I are still talking to each other,' laughed Brian. 'There has not been a single problem between us. The only swearwords are directed at minor technical problems. The one thing that annoys me is the dehydrated food. But if it's the only problem, I think we can survive it.'

The fresh food – meals cooked and vacuum-packed by the hotel in Château d'Oex – had run out after the first three or four days. It had been selected according to the pilots' own tastes; Brian Jones had salmon for example, while Bertrand Piccard had emu steak which he likes, and this food was heated by immersing it in a small water boiler. After that they had nineteen days of dehydrated rations such as pasta or potato which had been provided by the development department of the Swiss company Nestlé. 'When we ate it in the workshop before we flew we thought it was really good,' says Jones. 'But when we were flying it was awful. Well, initially it was okay but after two weeks it was becoming a little bland.' They also had a good supply of sweets and chocolate with them as the company had given them carte blanche to help themselves to whatever they wanted, although half of it had been left behind and most of the rest ended up being ditched in the Pacific.

Most meals were eaten separately to ensure that if there had been anything wrong with the food only one of the pilots would have been taken ill. 'We had our own sort of body-clock rhythm,' Jones says. 'Bertrand had an appetite like a horse, which is extraordinary as he is thin as a rake. I had very little appetite, so I had one meal every twenty-four hours apart from breakfast, while Bertrand probably had three. We missed fresh food of course, but it actually wasn't very important. There were lots of things that in normal life would take on an aura of importance, but we were so anxious to get as far as we could that the flight was the be-all and end-all. If we had been compelled to survive on only water and bread it wouldn't have been that much of a problem.' And to prove their good humour, the pilots turned their skills and spare time over the Pacific towards converting their redundant flight maps of China into paper hats.

*

By the twelfth day progress had become desperately slow. Shortly before dawn they had taken the balloon down to an altitude of 6,000 feet and for the first time in a week they opened the hatch to enjoy some fresh air. Advised by the meteorologists, Alan Noble had opted for the subtropical jet forming around Hawaii and for the next few days the balloon was forced to drift at a snail's pace at around only 30 knots. For the pilots this slow motion crawl was increasingly hard to cope with and Brian Jones recalled that at the time of the launch he had not really expected them to get around the world at all. 'I thought, 'Please God, let us get across the Pacific. If we could do that we would have set an impressive new record. If we can just make America.' And here they were, with thousands of miles of ocean still to come, going nowhere fast.

Their spirits were raised a little by a message from rival balloonist Steve Fossett wishing them a safe flight to Mexico and another from *Apollo 11* astronaut Neil Armstrong. And a few hours later Richard Branson e-mailed, 'Hats off to you for an incredibly bold flight. It really does look like you could do it this time. Look forward to greeting you in Europe. Have a safe and uneventful journey across the Pacific.'

Despite the lack of progress their days were seldom uneventful. With the hatch open it was time to do some housekeeping chores outside. 'Lying along the outriggers to get to tank valve no.14, with Bertrand holding my foot, was not much fun,' Brian observed. At 1700 GMT on day twelve *Breitling Orbiter 3* accomplished half of the circumnavigation when it crossed the 171° East longitude, although that still left half a world to fly round and two-thirds of the fuel supply now gone. Things were looking increasingly bleak and the following day progress became even slower over the endless stretch of water towards the Hawaiian Islands. For the second time in two days they took advantage of their low altitude to clamber out of the gondola to check over the equipment and take the air.

Because the balloon was flying unexpectedly close to the equator, satellite communications were becoming patchy as the overhang of the silvery envelope obscured the line-of-sight link to the Inmarsat satellite. They could communicate only with the ATC and then only via the HF radio. A long way from help or support of any kind.

'The Pacific was scary, really scary,' recounts Jones. 'We had lost contact with our people and we were doing less than 15 knots. Rescue would have been six days away, maybe even longer, so just imagine being in a single-man life-raft for that length of time. You'd be so ill that you would probably have dehydrated by day two. The capsule was designed to float of course, but all that metal work on top for the propane fuel system completely screwed that up. So there's no question that if we had gone into the water it would have inverted. Not a pleasant thought.'

To add to their misery it was getting incredibly cold in the capsule. 'People didn't realize – our Control Centre certainly didn't. I sent these faxes down, most of them humorous with a lot of banter – we had this strange humour where we were constantly insulting each other. But what actually gave them a good sense of when things weren't quite right was when I lost my sense of humour. It didn't happen very often. Not because of discomfort, but when things weren't going right or if I thought the Control was not giving us the support I wanted . . .'

It has long been recognized in the space business that on long flights a paranoia can build up within the crew that their Control Centre is not doing everything it can for them. This was what was happening in the Breitling capsule and thousands of miles from land the two men were learning to support each other. Theirs was a relationship where a simple touch on the shoulder or arm, or just a look sometimes, said, 'I know what it's like; believe me I'm going through it too.'

Dutifully they kept a regular video diary. Sometimes these sessions revealed moments of pure comedy as when Piccard unfolded the large map of the Pacific. 'All this is blue water – all blue.' And

he turned the map over to reveal another rectangle of uninter-
rupted blue. Then there were other times when their inner
thoughts came to the surface. 'We are afraid, Brian and I. We
talked about . . .' Briefly Piccard's words tapered off. 'The people
in the Control Centre understand and make reassuring faxes . . .'
and he drifted off again, lost in his own thoughts as he gazed out
at that expanse of blue that didn't look quite so funny after all.
Later he confessed that at that moment he felt that the flight
would fail.

On 14 March, after two weeks aloft, the balloon crossed the
International Date Line and the two pilots became one day
younger and, even more reason to celebrate, the communications
link was restored. One of the first messages to reach the Control
Centre came from Jones. 'Lord knows where I got it from, but I
have a cold. Fortunately Doctor Piccard has his remedy box and I
am now sipping hot lemon with honey.' Both pilots were also
demonstrating the symptoms of some sort of one-day migraine,
but fortunately not at the same time as each other.

The next day they got another psychological boost when they
realized that they had beaten Steve Fossett's ballooning distance
record and, best of all, at 1200 GMT the balloon entered the
mouth of the promised subtropical jetstream south of Hawaii.
Though voice communication with the Control Centre remained
troublesome, this increase in speed was the best possible tonic for
their flagging spirits. 'When the balloon was flying over Africa, I
started to love the desert,' observed Piccard. 'I now realize that the
worst desert is not sand but water. I must say that up until now,
the crossing of the Pacific has put us through some anguish . . . I
think the worst thing is anticipating what is to come. One begins
to imagine all sorts of things, and that can become disturbing. As
long as one manages to live the "here and now", one feels fine!
Hopefully our speed will be fast enough so as to reach Europe
before we run out of propane.'

This was a moot point. For some reason the balloon had consumed more fuel than on previous nights, which gave rise for

concern. 'We hope this is a one-off problem, possibly caused by the balloon passing through a few clouds,' commented Noble. If he was wrong the flight could still fail at the final hurdle as they might lack sufficient fuel to complete the Atlantic crossing. In fact the balloon was also forming its own little isolated cloud to acerbate the problem. Just as a jet airliner will leave a contrail in certain conditions, the balloon's burners were creating a cloud of water vapour every time they fired. But unlike a jet which leaves the contrail trailing behind, their cloud of vapour was travelling at the same windspeed and this meant that they had to burn more frequently than usual.

The Met men were proved right in their strategy, and when the balloon climbed to 33,000 feet it hitched a ride on one of the most powerful jets yet, racing them to Mexico at 150 knots. On 17 March *Breitling Orbiter 3* entered Mexican airspace at 34,000 feet – although by this time with a reduced speed of 45 knots as somehow the balloon had been ejected out of the jetstream much earlier than expected. It then began an unwanted southerly drift, but the meteorologists had known that the jet would dissipate and they were convinced that it would reform.

Understandably the pilots were nearing exhaustion and they shivered with cold as the temperature inside the capsule dropped to 8°C at times owing to the problem with the heaters. Piccard and Jones also reported breathing problems as fatigue overtook them. 'It's getting tougher and tougher,' admitted Piccard in an emotional phone call to his wife Michèle. 'After all this effort . . . We're never going to make it,' he sobbed. They knew that the finishing line was in sight and this was all that was keeping them going, but there were concerns among the ground team at the sound of Piccard's laboured breathing.

When Jones awoke he too struggled to catch his breath, and to his alarm he discovered his partner slumped against the bulkhead, gasping for breath. The two men were slowly suffocating, poisoned by the capsule's atmosphere, and it would be only a matter of time before they slipped into unconsciousness if something wasn't done about it. After consulting with the doctors Noble thought that their symptoms might be those of early pulmonary pre-oedema, an accumulation of fluid in the lungs caused by breathing a dry atmosphere over a prolonged period, and he advised them to increase the oxygen content of the atmosphere and, for a short period, to breathe from the constant-flow face masks. After fifteen minutes of this treatment the symptoms passed and for the remainder of the flight they were able to breathe normally. But it had been a close call.

Thursday 18 March, the Atlantic Ocean

Day eighteen. Although Piccard and Jones had completed three-quarters of the circumnavigation the Atlantic Ocean still lay ahead and it was no less inhospitable because it represented the home run. Alan Noble called up the two men for their daily conference and he outlined the options that they faced. Given that out of 32 fuel tanks they had already consumed 29, they estimated that they had adequate fuel for only about another two days aloft, although at their present speed it would take four days to reach Africa. It wasn't just a question of not reaching their goal, a ditching in the Atlantic was a daunting prospect, but Noble knew what the pilots' decision would be and Piccard and Jones had already come to an unspoken agreement between themselves – they would press on.

The first problem they faced was how to get back on track to avoid drifting further to the south-east along the coast of Venezuela. Piccard was at the controls while Jones slept. He consulted the weathermen who said to go higher, but Noble was concerned about the precious fuel a climb would consume. Gambling was not in his nature, but he knew that he had to take the balloon up to its limit – a manoeuvre that could have cost them the flight if he failed to find the right wind direction and speed higher up. But if they stayed low then the flight was probably doomed anyway. The so-called aviation experts were already queuing up on the television news to confirm that the Breitling balloon did not have enough fuel to reach Africa. Incredibly, in the last few hundred feet of altitude available Piccard found a wind which began to turn the balloon on a track of 85° – almost due east on the compass, straight to Africa. Nobody deserved such good luck so often, but the next problem would be getting there before the fuel ran out and with the balloon travelling at only 41 knots.

Next day, day nineteen, another record: this time it was the short-lived endurance record which they claimed from Andy Elson and Colin Prescot. Now the Breitling pilots were totally focused on their flight, estimating their fuel and reserves and calculating their anticipated consumption over and over again. But the sums wouldn't work out right – they had to pick up some more speed or they could still fall short of the finishing line. Worse still, they were over Puerto Rico and they had started to drift southwards again. With the balloon at its altitude ceiling the only option was to vent some helium and come lower.

'I was doing my utmost to work out all the what-if scenarios concerning the fuel,' says Jones. 'Did we have enough to get to the coast?' Fearing the worst, a humiliating splashdown so near to their goal, he put his calculations aside in despair, rubbed his weary eyes and checked their speed as indicated by the GPS. It was just over 40 knots, not nearly enough. And with failure staring them in the face he abandoned his calculations and continued to monitor the instruments. Incredibly the speed gradually increased as he watched; 50 knots, 60 knots, 70 knots . . . in the course of ten minutes it had increased to 100 knots – 'as if pushed by an invisible hand' (as the two would describe it later). Hardly daring to believe the evidence of his own eyes, Jones knew that they were still in with a chance. Silently they each thanked their greatest ally, the wind.

This was the last lap, but high above the Atlantic conditions inside the capsule were worse than ever. Outside the temperature was −50°C and inside it was −2°C. One of the heaters had packed in completely and even the inboard water supplies were beginning to freeze. But they had to stay high to force the pace, they had to eke out every mile from the last meagre drops of propane. At least they were back in the core of the jetstream and travelling at a very respectable 90 knots or so. Taking his turn at the controls once again, Piccard monitored their progress. It was fully dark as they approached the coast of Africa and he would wake Jones when they neared the invisible finishing line for their circumnavigation which ran north to south through Mauritania, a further three hours away. This was the lull before the storm and in the pit of his stomach Piccard felt anxious about what could still happen to rob them of their prize so close to victory.

Friday 19 March, Western Sahara

A new dawn over Africa. A glorious sunrise burst over the horizon and there was the African desert once more. Then suddenly both burners went out.

'*Merde!*' Piccard silently swore to himself. Biting his lip, he tried to ignite them, but there was nothing. This couldn't be happening. Not now! It was impossible – they couldn't fail like this with the finish line just 300 miles away. In desperation he tried once more to ignite the burners but nothing happened. He tried again and then again and with an almighty jolt they burst into life. The *Breitling Orbiter 3* hadn't given up on them yet.

With their speed creeping up to the 100-knot mark the last miles dashed by in a blur as they made their preparations for the historic moment. Alan Noble faxed them from the Control Centre with instructions on how they would handle the media. He ended with a heartfelt personal message: 'I'm proud of you both. Alan.'

Saturday 20 March

Having travelled an incredible 25,361 miles, at 09.54 GMT on 20 March 1999 Bertrand Piccard and Brian Jones became the first balloonists to encircle the globe non-stop. But aboard the tiny capsule high above the African hills, they were at a loss as to how they should mark the occasion. In disbelief the two men hugged each other and Piccard pounded his fist on Jones's chest. 'We've done it! We've done it!'

At this vital moment the satphone went dead and their first communication with Geneva was via the fax. 'We can hardly believe our dream has finally come true.' Shortly afterwards the voice link came alive again and when asked by the media how they would celebrate, Jones replied: 'I'm going to tell my wife I love her, and then I'm going to celebrate with a cup of tea like any Englishman.' In fact they celebrated by eating their first in-flight meal together, a tin of foie gras eaten with a Swiss army knife.

But this was no time to relax. Exhausted, the two men had yet to get the balloon down in one piece. 'If there is one thing to say after this flight it is to thank that invisible hand who guided us safely for the whole flight,' commented Piccard. 'I hope it will guide us also for a safe landing.' But the landscape of north-west Africa was far too treacherous to make an immediate touchdown – an obstacle-course of mountains, extensive minefields and even bandit country. With the fuel gauges barely registering the last remaining dregs of propane they had no choice but to fly on through another night with the intention of fulfilling Jones's original vision of a landing in Egypt at first light.

Sunday 21 March, near Dakhla, Egypt

500 feet, 400, 300 . . . Brian Jones was struggling to control the fall, but downward visibility through the tiny portholes was severely restricted, especially as the capsule was coming in to land backwards. Bertrand Piccard peered out through the bubbleglass hatch and he suddenly saw small stones close up in the yellowy brown soil. 'Look out,' he shouted. 'Hold tight! We're going to hit!' With an almighty thud the *Breitling Orbiter 3* pounded into

the edge of a lonely Egyptian plateau. Huge chunks of melting ice were thrown free by the sudden impact and they showered down onto the roof of the capsule. Inside the two pilots were jolted backwards and loose equipment was strewn across the floor.

Slender as an exclamation mark and exhaling its last gasps of helium, the envelope sagged downwards under the momentum. Abruptly relieved of its burden it sprang back upwards, lobbing the capsule high into the sky and leaving behind an oblong footprint in the desert like that of a visitor from another world. Three hundred feet back in the air Jones fired the burners to stabilize the balloon's descent until they reached a more level stretch of ground. Then Piccard helped him to haul in the control lines which operated a rip panel high in the side of the balloon to release the helium gas, and they bumped down again, bounced once and then came to a juddering halt.

Jones immediately retrieved the laptop computer from the tumble of equipment and unwittingly inspired by the lunar-like landscape at 6.01 am he faxed the Control Centre, 'The Eagle has landed! All OK. Bloody good. B.' After nineteen days and twenty-one hours their fantastic voyage around the world was over.

With tired and aching limbs they clambered out of the life-protecting pod for the last time. A single chase plane roared past, making low level sweeps around the balloon, but it was soon gone. Overcome by emotion, the two men stood in the middle of the desert and surveyed the scene. Behind them their silvery balloon still wallowed as it caught the morning breeze, looking more like a wounded jellyfish than the tall cocktail-shaker which had become familiar to millions of people around the world over the past three weeks. Using their knives they hacked gashes into the sagging envelope to prevent it from dragging the capsule across the sand. When they checked the fuel tanks they discovered how lucky they had been – a crusting of frost revealed just a few inches of cold liquid propane remaining at the bottom of the tanks, adding up to perhaps half a tankful in total. They calculated that at most they had landed with only a few hours of fuel still available. As the envelope slowly collapsed to the ground Piccard filmed the scene and as he walked around the balloon he talked aloud to the camera or to nobody in particular. 'This is fabulous! Thank you! Thank you!'

Bertrand Piccard and Brian Jones were two of the most famous people on the planet at that particular moment, but there was no one else there to share their joy – it would be several hours before they saw another face. For them it was enough to breathe the cool morning air, to absorb the silence of this remote spot and to enjoy the feel of the ground beneath their feet. No cheering crowds, no flashgun cameras, that was all to come. Two men alone in the desert – conquerors of aviation's last great challenge. By flying non-stop round-the-world Piccard and Jones had flown full circle in more than one sense. They had made the final step in a long journey of exploration and achievement; one that stretched all the way back to Joseph and Etienne Montgolfier's fragile craft sent aloft over two centuries earlier.

POSTSCRIPT

As I begin to write this postscript it is exactly one year to the day since I stood stamping my feet against the cold, watching *Breitling Orbiter 3* float off to keep its appointment with history. It was not without a little envy that I followed its gentle drift over the mountains and thought of the two men on board, for whether they flew to America or encircled the globe theirs would be the journey of a lifetime. In all honesty, very few of us present really believed they could successfully make a circumnavigation so late into the jet-stream season, so it was with a real sense of wonderment that we followed Bertrand Piccard's and Brian Jones's great adventure.

End of story? Emphatically not. For incredibly, on 22 February 2000 Kevin Uliassi, the 'other' global soloist, launched again in the *J Renee* and although initial progress was slow – it took a whole week to reach the coast of Africa – little by little Uliassi continued eastward. By 2 March he was over the Bay of Bengal heading for Myanmar, a magnet for global balloons, and then suddenly his Control Centre issued an enigmatic statement saying that he had landed without saying why. I immediately rang Alan Noble at Cameron's and asked him.

'Probably because he's dead,' came the no-nonsense response. 'During the night he stopped answering his phone and it looks likely that he may have had a problem with the oxygen while he was asleep. I may be pessimistic of course – we just don't know.' Half an hour later Noble was back on the phone. 'He's alive. The rescue party is with him.' In fact he had been almost right in his original prognosis, as Uliassi had experienced problems with his oxygen system and was suffering from altitude sickness when the balloon came down. Miraculously he had just a few bruises and the balloon survived intact. Only halfway round the world – but he had established a new solo endurance record: 243 hours 28 minutes.

But what did the success of *Breitling Orbiter 3* mean for all the other global hopefuls? Was it the end of the line for the likes of Branson or Fossett? Their cumulative expenditure has been estimated as something in the region of the combined sum of $40 million and as a result the planet remains littered with discarded hardware. Never to be seen again are the *Virgin/ICO Global Challenger*, Steve Fossett's *Solo Spirit* and *Cable & Wireless*, all of which languish at the bottom of various oceans, or Dick Rutan's *Hilton Global* which was destroyed by fire. Still in existence are the *Earthwinds* capsule (offered for sale by Larry Newman after a parachuting accident put him out of the picture) and Henk Brink's which is gathering dust in a Dutch aircraft hangar. At Per Lindstrand's factory in Oswestry sits the abandoned shell of the replacement *Virgin* capsule. Richard Branson halted all work following Breitling's success, although he briefly considered a solo attempt before his advisers talked him out of it. Meanwhile the *Team Re/Max* and *Spirit of Peace* teams both have complete balloons which have yet to fly at all. As for Breitling's clutch of capsules, two are used for exhibitions and promotional purposes while the most famous, *Orbiter 3*, has pride of place at the Smithsonian Air & Space Museum, Washington, rubbing shoulders with the Wright brothers' biplane, Lindbergh's *Spirit of St Louis* and the *Apollo 11* capsule.

So if the round-the-world flight has indeed been ballooning's Everest, what new mountains are there left to climb? The FAI has proposed a global race with several balloons departing together, but the logistics for such a project are enormous and sponsorship may prove elusive. It is possible that we shall see a successful solo bid.

For the Breitling pilots their triumph brought with it a whirl-wind of publicity as they were paraded before a succession of heads of state to collect a cabinet full of trophies – including the OBE presented to Jones by the Queen. Once the initial furore had died down Piccard returned to his work as a psychiatrist while Jones had plans to tour the lecture circuit. 'I can't stop talking about it. Interest may start to wane, but the achievement will never go away. Until the day I die we will still have been the first people to fly around the world in a balloon.' But he holds no ambitions to repeat the global experience. 'Flying a balloon around the world is bloody difficult and it doesn't get any easier just because we have done it. For me it was a one-off. It is a wonderful memory and I don't want anything to taint it.'

Perhaps the most lasting legacy of the *Breitling Orbiter 3*'s flight is the Winds of Hope Foundation*, the charity set up by the two pilots in response to their new-found respect for the planet. Launched with the $1 million Budweiser prize money, it aims to champion forgotten causes and to bring them to public attention. 'It is mainly for children anywhere in the world who are suffering and who are somehow not important enough to attract attention,' says Jones.

The other global balloonists, meanwhile, are casting their eyes to the heavens; Per Lindstrand, Colin Prescot and Andy Elson all have ambitions to fly to the edge of space. Steve Fossett has busied himself collecting more merit badges, including a successful round-the-world speed record flight with two other pilots in his own *Citation X* jet. For ballooning in general the global endeav-ours were a fitting climax to over two hundred years of pushing the boundaries of lighter-than-air flight. Today hot-air ballooning is a popular form of recreational and sport flying throughout the world, and the gas balloonists are still going strong, with increased interest in the Gordon Bennett races and other 'local' records falling like nine-pins. In the spring of 2000 'rookie' balloonist

* Website www.windsofhope.org

David Hempleman-Adams stole the limelight by flying a Cameron Rozière to the North Pole; definitely a name to watch out for in the future.

Undoubtedly there will be other new ballooning challenges and challengers in the twenty-first century, for the spirit of adventure is too deeply embedded in human nature to stop now. I feel privileged to have been involved with the global balloon adventure and to have met so many of the people taking part, but for all of us the round-the-world flight wasn't the end, it was a new beginning. Keep watching the skies . . .

JC

GLOSSARY

Appendix tubes
The fabric tubes that allow excess helium to escape. (See *Float altitude*.)

ATC
Air Traffic Control.

AWACS
Airborne Warning and Control System.

cubic feet
Balloon size is measured by volume in thousands of cubic feet or cubic metres (1,000 cubic feet = 28.3 cubic metres.)

EPIRB
Emergency Personal Identification Radio Beacon.

EVA
Extra-Vehicular Activity; a term borrowed from the spacemen.

FAI
Fédération Aéronautique Internationale; the governing body of aviation sports and record-breaking.

Float altitude
The point at which the gas has expanded to completely fill the cell because of reduced external air pressure or the effects of temperature.

fpm
Feet per minute, rate of ascent or descent.

GMT
Greenwich Mean Time, the reference point for international time, also known as Zulu or UTC (Universal Time Code).

Gondola
The traditional term for a

balloon basket, which was originally often shaped like a boat. The term *capsule* usually implies a sealed and pressurized gondola.

GPS
Global Positioning System, using fixes from a number of different satellites to establish an extremely accurate position.

HF
High frequency radio for long range.

Hyperbaric toilet
Airline-style toilet that relies on lower outside atmospheric pressure.

ICAO
International Civil Aviation Organization; the body for collaboration in the standardization of aviation rules and procedures.

INMARSAT/Inmarsat
INternational MARitime SATellite organization responsible for communications via satellites.

Knots
A speed of *1 nautical mile* per hour.
(A nautical mile = 1 minute of 1 degree of Latitude, or 1.15 *statute miles*.)

Omega
Long-range radio navigation aid covering the whole of the Earth.

Rozière
Combination gas and hot-air balloon in which the temperature of the gas can be adjusted to maintain or alter altitude.

TSM
Thunderstorm.

UHF
Ultra High Frequency radio transmissions.

Variometer
Instrument that measures rate of climb.

VHF
Very High Frequency radio transmissions – mostly for short range.

CHRONOLOGY

Including major ocean crossings and other significant long-distance flights
• *= global attempts*

1783 21 Nov **First flight**
Pilâtre de Rozier and the Marquis d'Arlandes fly the Montgolfier hot-air balloon.

1 Dec **First gas balloon**
Professor Charles and Noël Robert fly their hydrogen-filled balloon – 27 miles.

1785 7 Jan **First Channel crossing**
Pierre Blanchard and Dr Jeffries fly from England to France.

15 Jun **Channel: *Royal Balloon***
Pilâtre de Rozier and Pierre Romain are killed when their combination balloon explodes. The first casualties of air travel.

1836 7–8 Nov **Distance: *Vauxhall Gardens***
Charles Green flies 380 miles from London to Germany in 18 hours.

1859 1–2 Jul **Distance:** *Atlantic*
John Wise, John La Mountain, O. A. Granger and
William Hyde fly 809 miles in USA.

1873 7 Oct **Atlantic:** *New Graphic*
US gas balloon lands after only 3 hours.

1901 Oct **Distance:** *Centauri*
Count Henri de la Vaulx flies 1,193 miles from
France to Russia.

1913 **Distance**
Hugo Kauleu of Germany flies 1,756 miles to
Siberia.

1928 8–29
Aug • *Graf Zeppelin*
Airship flies from Lakehurst, New Jersey, to
Friedrichshafen in Germany, then Tokyo, Los
Angeles and back to Lakehurst – 21,000 miles in
just over 21 days. First lighter-than-air flight around
the world.

1958 12 Dec–
5 Jan **Atlantic:** *Small World*
Gas balloon takes off from Canary Islands; Colin
and Rosemary Mudie, with Arnold and Tim Eiloart
(UK). They ditch in the Atlantic and complete their
journey by sea.

1964 Apr • *Gulliver*
Journalist David Royce (USA) announces plan to fly
gas balloon *Gulliver* around the world, stopping
daily along the way. Also advertises for a balloonist
to go with him.

1968   10 Aug   **Atlantic:** *Maple Leaf*
Gas balloon ditches off Nova Scotia; Mark Winters and Jerry Kostur (USA). Rescued.

1970   20 Sep   **Atlantic:** *Free Life*
Hot-air/gas hybrid balloon lost in Atlantic. Malcolm Brighton (UK), Rod and Pamela Anderson (USA) not found.

1973   7–8 Aug   **Atlantic:** *Yankee Zephyr*
Bobby Sparks (USA) rescued after his Rozière balloon ditches off Newfoundland.

1974   18 Feb   **Atlantic:** *Light Heart*
Thomas Gatch (USA) disappears near Azores in helium cluster balloon. Not found.

        6 Aug   **Atlantic:** *Spirit of Man*
Gas balloon bursts near the coast, killing pilot Bob Berger (USA).

1975   6 Jan   **Atlantic:** *Windborne*
Launch of helium cluster balloon aborted; Malcolm Forbes and Tom Heinsheimer (USA).

        21 Aug   **Atlantic:** *Odyssey*
Bobby Sparks tries again with Haddon Wood (USA), the launchmaster who failed to let go and is hauled aboard. Ditches off Cape Cod after 2 hours 5 mins. Rescued.

1976   25–26   **Atlantic:** *Spirit of '76*
        Jun   Gas balloon forced down by storm; Karl Thomas (USA). Rescued.

5–9 Oct **Atlantic: *Silver Fox***
Ed Yost (USA) flies gas balloon to within 700 miles
of Portugal. Rescued.

1977 9–12 **Atlantic: *Double Eagle***
Sep Ben Abruzzo and Maxie Anderson (USA) fail in
their bid to fly gas balloon across the Atlantic. Ditch
off Iceland. Rescued.

10–12 Oct **Atlantic: *Eagle***
Dewey Reinhard and Charles Stevenson (USA)
ditch gas balloon off Nova Scotia. Rescued.

1978 26–30 **Atlantic: *Zanussi***
Jul Don Cameron and Major Christopher Davey (UK)
launch from Newfoundland in Rozière *Zanussi*; 96
hours 24 min later they ditch in the Bay of Biscay,
108 miles off the French coast. Rescued.

11–17 **Atlantic: *Double Eagle II***
Aug First successful crossing when Maxie Anderson, Ben
Abruzzo and Larry Newman (USA) fly gas balloon
to France.

1980 • *ICI Innovation*
Don Cameron (UK) announces plans to make
global flight in Rozière balloon, with Peter
Bohanna, Julian Nott and Leo Dickinson (UK).
Although cancelled, this project accurately predicts
the successful concept of a Rozière combined with
pressurized capsule.

1981 11–13 • *Jules Verne*
Jan Maxie Anderson and Don Ida (USA) lift off in gas
balloon from Luxor, Egypt. Land at Hansi, India,
after 48 hours.

9–12   **Pacific:** *Double Eagle V*
Nov   First Pacific crossing. Gas balloon flies from Japan
        to USA. Ben Abruzzo, Larry Newman, Ron Clark
        and Rocky Aoki (USA).

20 Dec • *Jules Verne*
        Anderson and Ida (USA) try again, launching from
        India, but land their leaking gas balloon after only
        20 miles.

1982   7 Nov   • *Jules Verne*
        Anderson and Ida (USA) launch from South
        Dakota, but land after 1,162 miles and before the
        Atlantic because of leaks. Both men killed the
        following year during the 1983 Gordon Bennett
        balloon race from Paris.

1984   14–17   **Atlantic:** *Rosie O'Grady*
        Sep   Joe Kittinger (USA) makes first solo crossing in gas
        balloon. Lands in Italy.

        Nov   • *Endeavour*
        Julian Nott (UK) claims a record-breaking test flight
        of super-pressure gas balloon in Australia. However,
        it has been suggested that the super-pressure
        equipment failed on take-off, leaving it a
        conventional gas balloon.

1985   25–27   **Atlantic:** *Flying Dutchman*
        Aug   Dutch balloonists Henk Brink, Evelien Brink and
        Evert Louwman fail in their attempt when their
        Rozière balloon ditches 900 miles from Europe after
        valve problems. Rescued.

1986 Jun •
Larry Newman (USA) announces plans for a
'Voyage of Peace' round-the-world flight with a
launch in January 1987.

31 Aug– **Atlantic: *Dutch Viking***
2 Sep   Henk Brink, his wife Evelien (first woman to make
crossing) and William Hageman (Netherlands) land
near Amsterdam in Cameron-built Rozière.

1987 Jun **Atlantic**
Don Cameron (UK) publicly challenges Per
Lindstrand (Sweden) to make the first hot-air
crossing, but following inflation problems
Cameron's balloon never flies.

2–3 **Atlantic: *Virgin Atlantic Flyer***
Jul   First crossing by hot-air; Per Lindstrand (Sweden)
and Richard Branson (UK).

1988 Mar • ***Operation SHARE***
John Petrehn with co-pilot Colonel Rowland Smith
(USA) attempt flight with pressurized capsule and
helium double balloon. Inflated at Mendoza,
Argentina, but one balloon damaged and flight
aborted. Petrehn had originally proposed a hybrid
hot-air and gas balloon combination to launch from
Perth, Australia.

• **Explorer**
Julian Nott (UK) says *Explorer* will be ready to fly in
November.

1989 25 Jan • *Explorer*
Julian Nott (UK) holds press conference to
announce launch of *Explorer* in the winter.

26 Nov   **Pacific:** *Virgin Pacific Flyer*
The first attempt to fly the Pacific by hot-air balloon is aborted when Per Lindstrand (Sweden) and Richard Branson's (UK) *Virgin Pacific Flyer* suffers envelope lamination problems after a night laid out in the frost.

1990   •
David Iggulden's book *Hot-Air Ballooning* reveals that Per Lindstrand (Sweden) was discussing plans for a round-the-world hot-air balloon before his departure from Thunder & Colt. (In fact Lindstrand says he has been discussing the project with Branson (UK) since their Atlantic flight in 1987.)

5 May   • *Earthwinds*
Richard Branson (UK) announces his intention to join the project with Larry Newman (USA). Reports say balloon will launch at the end of the year.

1 Oct   **England to USSR:** *Doctus*
Don Cameron (UK) and Gennadi Oparin (USSR) fly Rozière balloon *Doctus*. Not the first time a balloon has flown to Russia, but an important demonstration of the new Cameron 'Atlantic' type Rozières.

Nov   • *Earthwinds*
Two-thirds scale *Earthwinds* balloon launches from Tillamook, Oregon, for 34-hour test flight. Problems prevent the lower ballast balloon from being inflated.

1991   12 Jan   **Pacific**
Japanese balloonist Fumio Niwa dies after ditching his gas balloon 300 miles out from Japan on solo attempt.

15–17   **Pacific:** *Virgin Pacific Flyer*
Jan   First crossing by hot-air when Per Lindstrand
(Sweden) and Richard Branson (UK) fly from Japan
6,761 miles to Canada.

Nov   • *Columbus*
Henk Brink (Holland) announces project, initially
called *Columbus*, to fly round-the-world with a
Rozière balloon.

1992   14–17   **Atlantic**
Feb   First east-to-west crossing by Spanish team
Thomas Feliú and Jesús Gonzales Green. Reusing
the Rozière that flew to Russia in 1990, they
launch from the Canary Islands and land in
Venezuela.

21 Feb   • *Earthwinds*
Inflated in hangar at Akron, Ohio, but attempt
aborted because of surface wind; Larry Newman
(USA), Vladimir Dzhanibekov (USSR) and Don
Moses (USA).

16–22   **Atlantic: Chrysler Transatlantic Challenge**
Sep   First Transatlantic Balloon Race: Five identical
Rozière balloons take off from Bangor, Maine for
Europe:

Chrysler 1 (Belgium)
Wim Verstraeten (Belgium) and Bertrand Piccard
(Switzerland). Land in Spain to win event.

Chrysler 2 (Germany)
Erich Kraft and Jochen Mass ditch mid-Atlantic.
Rescued.

Chrysler 3 (UK)
Don Cameron and Rob Bayly land in Portugal.

Chrysler 4 (Netherlands)

Gerhard Hoogslag and Evert Louwman ditch off Land's End. Rescued.

Chrysler 5 (USA)
Richard Abruzzo and Troy Bradley fly to Africa and establish new endurance record.

Dec • *Earthwinds Hilton*
Now at Reno, Nevada. Plans to inflate balloon inside a massive inflatable tent abandoned after tent and inflated ballast balloon damaged by wind.

1993 12 Jan • *Earthwinds Hilton*
Balloon flies just 7 miles before crashing into mountains after failing to push through inversion; lower ballast balloon damaged; Larry Newman (USA), Vladimir Dzhanibekov (USSR) and Don Moses (USA).

16–18 **Australia: *Australian Geographic***
Jun Dick Smith and John Wallington (Australia) fly over 2,000 miles across Australia in Rozière R77, beating rival team Phil Kavanagh (Australia) and Brian Smith (UK).

5 Nov • *Earthwinds Hilton*
Launch abandoned after anchor bolts break during inflation – envelope damaged; Larry Newman (USA), Vladimir Dzhanibekov (USSR) and Richard Abruzzo (USA).

1994 • *Windstar*
Joe Kittinger (USA) is said to be firming up plans for his *Windstar* project.

12 Jan • *Earthwinds Hilton*
Fourth attempt – flies for 7 hours and 202 miles in the wrong direction before a ballast valve freezing

problem forces a landing; Larry Newman, Richard Abruzzo and Dave Melton (USA).

3 Apr   • *Odyssey*
Odyssey project announced. Troy Bradley, Bob Martin and Mark Sullivan (USA) plan to fly a massive high-altitude gas balloon; they start looking for sponsors.

Jun   •
Aerostat article lists active contenders: Julian Nott (UK); Per Lindstrand (Sweden), *Global Orbiter*; Henk Brink (Netherlands), *Columbus*; Bradley, Martin and Sullivan (USA), *Odyssey*; Larry Newman (USA), *Earthwinds*; Joe Kittinger (USA); and Dick Rutan (USA).

• *Aeolus 1*
Dick Rutan (USA) announces plans to fly *Aeolus 1* Rozière round-the-world. Originally to be solo; he later suggests a two-man attempt.

17–21   **Atlantic**
Aug   Steve Fossett and Tim Cole (USA) fly Atlantic in Rozière.

31 Dec   • *Earthwinds Hilton*
Takes off from Reno and lower balloon bursts at 32,000 feet; Larry Newman, Dave Melton and George Saad (USA).

1995   Jan   • *UNICEF Flyer*
Henk Brink (Netherlands) postpones launch, but says he will make attempt later this year (November); Brink, Hageman and Bakker.

17–21   **Pacific**
Feb   Steve Fossett (USA) flies Pacific solo in *R150* Rozière. Launches in Korea and lands near

Medicine Hat in Canada, 103 hours and 5,439 miles later.

9 Apr •

Newspapers reveal Branson's (UK) new attempt is in partnership with Per Lindstrand (Sweden). In May Lindstrand confirms that this is to be by Rozière balloon and not hot-air.

Jun •

Steve Fossett (USA) says he will make attempt using his existing Pacific balloon.

Jun •

Bertrand Piccard (Switzerland) and Wim Verstraeten (Belgium), winners of the Chrysler Transatlantic race in 1992, plan to make attempt using a Cameron Rozière.

Jul • *Virgin Flyer*

Per Lindstrand (Sweden) and Richard Branson (UK) reveal that their *Virgin Flyer* is to be a 700,000-cubic-foot Lindstrand-built Rozière, and their intention is to fly with a third person on board. They hope to be ready by the end of the year.

1996 15 Jan • *Solo Challenger*

Steve Fossett (USA) lifts off from the Stratobowl, South Dakota, but soon runs into trouble when the Mylar envelope splits. Other problems follow and he lands in New Brunswick rather than attempt Atlantic crossing.

Jan/Feb • *Virgin Global Challenger*

Richard Branson (UK), Per Lindstrand (Sweden) and Rory McCarthy (UK). Rain stops play at Marrakesh, Morocco and the Virgin team goes home.

1997 7 Jan • *Virgin Global Challenger*
Richard Branson (UK), Per Lindstrand (Sweden),
Alex Ritchie (UK). Second envelope and second
attempt from Marrakesh ends 20 hours after
launch. Locks on the fuel tanks had been left on
during inflation and an attempt to correct this
brings the balloon into severe rotor winds and after
several plunges they land in the Algerian desert.

12 Jan • *Breitling Orbiter*
Bertrand Piccard (Switzerland) and Wim
Verstraeten (Belgium) launch from Château d'Oex,
Switzerland, but after only six hours aloft the
balloon ditches in the Mediterranean. Fumes from a
kerosene leak have filled the gondola, making the
two-man crew ill. The cause is a small connector
clip.

13–20 Jan • *Solo Spirit*
Fossett (USA) lifts off from St Louis, Missouri, to
make the longest flight in the history of ballooning
to date. Having flown 9,594 miles in a little over six
days he lands in India, his fuel reserve too low to
cross the Pacific.

9 Dec • *Virgin Global Challenger*
At Marrakesh, Morocco, the third Virgin global
envelope breaks free during a daytime inflation and
lands 30 miles within Algeria. Crew should have
been Richard Branson (UK), Per Lindstrand
(Sweden) and Alex Ritchie (UK).

31 Dec–
5 Jan • *Solo Spirit*
Steve Fossett (USA) tries again. Launches from St
Louis, USA, and ends up in a muddy field in Russia
with inadequate fuel to make it all the way.

31 Dec
• *J Renee*
Kevin Uliassi (USA) lands after just 5 hours when helium cell of balloon splits shortly after taking off from Illinois.

1998 8 Jan
• *Breitling Orbiter 2*
Launch postponed when a suspension cable comes away and the capsule falls back onto its trailer. A lucky escape for Bertrand Piccard (Switzerland), Wim Verstraeten (Belgium) and Andy Elson (UK).

9 Jan
• *Hilton Global*
The season of global balloon fiascoes is rounded off with Dick Rutan and Dave Melton (USA) leaping from their balloon in the New Mexico desert 100 miles from their launch; the balloon continues without them.

28 Jan–
7 Feb
• *Breitling Orbiter 2*
Refused permission to fly into Chinese airspace, they land in Myanmar after a record-breaking flight of nearly 234 hours; Bertrand Piccard (Switzerland), Wim Verstraeten (Belgium) and Andy Elson (UK).

Jan/Feb
• *Virgin Global Challenger*
Despite building a replacement envelope in record time the Virgin team has to admit that time and the weather have run out for this season. Alex Ritchie (UK) seriously injured in a parachuting accident.

11 Apr Alex Ritchie (UK) dies.

7 May
• *Team Re/Max*
A new sponsor and a new name for the project that began life as *Odyssey*. A new crew line-up too with Bob Martin (USA), John Wallington (Australia) and Dave Liniger (USA).

7–16 • *Solo Spirit*
Aug Steve Fossett (USA) makes the first southern
hemisphere attempt and a last brave bid to make the
flight solo. He travels halfway round-the-world and
beats his own record – but severe storms bring him
down off Australia.

10 Nov • *ICO Global Challenger*
Steve Fossett (USA) joins forces with
Branson/Lindstrand team.

18–25 • *ICO Global Challenger*
Dec Richard Branson (UK) and Per Lindstrand
(Sweden) with Steve Fossett (USA) in the balloon
now known as the *ICO Global Challenger*. After six
days they face an impenetrable weather front and
splash down in the Pacific just off Hawaii.

1999 Jan • *Team Re/Max*
The high-altitude project is in disarray. Bad weather
at Alice Springs, Australia, causes 17 cancellations.
Bob Martin (USA) stands down when it is
calculated that the balloon cannot carry the full
three-man crew.

12 Feb • *Spirit of Peace*
Jacques Soukup (USA) decides that the weather
window has closed for this season.

17 Feb– • *Cable & Wireless*
7 Mar Unable to enter Chinese airspace, Andy Elson and
Colin Prescot (UK) take the slow southerly route. A
new endurance record is set, but after 18 days they
are forced to ditch off the coast of Japan. That leaves
Breitling the only global contender.

1–21 • *Breitling Orbiter 3*
Mar Bertrand Piccard (USA) and Brian Jones (UK)
become the first to pilot a balloon around the

world. Launched from Château d'Oex, Switzerland, *Breitling Orbiter 3* touches down in Egypt after 20 days aloft.

2000 22 Feb– 3 Mar
• *J Renee*
Kevin Uliassi (USA) sets a new solo duration record of 243 hours 28 minutes flying from USA to Myanmar.

28 May– 3 Jun
North Pole: *Britannic Challenger*
David Hempleman-Adams (UK) flies to within a few miles of the North Pole in a Cameron Rozière.

30 Aug– 4 Sep
Atlantic: *Conseil Régional de Lorraine*
First French crossing. Laurent Lajoye and Christophe Houver fly their Lindstrand Rozière from New Brunswick in Canada to Calvados, France.

2001 17 Jun
• *Solo Spirit*
Steve Fossett's sixth (and fifth solo) circumnavigation attempt is thwarted when the balloon is damaged by strong gusts during inflation at Kalgoorlie, Australia.

INDEX